Solly Ozrovech

CHOOSE LIFE!

Lux Verbi

For my family
for all their love, loyalty,
support and prayers

Copyright © 1989 Lux Verbi
P O Box 1822, Cape Town
All rights reserved
Set in 11 on 13 pt Plantin
Printed and bound by
National Book Printers
Goodwood, Cape
First edition, first print 1989
Second edition, first print 1993
Second print 1995

ISBN 0 86997 446 7

JANUARY

PRAYER

Heavenly Father,
At the beginning of this new year, I humbly come to You, the almighty and all-knowing God, who, from the beginning, can also see the end.
Before I set foot on this new, unknown road, I confess that I can only be safe and secure if You hold my hand every step of the way.
If the road ahead seems dark, let me proceed in the light of faith;
if much is hidden from my sight, keep me faithful and true to that which I am able to see;
if I cannot view my destination ahead, make me thankful for each step which I can see;
if I cannot fathom your holiness, help me to cling to your promises with the trust of a child;
if at times my faith is weak, let me never abandon hope and love;
if I have no insight into your divine plan for my life, let me follow obediently and never question your wisdom;
if I meet with success during this year, keep me humble, grateful and kind;
if I meet with disappointment and failure, keep me from despair and bitterness.
Whether my dreams and ambitions are realized, or whether my ideals fall shattered at my feet, dear Father, hold me in your love and teach me anew that all things work together for the good of those who love You.
Make me a joyful follower in the new year.
This I pray in the Name of Him, who by his death and resurrection made it possible for me to choose life – Jesus Christ, my Lord and Saviour.
Amen.

January 1 Deuteronomy 30:11-20

CHOOSE LIFE!
Choose life. Love the Lord your God, obey Him and be faithful to Him . . . (Deut 30:19-20)

Countless people have lost the capability to live meaningful lives. They have fallen into a rut and exist one dreary day after the other with no exciting expectations – the hope and joy of striving for a spiritual ideal have died.

This is so unnecessary, because Jesus said: "I have come in order that you might have life – life in all its fullness" (Jn 10:10). By his merit we have received the grace to live full and rich lives; to give freely of our love; to live creatively; to discover new dimensions of the spirit through growth; and to make this world a better place by the regeneration of our spirit.

To choose Christ is to choose life! He transforms an everyday and colourless existence into an exciting and new life. Living becomes a pulsating adventure.

Christ makes the essential difference – He transforms everything. He is the true origin of abundant life. He teaches us to live meaningful lives and in our turn to spread a fragrance which enriches the lives of others.

Lord, teach me to live in such a manner that each day will be meaningful, so that I may experience the abundance of true life – the life I chose in Jesus Christ – to your honour and glory.

January 2 Isaiah 40:27-31

THE FLIGHT OF AN EAGLE
But those who trust in the Lord for help will find their strength renewed. They will rise on wings like eagles . . . (Is 40:31)

Life can be full of pettiness, and irrelevant matters can easily be blown up beyond proportion. We can so easily become entangled in the trivialities of our everyday existence that our potential is limited and we are reduced in mind and action.

A positive Christian receives the grace to rise above irritations by trusting in the power of the living Christ. It is impossible to be petty and biased when the love of Christ is in your heart, your mind and your deeds.

To demonstrate the love of Christ means to be elevated to the heights where our heavenly Father desires his children to live.

Whatever the circumstances, never allow pettiness to warp your mind to such an extent that you become incapable of seeing the spiritual realities which bring depth, meaning and purpose to your life.

Once you become aware of the presence of God, you will be able to see life in its true perspective, and to recognise the things that are of real importance. Then you will rise on wings like an eagle!

I thank You, Lord Jesus, for the power and strength You impart so that I can rise above pettiness on the wings of an eagle.

January 3   Matthew 28:16-20

HIS CONSTANT PRESENCE

And I will be with you always, to the end of the age (Mt 28:20)

Life sometimes demands adjustments from us. One of the most difficult to make, is when death narrows the circle of your acquaintances and loved ones until you are left surrounded by aloof strangers. You feel like lamenting: "The sun still rises, and it still goes down, going wearily back to where it must start all over again" (Ecc 1:5).

One must guard against becoming morbid and bitter, or to fall into the trap of self-pity. To be able to adapt to a new phase of life in spite of your loneliness, demands a great deal of tolerance, especially with the new generation. Grant them the opportunities which you have had; appreciate their dedication, their honest intentions and their endeavour for that in which they believe.

Reconcile yourself with the fact that yesterday is past and done with and is of value only if it brings inspiration to the present and the future. Enjoy your beautiful memories, but don't allow them to chain you to the past.

There are, however, values which never change: faith, hope and love, and above all, Jesus Christ, who is always the same, yesterday, today and for all eternity. In this knowledge you can find the strength to adapt to any circumstance and to live a joyful life to his glory and honour.

Eternal and unchanging God and Father, I thank You for the inspiring memories You grant me. I trust in You for the unknown future as well.

January 4 Proverbs 16:1-9

AN UNFAILING PLAN FOR LIFE
Ask the Lord to bless your plans, and you will be successful in carrying them out (Prov 16:3)

He who fails to plan, plans to fail. Every person must have a plan according to which he approaches life. Such a life-plan need not be rigid, but it must indicate the course you are taking. Without it your life will be aimless and unsatisfactory.

It may be that you feel incapable of planning your future and simply accept things as they come. To drift along with circumstances in the hope of attaining success, leads only to failure and disaster. Success is not achieved overnight. No, the lift to success is out of order – you have to use the stairs.

To plan constructively, you must do so in co-operation with God. Be sure that your plans comply with the Lord's demands and that you are led by the Holy Spirit. Then you can expect the blessing of the Lord and act in confidence. With the help of the almighty God you can execute your plans and obtain success.

Lord Jesus, lead me and teach me to plan my life according to your holy will.

January 5 Psalm 55:1-23

ESCAPISM OR FAITH
I wish I had wings, like a dove. I would fly away and find rest (Ps 55:6)
Leave your troubles with the Lord, and He will defend you . . . (Ps 55:22)

In this psalm the writer mentions two ways of facing your problems. The fly-away method – to try and escape from your problems. Or the faith method – to face up to them boldly and to trust the Lord to help you solve them.

Jona tried to run away, but he only created grave problems for himself.

When, however, he followed the road of faith, he discovered that the Lord was providing for him in ways he could never have thought possible. He learnt an important lesson: they who cast their cares upon the Lord and follow Him by faith and trust, can conquer any problem.

There is no short-cut in solving problems, but when we act in faith, we receive the strength and courage to overcome any crisis. Then we make the startling and exciting discovery that the Lord has moved ahead of us to level the way.

Faithfully do your part and leave your troubles with the Lord. God is almighty and capable of supporting you in ways which are beyond your understanding.

Dear Lord, help me never to try to escape from my problems or my duty, but to tackle and overcome them in faith and trust.

January 6 Revelation 21:1-8

A SECOND CHANCE
Then the one who sits on the throne said, "And now I make all things new!" (Rev 21:5)

If your spiritual life has fallen into a rut, and lacks the sparkle which you once experienced, it is time to be absolutely honest with yourself. It is human to blame your faults on someone or something else and to refuse the Holy Spirit to lead you to look into your own heart.

You may profess that you have outgrown the need for a living faith and that you are self-sufficient. Possibly you have worldly friends and you are trying to emulate them. Or, by a lack of prayer and Bible study, you have allowed your love, enthusiasm and faith to languish.

However, Jesus' love for you never changes. His constant love does not depend on your changing moods or backsliding spirit. His love is eternally the same.

When you realize how far you have drifted away from Him, you are possibly too ashamed or embarrassed to return to Him. Do not agonize in self-pity over failures of the past. Make a new start – and do it now!

Jesus Christ does not expect you to build a new spiritual life on the ruins of failure. His promise is unconditional: "And now I make all things new!" He invites you to an exciting new life in his power, grace and love. Choose life!

Heavenly Master, in your power and love I will make a new beginning each day.

January 7 Isaiah 43:14-21

A NEW DISPENSATION
Watch for the new thing I am going to do. It is happening already – you can see it now! (Is 43:19)
Covetousness and selfish ambition has caused the degeneration of man: old values crumble before the onslaught of new demands. In his search for eternal values which give meaning to his life, he experiments with drugs, alcohol, free love and false religion. But it is an idle hope that he will find relief for the deepest longing of his soul in these things.

The only way to find new meaning in life, is to return to the trusted values and truths of Scripture. This is the first step on the road to a new life.

To be part of this inspiring new era, you first have to become a "new" person yourself. The presence and power of the living Christ must become apparent in your own life.

The greatest contribution you can make to the future, is to consecrate yourself to Christ. As a Spirit-filled child of God you must totally commit yourself to live to his honour and glory. This is how a new world is built.

Oh Lord, my Saviour, equip me through the work of the Holy Spirit to accept by faith the challenges of a new world and to be your witness.

January 8 John 21:1-9

CHRIST ON THE BEACH OF MY LIFE
As the sun was rising, Jesus stood at the water's edge, but the disciples did not know that it was Jesus (Jn 21:4)
The disciples had toiled hard, but without success, all through the night. At dawn they were nearing the beach, discouraged by their failure. Then Jesus arrived to transform their night of failure and desperation into a new day of hope and joyful expectation. "Young men, haven't you caught anything?" He knew of the fruitless efforts, their unfulfilled dreams, of the deepest yearnings of their hearts. He was waiting for them to confess it to Him. Then the Lord directed them from failure to success: "Throw your net out on the right side of the boat, and you will catch some." When the Lord demands a change of

direction from you, your obedience will culminate in success. You dare not allow yourself to be crippled by your failures.

With Jesus on the beach, your life generates new power. He said to his disciples: "Come and eat!" God will supply all your needs so that you can proceed. He says to you as He said to Elijah sitting in the shade of a tree in the desert, utterly despondent and spiritually defeated: "Get up and eat, or the journey will be too much for you" (1 Kgs 19:7). The Lord never demands of you to do a task for Him, without equipping and strengthening you. Standing on the shore of your life, He is always available.

Lord, I thank You for appearing to me on the scene of my failure and disappointment, to inspire me with new courage and power for the task You lay upon me.

January 9 1 Timothy 6:6-21

GO FOR GOLD!
Run your best in the race of faith, and win eternal life for yourself ... (1 Tim 6:12)

"Go for gold!" was the motto of the American team at the Olympic Games of 1984. Only the best would be good enough for them.

Each of us has an inherent desire to obtain success. Nobody deliberately wants to be a failure. Why then are there so many who fail?

It is amazing that so many people drift through life without a fixed purpose. And because they expect nothing from life, that is exactly what life gives back to them.

There are also people harbouring wonderful ideals, but they have convinced themselves from scratch that they will never be able to fulfil them. Later they complain bitterly that they have never had the opportunity, while in actual fact they lacked perseverance.

Success is not the fulfilment of a burning ambition, but rather the deep satisfaction of striving for a worthy cause. There are people who have attained everything the world can offer and yet they are unhappy and depressed, because they are longing for something which earthly wealth cannot supply. It is not what you have on the outside, but what you are on the inside, that leads to true success.

Therefore Paul encourages Timothy to fight the good fight of faith and to strive after "eternal life" – that is the gold! Constantly aim forward and upward, so that you may reach a spiritual level where you are so totally committed to God, that He can reach his purpose with your life.

I thank You, my Saviour, that my success does not depend upon the world and its standards, but upon the measure of my commitment to the Holy Spirit.

January 10 Hebrews 13:7-19

INTO THE FUTURE WITH CHRIST
Jesus Christ is the same yesterday, today, and for ever (Heb 13:8)
The unchanging Christ brings stability into the lives of his children. It seldom happens that our lives are free from cares and problems. Sometimes all things go well for us; and then suddenly, without any apparent reason, problems beset us.

One moment you are riding the crest with exuberant joy, and the very next moment you plod through the valley of despair.

You are constantly fluctuating between the extremes of hope and despair; of joy and sadness. For this reason you need a stabilizing influence in your life – the living Christ.

Christ is eternal and He never changes. Even though we are temperamental, with feelings that change according to our circumstances, we discover unknown stability when Jesus is the Lord and King of our lives and the Holy Spirit dwells within us.

Then you are not flung around by every wind of change. You experience a joy in life which is so great that it cannot be expressed in words. When you hold on to his loving and comforting hand, you can face the future with courage and self-assurance.

Holy Master, by faith I accept your Spirit's guidance. I want to live according to your will, so that I can have stability in my life.

January 11 Matthew 16:24-28

A FORMULA FOR LIVING
Will a person gain anything if he wins the whole world but loses his life? (Mt 16:26)
To stay alive one needs food, clothing and other material things. However, these things must never be elevated to the highest good, because then you become like the rich fool who loved his earthly possessions so much that he neglected his soul.

To live a rich and full life one needs somebody to share your life with. Family, friends and loved ones are necessary for a happy and contented life. They help you to discover yourself. It is a lucky person who can say of his friends: ". . . every time I pray, I mention you and give thanks to my God" (Phlm 1:4).

You must also have something to live for – a task demanding your talents, your love, your energy and dedication; a work which brings pride and joy to your heart.

You must have a living faith which raises you above yourself and gives purpose and meaning to your existence. Otherwise your life becomes a labyrinth of blind passages. With faith in your heart all things are possible, because to have faith, is to be sure of the things you hope for and to be certain of the things you cannot see.

Eternal Source of all true life, teach me to approach and accept, to use and handle the precious gift of life with great responsibility.

January 12 Ephesians 4:1-16

STRIVING FOR ADULTHOOD
. . . we shall become mature people, reaching to the very height of Christ's full stature (Eph 4:13)
Nature has its way and human beings develop and grow from infancy to old age. It does not follow, however, that a person's mental and spiritual development keeps pace with his body. This calls for dedicated work on our part.

In our quest for maturity it is necessary to have a norm by which progress can be measured. To Paul this norm was nothing less than the perfection and maturity of Jesus Christ himself.

It may seem arrogant to look up to Jesus Christ and to decide to emulate Him and to reveal his perfect balance and maturity in your daily life. But to strive for anything less, is to lower the standards of Christian discipleship. The challenge to reach such a high and perfect ideal should be both an inspiration and a comfort. When you realize the difference between what you are and what Christ is, you may become so despondent that you may cease trying.

However, through his love and the Holy Spirit, He works the strong desire in your heart to strive for perfection. You have only to be constantly aware of your total reliance upon Him and draw your strength from the source He makes available to you every day.

Lord Jesus, thank you that by your example and grace I can know the joy of a life of victory.

January 13   Proverbs 3:1-10

PLANNING WITH GOD
Trust in the Lord with all your heart. Never rely on what you think you know. Remember the Lord in everything you do, and He will show you the right way (Prov 3:5-6)
One can live only for today, or you can ignore your immediate needs and plan only for the future. Both methods are foolish.

To neglect using the present constructively, is to lose many opportunities. Many people dream great dreams for the future, but forget that the foundation of future happiness is created in the present.

Blessed is that man who sees visions of what he desires to accomplish and then prepares himself by doing the mundane but necessary tasks of every day.

Christ is not with you only in the present – He is also with you in the future. He sees your total life in full perspective. This truth should encourage you to plan your future in such a way that it will always be in harmony with his holy will.

To plan with God, often means to do a menial duty without immediately seeing the results. But during this time God is constantly busy accomplishing his will with your life.

Sometimes it is difficult to know what God plans for you. Especially at such times you must be loyal to Him and be prepared for any door which He might open.

Master, I accept your Kingship regarding my whole life, and pray that You will keep me aware of your guidance from day to day.

January 14 — Psalm 28:1-9

THE POWER OF PRAYER

Give praise to the Lord; He has heard my cry for help. The Lord protects and defends me; I trust in Him. He gives me help and makes me glad; I praise Him with joyful songs (Ps 28:6-7)

In spite of the unbelief and cynicism of modern man, God still works miracles. Each time someone is healed in answer to prayer, God has performed a small miracle.

Every time you find peace of mind after a period of dire stress; whenever your sorrow and affliction becomes bearable or is transformed into a song of praise – then a miracle has occurred.

Many people pray to God in a moment of crisis, but when the situation has normalized, they forget that they cried out to God and that He answered their prayer.

Many modern-day Christians have firsthand experience of miracles which have taken place in answer to prayer. Lives are transformed; the sick are healed; destructive habits are conquered; distorted human relationships are rectified. Untold numbers of people have experienced the guidance of God in answer to prayers of faith.

Bring every problem to the Lord in prayer and faithfully wait upon Him to act. If there is something you have to do yourself, do it without procrastination. Never be overwhelmed by despair, even in your greatest need. At the right time, and according to his wisdom, God will answer your prayers and you will kneel in humble adoration and surprise because of the way in which God comes to your help.

God and heavenly Father, I know that You are almighty and powerful to do so much more than we can imagine or pray for. Let this joyful truth lead me from day to day and put a song in my heart.

January 15 Jeremiah 18:1-17

TO KNOW GOD'S WILL
Go down to the potter's house, where I will give you my message (Jer 18:2)
Many people find it a real problem to know what the will of God is for their lives. But in his own good time and way God reveals his will to you. It often happens in the most unexpected place and in a singular manner, as in the case of Jeremiah.

You can seek the seclusion and quiet of a church, where past generations sought and found God. You can seek the quiet and peace of nature. You may have your own special place where, in the past, God has often become a reality to you.

God reveals Himself to those who search for Him – and it is definitely not dependent on a specific place. God can meet you in any place and under any circumstance. It may be on the mountaintop, where you glimpse his glory. Or it may be in the darkest valley, where you wrestle with your weakness and disbelief.

Jeremiah had to go to the potter's house to hear the voice of God. How powerfully God revealed Himself to Jeremiah in those strange circumstances. He was deeply convinced of the high calling and the responsibilities which the Lord had bestowed on him.

If you are sensitive and obedient, you will hear his voice and discover his will for your life.

I thank You, Lord, that I can speak to You at all times and under all circumstances. Make me sensitive to hear your voice and obedient to do your will.

January 16 Genesis 28:1-15

JOURNEYING INTO THE FUTURE
Remember, I will be with you and protect you wherever you go . . . (Gen 28:15)
Today is a new beginning, a point of departure! The decisions you make today, will influence all your tomorrows. It is only when you make a balanced evaluation of each separate day, that you can build constructively for the future. This kind of building calls for a plan. It is imperative to have goals in life to prevent you from becoming a traveller to nowhere.

If you intend living a worthwhile life, your ideals or goals must be great enough to serve as a challenge to make you rise above yourself and work towards them with single-minded purpose. Do not shirk trying to accomplish something extraordinary or novel. It is the only road to satisfaction, spiritual growth and maturity.

Your everyday tasks create unlimited opportunities to practise your faith in an ever-present God. Then even the most humble task becomes a divine calling.

Your faith becomes a practical reality when you strive to do God's will at the very spot where He places you in life. Then your faith is not simply an emotion reserved for Sundays. It is a powerful motivation to place all your talents at God's disposal and to live in the constant knowledge that you have the unchanging promise of his daily support and protection.

In this way you live from day to day with God – and for God!

Teach me to do your will every day and to tread your path, oh God, so that I will do my duty with joy and fulfil your purpose with my life.

January 17 Philippians 2:12-18

IN PARTNERSHIP WITH GOD
Keep on working with fear and trembling to complete your salvation, because God is always at work in you to make you willing and able to obey his own purpose (Phil 2:12-13)
What an overwhelming thought, full of inspiration and excitement: God is working in you! The challenging question is whether you are working with Him, or whether you are an obstacle to Him?

You may be vaguely aware of your purpose in life, but it may just not be clear enough for you to travel the road God has planned for you. Then you live according to your own desires and choices and not according to the divine will of God. This self-chosen road inevitably leads to disappointment and frustration. You plod along in your own insufficient strength along a path your own blind heart has planned, more aware of dismal failures than of glorious victories. Life itself loses its splendour and you fall into a dismal, humdrum routine.

When you admit with conviction that God is working in you, and you decide to obey Him steadfastly in all matters, you become a co-worker of God. When this happens, unbelievable and unexpected wonders occur in your life. Previous obstacles suddenly become opportunities when you approach the future in partnership with the living Christ.

Lord Jesus, on whom our faith depends, grant me dedication and consecration and a willing ear for your commands, so that I may constantly be aware of your will for my life.

January 18 Luke 9:23-27

SPIRITUAL UNDERNOURISHMENT
Will a person gain anything if he wins the whole world but is himself lost or defeated? Of course not! (Lk 9:25)
Everybody wants to achieve something in life; to taste the satisfaction of not having lived in vain. For this reason people set goals for themselves and work diligently, with the input of all their strength and talents, to realize that which they consider essential for success.

Many people acquire all that money and social prestige can offer: a steadily increasing income which generates a feeling of success; friends who can help to reach goals and positions and open doors to the correct social circles – these things become increasingly more important.

Nevertheless it so often happens that people who have achieved everything possible and who possess all the luxuries one can think of, still feel discontented. They become aware of a feeling that something of great importance is missing in their lives.

When possessions and material things become more important than God; when tangible things are more important than spiritual values; when a balance sheet becomes more important than honesty and integrity – then you are the victim of spiritual undernourishment.

No person who ignores God when planning his life, can be truly successful. It is when you grow to spiritual maturity in Jesus Christ that you come to understand the true aim and meaning of life.

Dear Lord, thank you for making it possible through your Holy Spirit to find sense and meaning in life and to be able to discern those things that really matter.

January 19 Ephesians 3:14-21

A GLORIOUS TRUTH
I ask God from the wealth of his glory to give you power through his Spirit to be strong in your inner selves, and I pray that Christ will make his home in your hearts through faith (Eph 3:16-17)

The riches of a life united with God transcends our wildest expectations. When you feel filled to capacity with his love, peace and power, you have only scratched the surface of the gold reef of his grace.

The only thing that can keep you from a richer experience with God, is your own inability to receive it. The greatest gift you can receive from God is a constantly growing yearning for Him. It sounds like a contradiction: if you know God, you experience his fullness, and as a result of this very fullness your desire grows to know Him more intimately. This is the work of the Holy Spirit in your life.

It is not only a passing emotion which settles upon you when you feel religious. It is a concrete act of faith in the indwelling power of the Spirit of Christ at those times when life seems to be falling apart.

You must continuously remind yourself: "Christ lives within me through his Spirit!" In due course you will believe it and will start living in his power. The Holy Spirit is the source of your inner power and strength. Praise the Lord for this glorious truth.

How will I ever be able to thank You adequately, oh Lord, that You have sent your Spirit to dwell within me. Give that this will become evident in my life and work.

January 20 Psalm 8:1-9

SELF-CONFIDENCE
Yet You made him inferior only to Yourself; You crowned him with glory and honour (Ps 8:5)

The Bible teaches us that conceit and arrogance are sins before God. But you can also sin to the other extreme: you can think too little of yourself. You can compare yourself to others, saying: I am not as clever, as strong, as handsome, or as talented as they are.

No person can live positively or constructively without self-confidence. Neither can you perform your God-given task.

Think of Joshua who received the practically super-human task to lead God's people after the death of Moses. How would he have been able to lead his people if he had constantly compared himself with the imposing Moses? How would he have been able to lead God's people into the promised land if he had always thought: I am not as great a leader as Moses. He was a true and great leader, a prophet, a man of God such as there had never been before. How can I, Joshua, take his place?

But God continuously encouraged him: Be strong and of good faith!

This encouragement should be reason enough for anybody to be self-confident – not because he thinks he is something special, but because he knows that God Himself has laid the task upon him. He also imparts the strength, the courage and the self-confidence to execute the task. "You give me strength to attack my enemies and power to overcome their defences" (Ps 18:29).

Compassionate Father, show me through your Holy Spirit what my task is and give me grace to do it in obedience and to your honour and glory.

January 21 James 1:19-27

A SENSITIVE EAR
Remember this, my dear brothers! Everyone must be quick to listen . . . (Jas 1:19)
The wise man Zeno said: "Man has two ears and one mouth to be able to listen twice as much as he speaks." Many people find it far easier to speak than to listen. Moments of silence embarrass them and they try to fill them with meaningless words and phrases. If one does not understand another's silence, one will never understand his words.

Scripture teaches us that there is a time to talk and a time to be silent. To find a healthy balance between the two requires real wisdom. Mere silence is meaningless. We must be constructively silent. This implies the ability to listen intelligently and with understanding.

This is especially true concerning our relationship with God. Prayer is not a monologue on my part. I must learn to listen to God so that my prayers may become an elevating and inspiring dialogue with God. If you develop the art of listening to God in the quiet, your inner ear will catch up his voice and you will regularly and expectantly plead: "Speak; your servant is listening" (1 Sam 3:10). His plan for your life will become clear and you will become more and more sensitive to his voice. In the silent hour with God you will hear wonderful things, if you are but willing to listen.

Living Lord, I thank You that I am taught by your Holy Spirit to listen. Let me recognize your voice clearly when I meet with You in quiet moments, and may listening to You be my greatest joy.

January 22 Isaiah 59:1-8

PRODUCTIVE PRAYER
Don't think that the Lord is too weak to save you or too deaf to hear your call for help! (Is 59:1)
For many of God's children prayer and meditation are hurriedly conducted and done with. This is the recipe for an unproductive prayer life.

Prayer is often considered one of the spiritual disciplines which can only be practised if one has sufficient time – a sort of insurance against accident and disaster.

Prayer is primarily the way to seek God's will for our lives, and not a means to bend the will of God to suit our own desires.

Before the full blessing of prayer can be experienced, the technique of prayer has to be mastered and practised regularly.

It is true that you can pray in any situation. It is also undoubtedly true that any task conscientiously completed, is a form of prayer. It is possible to become aware of God through a silent prayer even in the turmoil of city traffic.

But time spent alone with God in prayer is the foundation of a productive prayer life.

After a time of solitary communion with God, you can approach life with a calm and balanced mind. The moral issues of life become clearer and you are more aware of God's will for your life. You also gain the confidence to meet any crisis which may come upon your way, and to proceed on your pilgrimage with a song of joy in your heart.

Lord, let nothing rob me of the precious time I spend alone with You. I ask this through Jesus Christ, who is my Mediator and Saviour!

January 23 Psalm 90:1-17

CARPE DIEM
Teach us how short our life is, so that we may become wise (Ps 90:12)
Today is a precious gift from God to you. This does not necessarily mean that everything will run smoothly and that you will be free of temptation and affliction. But if you accept this gift of the Creator with gratitude, you will become aware of the grace and love He bestows upon you. He soothes your pain and straightens your path.

One can count one's years according to number or according to quality. When quality is the norm, a long life might in fact be short, and a short life long. When measured according to God's standards a long life without faith, blessing to others, love, labour and grace, will be very short. The quality of life depends on how each moment of every day is spent.

In his infinite grace and mercy, God allows you to decide what your "today" will be like. Possibly you have already thought of everything that can go wrong and started out with fear and trembling in your heart. Perhaps you are discouraged and despondent, even before your day has started. This pattern of thinking is counter-productive and forces you to agree with Job: "Everything I fear and dread comes true" (Job 3:25).

Trust in the Lord and thank Him for each new day!

Good Master, I thank You for the privilege of living this day to your honour and to share it with others. My times are in your hand. I praise your holy Name.

January 24 Esther 4:1-17

UNIQUE CREATION OF GOD
Yet who knows – maybe it was for a time like this that you were made queen! (Esth 4:14)
"Who am I?" is a question that cannot be avoided – one that is asked from the tender teens up to the ripe old age. The answer is simply this: You are the creation of God; He created you according to his image – even though sin has desecrated that image. You are royalty, a prince or princess, and you are called to live worthy of your royal heritage.

You are unique – God makes no duplicates. Scientists profess that no two leaves of a tree are identical. Would God not give his children an own identity, nature and personality? Nobody on earth can take your place. Therefore you may never allow your own unique person to be neutralized by a nameless, faceless mass.

The instruction to be yourself is not an excuse for vanity or self-exaltation, but is pure grace of God and a summons to live worthy and in self-confidence. You need not imitate somebody else's lifestyle. Christ is your perfect example.

A practical faith in Jesus Christ leads to the discovery of your true self. False vanity, inferiority which impede your spiritual growth, warped values which spoil your perspective on life – all these vices are conquered and purified by the power you receive from the living Christ.

I kneel in adoration and worship, Lord Jesus, so that You can teach me, through your Holy Spirit, to be myself.

January 25   1 Corinthians 12:12-31

EVALUATION OF THE BEST
Set your hearts, then, on the more important gifts (1 Cor 12:31)
It is only natural to covet the best in life. However, it is imperative to know what the "best" is, and to refuse to accept a substitute or to be satisfied with the second best. People often strive for a purpose which they consider to be the best, while God has a better and nobler calling for them.

A false sense of values often leads you to accept the second best. Thus you may consider possessions more important than a noble character; to receive better than to give. Or you may believe that you must extract as much as possible from life without putting anything back; that the end justifies the means; that only fools serve out of love!

To know what is best for you, you must know yourself. You must know what you are capable of doing, who you are, and what your potential is. It demands courage of a special quality to accept and acknowledge your limitations; to understand your faults and to confess them; to be resolute in your decision to live according to God's standards and aims: love, purity and unselfishness.

You will not always be able to comply with these high standards, but it will have such an impact on your life that you will discover that God's best for you excels everything you could desire for yourself.

Give me the wisdom, dear Lord, to be satisfied only with the best by striving after your values and principles.

January 26   Ecclesiastes 12:1-8

THE FUTURE IS DETERMINED BY THE PRESENT
So remember your Creator while you are still young, before those dismal days and years come when you will say, "I don't enjoy life" (Ecc 12:1)
If you are harbouring unworthy thoughts and living a life of fraud today, you must not expect to experience peace, truth and prosperity in the days ahead.

The law of cause and result is relentless, even for God's children. You cannot sow negative thoughts and expect to reap positive acts. Many people do not live – they simply exist. They cherish the idle hope that in one way or another, sometime in the future, life will grant them joy and fulfilment. Your future happiness depends directly upon how you think and act today. The present is a product of the past and it is already determining your future.

Today is actually the most important day of your life. For this reason you must develop your potential to its maximum each day. In this way you lay a strong foundation for the future. You also create happy memories for the day when today is part of your past.

Then you approach the future in a positive manner. With the living Christ as the focal point of your thoughts and emotions you begin to live creatively and enterprisingly. Your approach to the future is trusting, dynamic and positive.

Lord, help me to use today as a stepping-stone to the future through the guidance of your Holy Spirit!

January 27   Psalm 139:1-24

ENFOLDED BY GOD
You are all round me on every side; You protect me with your power (Ps 139:5)

It is a grace of God which denies expression: that He encompasses us with his love, that we may rejoice: "Immanuel" – God with us! How these words warm our hearts every time dark clouds of strain and affliction threaten to drive us to depression and despair.

The presence of God is not just a theory, but a concrete, practical reality:

God is above you – to protect you against the heat of the sun in the struggle of each day; also against the scorching rays of temptation;

God is behind you – to protect you against backsliding and to strengthen you to go forward in his power;

God is beneath you – to hold you up and to support you with everlasting arms when the battle rages around you;

God is in front of you – to lead you in the path of righteousness;

God is around you – to encompass you with his love and to protect you against visible and invisible enemies;

God is within you – to be the Way, the Truth and the Life, to supply all your needs according to the riches and glory of his mercy. God is everything to you, every day!

God is Immanuel – God with us – in Jesus Christ our Lord!

Lord, I kneel in speechless adoration before the knowledge of your royal presence in my life. I thank You that I may be your child.

January 28 Psalm 32:1-11

GOD HAS A ROAD
The Lord says, "I will teach you the way you should go; I will instruct you and advise you" (Ps 32:8)
God has laid down rules which govern your life. As an obedient child of God your aim must constantly be to follow his guidance.

God is a God of order and not of chaos. The confusion of humanity today is the direct result of disobedience to the laws of God. When you have committed yourself totally to God and diligently sought his will for your life, you will discover that your spiritual life will gain in depth and in growth. Your duty is to co-operate with the Spirit of God through Bible study, prayer and meditation.

Progressively you will attain a better knowledge of God and allow Him to control more and more of your life as his will for your life becomes clearer. Then you travel the road He has plotted for you.

At the outset his will may not be so clear and you will have to walk by faith. However, accept unconditionally the sovereignty and guidance of your heavenly Father, and you will be able to face the future with unbounded confidence. You will stand strong in the knowledge that God is leading you and watching over you.

Loving God and Father, help me to know your will for my life, so that I can obediently and joyfully be what You intended me to be.

January 29 Josua 1:1-9

A RECIPE FOR CONFIDENT LIVING
Remember that I have commanded you to be determined and confident! Don't be afraid or discouraged, for I, the Lord your God, am with you wherever you go (Josh 1:9)

Joshua was called by God to lead his people into a foreign country and to conquer it in the Name of the Almighty. What a super-human task! But God promised to be with him and to support him.

Ahead of you lies an unknown year and there may be hestitation in your heart. For some of us it will bring hardship and for others joy and happiness. Experience has taught that each year contains a mixture of both: the good and the bad.

Many of us will find ourselves on the mountaintop, riding the waves of success and prosperity. Perhaps we may experience the despair of travelling through a dark valley. As the year unfolds we will probably receive our share of joy and sorrow.

We must know how to cope with the different situations we will encounter. Only in this way can we approach the future with confidence.

There is only one sure way to approach the future without fear: we must live from day to day in the presence of the risen Christ. We must commit ourselves to Him from day to day; consecrate our lives to Him; seek his will for our lives and obediently live accordingly.

If you are willing to do this, you will not fear the future and you will proceed confidently and in the power and peace of God, your Father through Jesus Christ.

Lead, kindly Light, amidst the encircling gloom, lead Thou me on. Make me willing and obedient to follow You step by step.

January 30 Matthew 6:24-34

FIRST OF ALL, THE WILL OF GOD
Instead, be concerned above everything else with the Kingdom of God and with what He requires of you, and He will provide you with all these other things (Mt 6:33)

Some people cause themselves great unhappiness because they are extremely keen to solve the problems of the whole world. They believe that their convictions are the antidote to all the ills of our time. In their burning enthusiasm they forget that imperfection is part of fallen man's sinful nature.

It is impossible to build a new world without new people. Neither will it help to try and reform everybody else. The best reformation and healing begins with yourself. Draw a circle in front of your bed, kneel in the centre of it and pray to God to start a reformation within that circle.

It is difficult to face this truth, but before you are in spiritual harmony with God, it will be impossible to reform others. Jesus must first become King of your heart and life, and this will be revealed in your actions of every day and in your character. Only then will you start having a real influence on others. You must strive towards perfection in your own life, even though you often fall short.

You may never use the imperfection of human nature as an excuse. The ideal of perfection must be kept alive.

Let the Kingdom of God become a reality in your life and strive to serve Him in obedience and love, before you try to rectify the whole world. Not in your own strength, but in the power and grace of Jesus Christ alone will you succeed.

Lord, I place You in the centre of my life in the knowledge that all other things will then fall into correct perspective. I thank You for granting me the power to be victorious.

January 31 1 Thessalonians 5:12-18

GREET THE DAY WITH GRATITUDE
... be thankful in all circumstances. This is what God wants from you in your life in union with Christ Jesus (1 Thes 5:18)

It is of the utmost importance that the Christian should have a positive attitude towards life. There are, however, many factors which may cause one to have a negative view of life.

Lack of sufficient bodily rest may cause irritation and warp your whole outlook on life. Ill health may influence you in such a manner that it becomes difficult for others to live with you. On the other hand there are many invalids who set a striking example of joy and gratitude.

Your attitude towards life is of vital importance to yourself and to those with whom you share your life. The correct attitude to life is not simply a matter of course. From the moment you awake in the morning, you fall prey to your emotions. If you have slept badly, you face the new day with a jaundiced approach, and you are full of complaints and grumbles before your feet have even touched the floor.

It is imperative that you take positive control of your thoughts and emotions from the moment that you awake. Thank God for the glorious privilege of starting a new day. Remember consciously every blessing from his loving hand, which you often take for granted: your home; your loved ones; your work; your friends; and the multitude of other things for which you can thank God. Count your blessings and name them to God with a joyful heart.

When your heart is filled with gratitude, you can start the day with peace and joy.

Loving Father, grant me the desire and the wisdom to start each day with a thankful heart. Through Jesus Christ, my Saviour and joy.

FEBRUARY

PRAYER

Everloving Father

Only thirty-one days of the year have gone by, and here I am standing before You in shame to confess that so many of my good intentions for the new year have already ended in failure. "Neglect" can be written over so much of my precious time: I could have spent more time with You in prayer, to talk to You and to listen to your voice; I could have read from your holy Word more often so that my life could have been enriched beyond recognition; I failed to seek your will and do it obediently and joyfully. Thank you, Lord, that you do not only forgive, but, through the Holy Spirit, you create the desire in my heart to live victoriously –

to obey You better each day;

to follow You more closely on the way;

to serve You more loyally and

to love You without reserve.

Thank you, God, that through Jesus Christ, You have forgiven my past failures and have made all things new. Lead me through this month by your Spirit and for the sake of Jesus Christ, my Redeemer.

Amen.

February 1 Romans 12:1-8

WHAT IS GOD'S WILL FOR MY LIFE?
Do not conform yourselves to the standards of this world, but let God transform you inwardly by a complete change of your mind. Then you will be able to know the will of God – what is good and is pleasing to Him and is perfect (Rom 12:2)

It is easy to discuss the will of God, but it is an entirely different matter to know and to do the will of God. Some devoted children of the Father experience a very special relationship with Him, and they have no doubt at all as to his will for their lives. Others again, perhaps just as devoted, seem to be in a labyrinth of uncertainty as to God's expectations for them.

If you are busy seeking the will of God, stop for a moment in your desperate search. Ask God sincerely for "a complete change of your mind". Concentrate your thoughts and spirit upon Him. You must know God before you can know his will. Only then will you discover his way and follow Him obediently.

But above all – you must love Him with all your heart. Love is the key which unlocks the portals leading to his way for you. It gives you confidence to know that however great your love for Him may be, his love for you is greater.

When love for the Master and unswerving trust in Him, control your mind and make you spiritually sensitive to his guidance, his will is unfolded to you.

Wait patiently and prayerfully when you have doubts about God's divine will for your life. God guides those who do not become impatient.

Shepherd Lord, by love and trust I seek your divine purpose for my life. Let your Holy Spirit work freely in me.

February 2 Psalm 42:1-11

WHAT ABOUT TOMORROW?
I will put my hope in God, and once again I will praise Him, my Saviour and my God (Ps 42:5)

People want to know what the future holds so that they can prepare for it. There are so many things which people fear: old age, loneliness, distress, sickness . . . and death!

If, however, we could know what was going to happen in the future, we would possibly be so afraid that we would not be able to live in the present. God does not reveal the future to his children, but He teaches us in his Word how to cope with it.

Because God is eternal, there is no past, present or future to Him. Faith is to trust God with all your tomorrows with unyielding assurance. It banishes worry from your life and makes it possible for you to appreciate and enjoy the present in the knowledge that the future is in God's almighty hand.

You can live with the assurance that, if you are obedient to Him, there is a constructive and fulfilling life ahead of you. You are elevated above anxiety or petty speculation. You live in joyful expectation, ready to receive all the undeserved blessings which God has prepared for all his children in the future.

Live in the present: one day at a time! Become increasingly aware of Jesus Christ as a living presence, and you will not fear.

Loving God and Father, I know that You control the future. Teach me to live out this faith in a practical manner. Let me follow You into the future with faith in my heart. This I pray in the glorious Name of Jesus Christ.

February 3 Ephesians 3:14-21

INNER STRENGTH
I ask God from the wealth of his glory to give you power through his Spirit to be strong in your inner selves, and I pray that Christ will make his home in your hearts through faith (Eph 3:16-17)

It is astonishing to notice how many people neglect their spiritual growth. They will take infinite pains to develop their bodies and minds, while they totally ignore the needs of their spirit. They seem to be ignorant of the fact that the great motivating power of our lives is seated in our spirit.

A mean and petty person can never imagine the warmth generated by a knowledge of the love of God. In this way he misses one of the great experiences of life. He robs himself of a source of power and inspiration which can be equalled by nothing and nobody else.

When a person acknowledges the presence of God, he experiences his power and becomes aware of the beauty and riches of life.

If Christ is present in your life, it is impossible not to make yourself available to the influence of the Spirit of God. It is a life-changing experience with untold blessings. Your faith becomes a practical and exiting experience. Christ starts to live in and through you. Just as the branch obtains its strength from the vine in order to bear fruit, so you are attached to an inexhaustible scource of power. Christ controls your thoughts, emotions and actions. You discover an entire new dimension of living, because the Spirit of the living Christ gives you the inner strength to live to his glory.

Merciful Master, You are the real vine; may the power and love I receive from You be expressed in my life of every day.

February 4 Psalm 90:1-17

LIVE ONE DAY AT A TIME
Teach us how short our life is, so that we may become wise (Ps 90:12)
Yesterday is but a memory which we will never be able to bring back; tomorrow is a promise of which we are unable to know the content. All we essentially own, is today.

We should not be concerned about yesterday. Together with Paul we must forget the things which are behind us. Yesterday with its faults and anxieties, with its failures and disappointments, with its sorrow and heartache, irrevocably belong to the past. There is no hope of recalling them. To try to live in the past is self-destructive foolishness.

We dare not be concerned about tomorrow either. Tomorrow is in the hand of God. Perhaps there will be burdens to bear, afflictions, sorrow and pain, but when the time comes, God will supply the strength to cope with them. Tomorrow the sun will rise in glory – even though it be now hidden behind ominous clouds. Until it arrives we have no right to it, because it is still unborn.

Today is all that matters. No human being can handle more than one day at a time. It is not the experiences of today that cause us to crack: it is the self-reproach and remorse, the bitterness of things which happened yesterday, or the fear of tomorrow which ruin our lives. When we try to add the unbearable burden of yesterday and tomorrow to that of today – then we fall into despair and depression.

Grant me your grace, o Lord, just for today. I do not desire too see into the future – I want to walk the road You planned for me step by step and leave the past in your loving care.

February 5   Romans 8:18-30

GOD OF ETERNAL HOPE

I consider that what we suffer at this present time cannot be compared at all with the glory that is going to be revealed to us (Rom 8:18)

It is just natural that there will be sorrow when death enters a family circle. It is only human to love your own passionately and to experience their loss with pain and anguish. As Tennyson aptly stated: "But o for the touch of a vanished hand, and the sound of a voice that is still!"

It is the gift of grace and hope in your heart which, on such a sad day, changes your sorrow into silent joy, your doubt into assurance, and your loneliness into a holy communion of faith: ". . . so that you will not be sad, as are those who have no hope" (1 Thes 4:13). Hope is that expectation which fills our hearts with joy. It is the Christian's unswerving trust in the eternal goodness of God. Hope is one of the three immortal values, with faith to the left and love to the right-hand side of it (1 Cor 13:13). Hope is Christian optimism in its noblest form.

Without hope, faith is hollow and love without meaning. It is the anchor to which you can cling in any storm. It is the thin thread which keeps life from falling apart.

Hope gives you an invincible spirit. When hope lives, all things live. Hope ensures you that this life is but a prologue to the exciting book of eternal life.

When the world asks: "Are you afraid?", hope answers: "No, because the Lord, my God, is there."

God of hope, from whence I come and to whom I return, thank you for your Word which always brings new hope when storms threaten my very existence. Strengthen me in my undying hope, which is the legacy of your children.

February 6 2 Peter 1:3-7

A SOURCE OF DYNAMIC INNER POWER
God's divine power has given us everything we need to live a truly religious life . . . (2 Pet 1:3)
Each person needs a source of inspiration which will brighten up his life and be an elevating power when depression settles upon him. This source differs from person to person. Some find it in art and music; some find it in beauty and nature; yet another finds it in service to the community.

It is good to have a place, a person, a fountain of strength in times of spiritual weakness. Through Jesus Christ, God gave us the Holy Spirit to be our source of strength.

The spirit-filled child of God soon discovers that the Spirit is a limitless fountain of power. True strength and inspiration start when you meet Jesus and commit your life to Him. He is the perfect origin of power. When you know Him and love Him, you start to worship in spirit and in truth and your whole life becomes a hymn of praise to his honour.

Your faith in Jesus and your love for Him is constantly fed by the flame of the Holy Spirit. This is the foundation upon which your spiritual life is built. It is the origin of your inner power. From here his strength and love flows to every separate part of your life. In times when you are bearing a heavy burden, the Holy Spirit will grant you guidance, new hope and courage from day to day. Christ has promised: "When the Holy Spirit comes upon you, you will be filled with power" (Acts 1:8).

O Holy Spirit, fill my heart with power from on high, so that I will live in faith and love to God every day of my existence.

February 7 Philippians 1:1-11

GOD, THE MAIN ITEM ON MY LIFE'S AGENDA
I pray that your love will keep on growing more and more, together with true knowledge and perfect judgement, so that you will be able to choose what is best (Phil 1:9-10)
There are so many important matters demanding your attention and strength from day to day. There is the business you conduct; full-time

study for a career; the humdrum of housekeeping; the raising of a family; the care for the sick and elderly, and many other things.

However, one must never exalt these things to the highest good in life. You must place God first on your agenda of each day. He is in fact the First and the Last, "for all things were created by Him and all things exist through Him and for Him. To God be the glory forever" (Rom 11:36).

He deserves the highest priority in your very existence, not only because He has the right to it, but also because only then your life reaches its highest purpose and attains depth and quality.

If God is the prime fact of your life, He will influence every department of your being which is subjected to his will.

Honour God with your time, your talents, your possessions and your plans. Allow Him to reign supreme over every aspect of your existence. Then you will make the exciting discovery that, when God is placed at the top of your life's agenda, you gain a healthy perspective on living. This will bring peace of mind to you and your life will blossom.

Heavenly Father, teach me by your Holy Spirit that my primary task in life is to place You first. Do this in my life by the merit of Jesus Christ, who lived and died to bring honour to your holy Name.

February 8 Romans 8:31-39

A MIGHTY ALLY
If God is for us, who can be against us? (Rom 8:31)
You are possibly, at this moment, battling to overcome a sense of inadequacy and failure. The devil is so strong that you feel like a man fighting with one hand tied behind his back. You know that you must rise above each threat and yet you are afraid of imminent failure.

You will have to change your thinking entirely. You must concentrate on victory instead of on failure. You will have to convince yourself that, though Satan may be mighty, God is Almighty. If you want to live a truly victorious life, make sure that you are on God's side.

One cannot travel the road which your own foolish heart ignorantly plans and then expect God's blessing on your actions. Seek his will first and then order your life and actions accordingly. Your obedience and his power can gain untold victories.

Working in harmony with God, does not only cause singleness of purpose, but also cultivates the characteristics which are necessary to live a life of strength and conquest.

This joy you draw from the Source of all true happiness. You experience peace with God which no power on earth can destroy. Even in the most trying moments you enjoy the peace of God which passes all understanding.

Grant me the faith and sprititual courage, Lord, to anchor my life to You inseparably, so that I can live victoriously through your power.

February 9 Matthew 10:16-25

COURAGE – A CHRISTIAN VIRTUE
Everyone will hate you because of Me. But whoever holds out to the end will be saved (Mt 10:22)

Christ never promised that the Christian's way would be an easy one. On the contrary, He often speaks of bearing a cross. Possibly you have sometimes wondered whether it is worth your while. And yet, to whom else shall we go? If you have once had a true spiritual experience with the living Christ, you will never again be satisfied by the second best.

When you are passing through a dark period of depression in your life and you feel tempted to deny your faith, do not over-react. Identify the cause of your losing your grip on spiritual values. Be absolutely honest with yourself. Is it possibly a neglected prayer life? Or a lack of Bible study? Are you caught up in the company of people who do not benefit your spiritual growth? Has your consecration to the Master weakened? The fault, if you have courage to admit it, is never with God, but always with yourself.

In the renewal of your faith you must develop wings to lift you up to Christ. Leave behind all excuses and arguments which cause confusion in your spiritual life. Christ will never let you go. Reaffirm your faith in the living Christ. Be courageous and persevere, believing and trusting in the undying love of your Redeemer.

Dear Father, by your unlimited power and mercy I shall persevere and reaffirm my faith by a life of total consecration and commitment. Enable me through the power of the Holy Spirit in Jesus Christ my Saviour.

To have faith is to be sure of the things we hope for, to be certain of the things we cannot see.

February 10 Hebrews 11:1-6

STORM-BEATEN FAITH
No one can please God without faith, for whoever comes to God must have faith that God exists and rewards those who seek Him (Heb 11:6)

More than ever before, we are living in difficult and dangerous times. There is a universal feeling that the world is moving towards a climax. It is therefore necessary that you possess an immovable faith when everything around you starts crumbling. Only a person with an irresistable faith in the purpose of God with this weary world, can approach the future with confidence.

They who ponder life seriously, become increasingly aware of the fact that we are living in an unique and unparalleled time in history. All over the world humanity is yearning for the assurance that God knows, that He cares and that He is capable of doing something. Even though it seems impossible, this is still God's world.

In his search for spiritual assurance man has followed many paths and many creeds, and the teachings of Jesus of Nazareth have been interpreted in many ways. Many disciples of the Master live in great confusion. But Christ did not come to teach a new dogma or theological philosophy. He came to offer a new life to them who would accept it. He also offers the power of faith – a faith which will survive the onslaught of the Evil One.

When Christ is given the central place in your life and his Spirit controls your life, you have a foundation upon which you can build with purpose and assurance. The structure which arises on this foundation will withstand the powers of darkness.

My living Lord, thank you for the privilege of experiencing your peace in quiet moments. Strengthen my faith and lead me on your way.

February 11 1 Timothy 4:6-16

THE COURAGE TO TESTIFY
Keep yourself in training for a godly life (1 Tim 4:7)

It is impossible to be a secret follower of Christ, like Nicodemus tried to do. Either the secret destroys your discipleship, or your discipleship destroys the secret. Some people are afraid of talking about their faith.

Their religious convictions are so intimate that they are hidden even from their closest friends.

There may be many reasons for this attitude: some people are inherently shy and withholding; or the company in which you circulate may ridicule anything vaguely connected with religion; the danger may be real that you will be excluded from certain circles because of your religious convictions, or enthusiasm regarding your spiritual experiences may be the cause that you are branded as unbalanced. As a result you remain absolutely quiet about the most important aspect of your life.

If your faith is a cherished reality, you will be unable to keep it secret. Your life will reflect it. It is only when a person's life does not concur with his convictions, that he tries to hide the fact that he is a follower of Jesus Christ.

When Christ occupies the central position in your faith and religious expression and you are aware of your relationship with Him – like the branch in the vine – it is no longer important what others say or do. You know that you live through Christ and your ideal is to obey Him. It will be impossible to hide your joy and excitement and you will constantly be sharing the glory.

Jesus Christ, you are the Source of all my joy. Thank you for being a living presence in my life from day to day.

February 12 — Romans 7:12-25

DANGEROUS SELF-CONTEMPT

What an unhappy man I am! Who will rescue me from this body that is taking me to death? (Rom 7:24)

There are many people who feel inferior even before they start a new enterprise, convinced that they are doomed to fail. They believe they are totally incapable of spiritually becoming what God had intended them to be. They approach life with the assumption that they have already failed.

To persevere with such a negative self-image, is to rob yourself of the renewing power which the love of God generates in your life. If you continue in self-contempt because of sins which already have been forgiven, you cannot share in his healing love.

If you accept the forgiveness of God and rejoice in your redemption from sin, you have no right to condemn yourself. You are a redeemed child of your heavenly Father and you must approach life courageously and with self-assurance. You must proceed further than: "What an unhappy man I am", and reach: "Thanks be to God, who does this through our Lord, Jesus Christ."

When your self-confidence has been restored in this manner and Christ becomes a living reality in your life, you will be able to confess with Paul: "No, in all these things we have complete victory through Him who loved us" (Rom 8:37). Nothing, not even a weak self-image, can separate you from the love of God in Jesus Christ our Lord.

Lord and Saviour, in your power and by your forgiveness I do not despise myself any more, but I rejoice in my redemption from day to exciting day.

February 13   1 Timothy 1:12-20

A RECIPE FOR SUCCESS
I give thanks to Christ Jesus our Lord, who has given me strength for my work. I thank Him for considering me worthy and appointing me to serve Him . . . (1 Tim 1:12)

Certainly everybody wants to achieve success. Nobody deliberately wants to be classified as a failure. In modern society "success" means to reach your goals and as compensation, to receive and enjoy prestige and wealth.

There are many people who do not rise above the average in their profession: people without great bank balances, and yet they earn the respect of their fellowmen. Success is desireable and something to strive after, but it is much more than money, prestige or power. It is a quality of life which is cultivated through a nobility of spirit and obedience to God.

The Bible does not classify "success" as the highest aim or virtue in our spiritual lives. There are other qualities of greater importance in the eyes of the Lord. Before God declares a person a "success", He demands obedience and loyalty from him in all matters. God ignores human assessments and judges true success in terms of commitment and consecration to his divine will.

One can be a success or a failure in the eyes of his fellowmen, but in the final analysis the question is: has God found me faithful?

My greatest joy, dear Lord, is to do your holy will and to be faithful to You under all circumstances.

February 14 John 15:1-8

BUILD UP YOUR RESERVES
Remain united to Me, and I will remain united to you. A branch cannot bear fruit by itself; it can do so only if it remains in the vine. In the same way you cannot bear fruit unless you remain in Me (Jn 15:4)

Dynamic discipleship means to live in a "vine-branch-relationship" with the living Christ from moment to moment.

This does not only mean that you are totally dependent upon Him, but also that you are continuously growing dynamically. The life of a Christian disciple is never static or stagnant, but constantly growing in the awareness of the presence and the power of God.

It also means that you have a reserve of faith to uphold you in dark and difficult days ahead. Just as the magnate builds up financial reserves, they who are serious about their spritual life also build up reserves. If you remain in the vine like a branch, you are not dependent solely on your own reserves, but you can depend upon the vine in time of need.

No Christian is absolved from times of depression. Time when it seems as if God is far away and a God in hiding. To have assurance and faith at such times, you must have a reservoir of power from which you can draw freely. That is why you must remain concealed in God like the branch in the vine, so that his power may flow through you without obstruction and you may bear the fruit He expects from you.

Strengthen me, o Fountain of strength, and build my reserves in such a manner that I will be strong in times of testing.

February 15 Matthew 16:24-28

THE PRICE OF DISCIPLESHIP
Then Jesus said to his disciples, "If anyone wants to come with Me, he must forget self, carry his cross, and follow Me" (Mt 16:24)

Christ never sought popularity. When the crowds wanted to proclaim him king, He silently disappeared. When a talented, rich young man came to offer his services, Jesus confronted him with a challenge he would not accept. He sadly turned away from Jesus. Through the ages Christ challenges his followers to be disciples of the truth. Never did He make any allowance to convince anybody.

Whether the Master has called you to a specific field of labour which demands great sacrifices, or whether He called and placed you in familiar circumstances where you must serve Him in humility and without glamour – his standard remains the same. He asks for total commitment and obedience to accept anything the future may hold in store. This means you must trust Him unconditionally.

To consecrate your life to Christ is not always easy. The act of commitment is not a single, emotional act, but a living dedication from moment to moment – your whole life long. He who accepts this challenge, confesses that the Lord's way receives top priority and not his own. When you joyfully bear your cross and follow Christ unconditionally, you discover to your surprise that the cross was all along the instrument of your redemption and spiritual growth.

I want to bear my cross to your honour and glory, Lord, so as to be physically and spiritually strengthened to do your work.

February 16   Nehemia 6:1-14

MAKING CHRISTIAN DECISIONS
I answered, "I'm not the kind of man that runs and hides. Do you think I would try to save my life by hiding in the Temple? I won't do it" (Neh 6:11)
When one has to make difficult decisions, one is inclined to postpone or avoid them as long as possible. However, this attitude only results in uncertainty and self-reproach. To know a life of tranquility and peace of mind, you must look up prayerfully to the Leader and Finisher of your faith and make your decisions resolutely. The longer your postpone, the heavier the burden on your mind becomes. Then life becomes an agony and you easily fall prey to dejection and depression.

When you have to make an important decision, you must not turn away to try to evade it. It won't simply go away. Confide in God. Discuss it with Him prayerfully and in faith. Keep an open mind for the work of the Holy Spirit. He will lead you to discover God's will for you. He will also strengthen you to make the correct decisions and give you the courage to execute them.

There is a time to make decisions. If it is neglected through doubt or procrastination, the opportunity will pass with possibly indelible negative results. To decide and to act in obedience to God is the recipe for peace of mind.

Heavenly Father, I come to discuss with You the vital decisions of my life and pray that You will guide me through the Holy Spirit.

February 17 Lamentations 3:21-30

IN THE SCHOOL OF PATIENCE
The Lord is good to everyone who trusts in Him, so it is best for us to wait in patience – to wait for Him to save us . . . (Lam 3:25-26)

It often occurs that people become impatient with God. How terrible it would be if it were the other way round. People often feel, though they will never admit it, that they are losing patience with God. When they pray and their prayers are not answered within a fixed period of time, they doubt God's willingness and power to answer their requests.

Sometimes they become so impatient with God that they express their discontent with a Lord who does not seem to care.

To devise you own plans and then to pray for God's blessing upon them, is simply to use God as a rubber-stamp to legitimate your own desires. If you want the blessing of the Almighty, you will have to accept his conditions.

If the pace at which God works, causes you to become impatient, it is an indication that you prefer to act according to your own devices. When God lets you wait for an answer, it is possible that He is teaching you a lesson – a lesson which is of major importance to your spiritual development.

When you have learnt the precondition of subjecting yourself to the will of God, it brings fulfilment to your personality and enrichment of your Christian character. If God sometimes lets you wait for an answer to your prayers, be grateful and learn the lesson which God is teaching you.

God of grace and mercy, grant me patience while You are busy revealing your will to me.

February 18 Psalm 103:1-22

PRAISE THE LORD
Praise the Lord, my soul! All my being, praise his holy Name! Praise the Lord, my soul, and do not forget how kind He is (Ps 103:1-2)

It is good to sing praise to our God. Songs of praise should be heard in our worship, in our homes, in our gatherings, in our prayers and Bible study. God should be praised in our literature which is printed in such vast volumes, as well as in our discussions and our songs of joy. This should veritably be so, because that is the aim of creation. God is worthy of the highest praise. It is the duty and privilege of the Christian to glorify his Name.

Scripture is full of invations to glorify and praise God. The consecrated Christian has a burning desire to praise and thank God and to worship Him as the Almighty, the Creater and Recreator.

The Christian must understand why he praises God, otherwise his words are meaningless and irrelevant. Your circumstances may seem confusing and incomprehensible, but then praise and worship has a special meaning. You praise God because He is always with you, because He controls your life, and because He makes all things work together for the good of those who love Him.

Then your song of praise fuses with that of all creation in heaven and earth to become a never-ending and resounding chorus to his glory and honour:

"Praise the God of our salvation;
Hosts on high his power proclaim;
Heaven and earth and all creation;
Laud and magnify his Name" (Neander).

I will praise you, o Lord. As long as I live I will praise your holy Name.

February 19 1 John 2:28-3:10

CHILDREN OR ORPHANS
See how much the Father has loved us! His love is so great that we are called God's children – and so, in fact, we are (1 Jn 3:1)
Many people who pray "Our Father!" on Sunday, live like orphans during the week.

The Fatherhood of God is a thrilling Christian truth. It erases all differences and elevates a person above sin. Instead of simply being a number on a computer, you become a unique individual created in the image of God.

Unfortunately many people are unaware of this divine relationship and their inheritance, and spend their lives in ignorance as to what the power of God is capable of. Their lives are governed by the fear that they may deny themselves if they hand over their total life to God. As a result they are frustrated and live without inspiration for the present or hope for the future.

It is a tragedy to be created in the image of God, having the right to call him "Father!", and yet to struggle along from day to day as if He does not exist. All that is needed is to claim your filiation, to accept Him unconditionally and have faith in Him.

Your life will be so much easier and compensating if you stop being a spiritual "orphan". Accept Him as your heavenly Father. His loving arms are stretched out to enfold you and make you his own.

Father-God, let me rejoice in the blessed assurance that, through Jesus Christ, I am eternally your child.

February 20   2 Corinthians 5:11-21

ABOUT GROOVES AND GRAVES
When anyone is joined to Christ, he is a new being; the old is gone, the new has come. All this is done by God, who through Christ changed us . . .
(2 Cor 5:17-18)

There is only a difference in depth between a groove and a grave. That is why it is so dangerous to allow monotony to overshadow your life.

A positive way to guard against this danger, is to become intensely aware of life around you and of everything that is happening. Never ignore the welfare of your neighbour. Be courteous and notice the consideration other people show you. Never take the beauty of nature for granted. Appreciate every gesture of kindness because this can lead to lifelong friendship.

If you find life monotonous and without colour, you have only yourself to blame. Don't be uninvolved and insensitive to the excitement and wonder of life around you.

Steadfastly believe that, through the indwelling presence of the living Christ, you have the power not to fall into a devastating groove and that you can transform the monotony of each day into an exciting experience. If you are united with Christ you can never be cut off from the world around you.

Allow the Spirit of God to lead you and you will discover that the monotony will disappear from your existence – Christ renews everything every day and lifts you out of the groove before it becomes a grave.

I thank You, merciful Lord, for the full and exciting life I have come to experience through You, my Saviour and Master of my life.

February 21   Titus 2:1-15

THE POWER OF THE HOLY SPIRIT
He gave Himself for us, to rescue us from all wickedness and to make us a pure people who belong to Him alone and are eager to do good (Tit 2:14)
You may often be concerned about your lack of spiritual growth, but find it extremely difficult to admit it to yourself. Do you honestly and sincerely ask: "How can I improve my spiritual activity and stimulate my growth towards the likeness of Jesus Christ?" Nobody less than Jesus Christ replies: "What gives life is God's Spirit; man's power is of no use at all" (Jn 6:63). This is the great secret of growth and development.

While your knowledge and experience of the indwelling Christ deepen, his image is revealed in your life more and more each day. However, it only happens in direct proportion to your devotion and consecration to the Holy Spirit. When a tiny seed germinates, it has the potential power to tear rocks asunder and to overcome unbelievable obstacles in its growth to fruitbearing. Leaven also works in silence, but with dynamic power and effectiveness.

The source of this power is the Holy Spirit. The Spirit is the most practical and dynamic power in the universe. Thus you dare not plod along from one drab day to the next. The Spirit supplies the energy for spiritual growth. No supernatural experience is required to prove the truth of this – it is a gift from Christ to all his children.

Spirit of power and growth, come and dwell in me and support me in my growth to Christ.

February 22 Matthew 6:5-15

OUR FATHER ...
Our Father ... (Mt 6:9)
When we pray to God as "Father", we confess the quality of our faith. We acknowledge that there is but one God who cares for us.

The greatest liberation the gospel brings to the heathen, is the assurance that there is but one God and Father.

Previously they were enslaved to a multitude of frightening and hostile gods and spirits. Natural phenomena such as lightning, thunder, rain, fire and numerous other gods were worshipped. The child of God, however, need not live in the constant fear that perhaps he has inadvertently sinned against a host of unknown gods. He finds peace of mind in the knowledge that there is but one true God – the God of love whom we may call "Father".

When things such as danger, affliction, sorrow, suffering and death confront him daily, the Christian knows that his life and times are in the hands of a loving and caring God. Helmuth Thielicke says that man's life can be compared with that of a child wandering through a terrifying forest: there are frightening sounds, mysterious dangers and dark shadows. Man feels small and insignificant in his fear and anguish. He realizes that he needs somebody to walk with him and whom he may call "Father".

But we are not only taught to pray "my Father", but "our Father". Nowhere in this prayer we find "me" or "my". To be able to pray this prayer, one must confess one's relationship with all humanity. Jesus replaced the selfish "I" with the loving and intimate "our".

When we pray "Our Father", we also realize our true worth, because God has considered us worthy to call us his children. However many weaknesses we may have, we dare never despise ourselves.

I kneel in amazement before You, our Father, through Jesus Christ.

February 23 Matthew 6:5-15

IN HEAVEN ...
Our Father in heaven ... (Mt 6:9)
The words "in heaven" remind us first and foremostly of the holiness of

God. The Greek word *hagios* and our word "holy" both means "different" or "set aside". Therefore we should treat God's Name differently to all other names. His Name must receive a place which is absolutely unique.

In Hebrew a person's name is not only a word by which he is called. It indicates his nature, character and personality. Even though God is our Father, we must remember that He is in heaven and is elevated far above us. We can approach Him as Father with love and joy, but always with respect and worship, adoration and humility.

To pronounce that God is our Father "in heaven" also indicates the omnipotence of God. We acknowledge Him as all-powerful, righteous and holy. Human love can be intense – and yet powerless. In this prayer we join the love of God with his omnipotence. We may love somebody and yet be unable to help him. God's love is boosted by his divine power, which makes it possible for Him to do anything He wills at all times.

Consequently, when we think of our Father "in heaven", we kneel before his divinity and holiness, and we rejoice in his omnipotence which makes all things possible.

Holy Father, make me deeply conscious of your love which is supported by your divine power. It greatly encourages me in my struggle to live according to your holy will.

February 24   Matthew 6:5-15

HOLY IS THY NAME
May your holy Name be honoured . . . (Mt 6:9)
Here we are called upon to treat God's Name entirely different to all other names. "Holy" in fact means "different" or "set aside from all others". We are actually saying here: "Give us the grace to give your Name the unique place which your character demands and deserves."

This means that we must approach God with deep respect. The knowledge that God is my Creator and Sustainer, urges me towards Him and makes me look up to Him as the entirely different One, the holy One who proclaims: "I am who I am" (Ex 3:14). Then we know with assurance that we were created for Him and that our hearts will find no rest in the whole of the universe, except in Him.

We must realize who the God is that we worship. We must be aware of his holiness, righteousness and love. It will compel us to bow before his omnipotence in humility and to plead only upon his mercy.

We must have a constant awareness of his holy presence from moment to moment in our lives. It must be a tangible and real experience.

We must subject ourselves to his will and be obedient to Him. In this way we honour his Name. It has absolutely nothing to do with fear. God must receive the honour which his Name and character deserve. Not only in my prayers, but also in my life.

Thank you, Holy Father, that I know You are there; that You are holy and different; that You are always with me and that I can follow You obediently.

February 25 Matthew 6:5-15

GOD'S KINGDOM AND GOD'S WILL
... may your Kingdom come; may your will be done on earth as it is in heaven (Mt 6:10)

God's Kingdom originates on earth, where his will must be done just as perfectly as in heaven. To be a citizen of the Kingdom of God, we must be willing to do the will of God obediently. This is why Christ said that the Kingdom of God is within us. It demands the surrender of my will, my heart and my life. It is to say after the example of Jesus Christ: ". . . Your will be done" (Mt 26:42).

You can also say it in hopeless defeat, because you have nothing else to say. It is fatalism to believe in a blind destiny which manipulates people like pawns in a game. God is omnipotent. Therefore it will be futile to say or to do anything else.

You can also say it in bitter rebellion. Then you see God as your enemy, but an enemy who is invincible and cannot be conquered. You accept his will, but with reluctance and suppressed anger.

You can, however, also say it in love and trust, with the sincere desire to do his will as perfectly as it is done in heaven. Then you are assured in your mind of the wisdom of God and that He will do that which is the very best for you. You are also sure of the love of God – a love which wishes only the best for you. Then his Kingdom and his will become the highest good in life.

Lord, let your kingdom come; may your will be done in my life just as it is done in heaven.

February 26 Matthew 6:5-15

BREAD FOR EACH DAY
Give us today the food we need (Mt 6:11)
When we pray this prayer, we confess that we believe that God cares for our physical well-being. He is not only interested in the soul of man, but in all the facets of his existence.

We need not be anxious, because God cares for us each day – even in the desert he provided manna and quails, enough for every day. It is, however, not so easy to trust in God just for today, because the spirit of materialism demands that one will be sure of where tomorrow's bread will come from.

When we pray to God for food we need "today", we give Him in fact the central place in our existence and confess that we receive all the good gifts of life from Him. With this prayer we acknowledge our total dependence upon the Lord.

However, this does not mean that we can just sit back and do nothing. Prayer and labour go hand in hand. God has ordained that we shall earn our bread in the sweat of our brow. God supplies life and growth; we have to supply the labour. Only then can we ask our bread from God.

We must also remember that we are asking: "Give us today the food *we* need." From the abundance which God supplies to us, we have to share in love with those who are not as fortunate as we are.

Heavenly Father, I thank You sincerely for my daily bread. Please also supply in my need for the Bread of Life – Jesus Christ.

February 27 Matthew 6:5-15

FORGIVENESS – RECEIVED AND GRANTED
Forgive us the wrongs we have done, as we forgive the wrongs that others have done to us (Mt 6:12)
The first part of this petition restores our broken relationship with God, because He promised: "He will forgive us our sins and purify us from all our wrongdoing" (1 Jn 1:9).

The second part of this petition restores the broken relationship with our fellow-men. What we literally ask is: Lord, forgive us our trespasses in direct relationship to that which we forgive them who do wrong to us. There is usually a reason why a person acts in some special way: a difference in temperament; anxiety or pain; misunderstanding; heredity or environment.

We must learn to forget. As long as we brood on an injustice, there is no hope that we will ever be able to forgive. Only the Spirit of the living Christ can free us from the bitterness which prevents us from forgiving.

We must learn to love. This love enters our lives when we commit ourselves to Christ. He not only *told* us to forgive – He *demonstrated* it when He prayed for his persecutors while dying on the cross.

We have received so much forgiveness. How can we withhold it from others and still be children of God?

Loving God, I rejoice in the abundant forgiveness You have granted me. Grant that it will always be my desire to forgive those who trespass against me.

February 28   Matthew 6:5-15

DELIVERANCE FROM TEMPTATION
Do not bring us to hard testing, but keep us safe from the Evil One (Mt 6:13)

Nobody is exempted from temptation. It is a test of the authenticity of our faith and obedience. The very fact that we pray this petition, is a confession that we cannot conquer temptation in our own power. We can, however, triumph through the power of God. Each temptation we overcome by grace and in his Name leads to spiritual growth.

In this petition we pray for God's protection from the temptations of our own sinful nature and from seduction by others. God is not a powerless spectator at the scene of our temptations. He controls every situation and He has the power to save to the utmost. Satan has no other power than that which God allows him (Job 1:12; 2:6). Thus we pray that God will lead us in such a manner that Satan will have no dominion over us. We must know God's will for our lives so well that we will avoid dangerous and forbidden territory.

This petition pleads for protection and for the strengthening of our resistance against temptation. Only God can redeem us. We have no other refuge and that is why we confess our weakness and plead for protection against this danger. There is no temptation or seduction which we have to fear while God is our Protector.

Almighty God, thank you that I can approach life in the knowledge that You are my strength against the attacks of Satan, by the glorious work of my Redeemer, Jesus Christ.

February 29 (Leap Year)　　　　　　　　　　　Matthew 6:5-15

A SIGNIFICANT SUPPLEMENT
For thine is the Kingdom, and the power, and the glory, for ever. Amen (King James Version Mt 6:13)
According to authoritative scholars this verse was not present in the earliest texts of the Bible. Probably an enthusiastic translator could not resist to exalt the omnipotence, glory and greatness of God after translating Christ's beautiful model prayer. This is a significant addition to remember on this day which is added to the calender every leap year to adjust the time. An extra day to laud and glorify God.

　　God is King. King of the universe; King of heaven and earth; King of time and space. He reigns forever in his creation and in the hearts of his children. Everything is subjected to his will. He holds everything in his protecting hand.

　　When this dominion and care becomes a reality in our lives by the redeeming work of Jesus Christ, it brings peace and security to our lives. He has conquered sin and death. In his almighty power He raised Christ from the dead and thereby guarantees eternal life for his children. We eventually become heirs of the glory of God.

　　"Praise, glory, wisdom, thanksgiving, honour, power and might belong to our God for ever and ever! Amen" (Rev 7:12).

My heart desires You as King, o God; through Jesus Christ I live under your dominion of love; your mighty power carries me from day to day. My love for You is not a supplement, but an essential part of my worship.

MARCH

PRAYER

It is autumn, dear Lord, with its maturity and mellowness, with a brilliance of colours and shades.
Thank you for spiritual growth which takes place during the days of peace and fulfilment in the autumn of our lives.

O, Man of Sorrows, this is also the time of the year when we follow you on your "Via Dolorosa" – your road of suffering! Yes, it was for the whole world, but it was also for me. All your sorrow and derision, all your pain and affliction, each word from the cross of Calvary – even your God-forsakenness – was on my behalf. You sacrificed your life for me, even though I was not worthy of it.

In genuine gratitude I once again consecrate my life to you: body, mind and soul! Lead me through this month; help me to be a dedicated disciple and a courageous witness to your Name.

Through the cross, make me conscious of the vileness of iniquity and let me flee from sin forever. Through the cross, make me conscious of your eternal love in Jesus Christ, and let me lose myself in You.
Amen.

March 1   John 10:1-21

MY CUP RUNNETH OVER

I have come in order that you might have life – life in all its fullness (Jn 10:10)

Many people have the misconception that the Christian faith places restrictions on everything which gives pleasure in life: beauty, spontaneous laughter and every form of enjoyment. They think that if something gives you joy, it has to be sinful.

In a certain sense faith is restrictive, because it demands from you to repudiate matters which are detrimental to your spiritual life – those things which offer transient fascination and satisfy our senses, but eventually harm our spiritual growth and rob our Christian life of its quality.

When the Lord grants you the fullness of life, He demands that you acknowledge Him as Lord and Master of your life. He expects your total commitment to Him.

To many this demand seems impossible and unfair. Why be "religious" while you can enjoy life? A cruel disillusionment awaits those who think they can live according to their own desires without considering the consequences. Everything has a price and pay-day can become a dreadful reality.

When Christ has control of your life, you are able to look beyond the fleeting moment and find peace and spiritual power. Then you have abundance in Christ and you can joyfully say: "My cup runneth over!"

Grant me the wisdom, o Lord, to follow You obediently so that the profusion of your mercy can flow through my life.

March 2   Isaiah 55:1-13

RESIGN YOURSELF TO GOD'S TIME

"My thoughts," says the Lord, "are not like yours, and my ways are different from yours" (Is 55:8)

If you turn to God for help you must allow Him to answer in his own good time. God handles your crises and needs in an entirely different manner than you would.

Often we panic and turn to God in our distress. We murmur a hasty prayer and then expect God to perform the impossible in answer to our pleas.

When you put the power and strength of God to the test, you must faithfully wait upon his answer. He will never disappoint you. Don't simply prayerfully wait upon God's guidance, but be sensitive to his will for your life. You dare not prescribe to God. What He prescribes, you must adhere to scrupulously.

Such an obedience opens up new horizons time and again. Things start happening in your life which you have never even considered possible. You will experience God at work in an amazing fashion, and this will spiritually inspire you to new heights of achievement. Along the way you will discover the will of God and his presence will become a glorious reality in your life.

Loving and omniscient Father, teach me not to anticipate your will for my life or to bend it according to my plan.

March 3 — John 1:1-18

CHILDREN OF THE KING
Some, however, did receive Him and believed in Him; so He gave them the right to become God's children (Jn 1:12)
When the full impact of these words strike you and you experience their truth in a personal sense, it will give wonderful meaning to your life.

Maybe you feel dismally alone at this moment. Perhaps you are facing a bleak future and your self-assurance is at an all-time low – even depression threatens to engulf you. Now is the time to remember that you are a child of the almighty God – and this knowledge will change your negative attitude radically.

Because you may call God your Father through Jesus Christ and because He loves you and desires your love and obedience, the responsibility is yours to reflect his glory in your life through your total consecration to Him.

The more you live according to his will, the stronger the bond between you will develop. You will increasingly experience the joyful assurance that He is indeed your Father and that you are irrevocably his child. Never again will you be alone! In the love of your Father you will be able to see new horizons beckoning and find a new self-assurance which will change your depression into never-ending joy.

Heavenly Father, thank you for your immeasurable love which constantly surrounds me. I kneel in absolute amazement before the wonder and the privilege of being your child. I rejoice that this has become possible through Jesus Christ, my Redeemer.

March 4 James 5:13-19

PRAYER EASES THE BURDEN
Is anyone among you in trouble? He should pray (Jas 5:13)
If the many burdens and anxieties of humanity were to be pooled and then distributed equally among all the people, it is – according to the Greek philosopher Socrates – quite possible that we, who previously thought we had an unbearable burden, would prefer to have our own again.

Another wise man said: "I complained because I had no shoes to wear, until I met a man who had no feet!"

There are visible and invisible burdens. The physical ones can easily be seen: declining strength, old age, sickness, crippleness and disablement. The burdens of the spirit and the mind are not that easily recognisable, but they are therefore not less severe: lost happiness, foiled ideas, disappointment and worry, burning temptations and the unbearable weight of sin.

When your load becomes too heavy to bear, the best position to be in is on your knees. No way else can we be released from this destructive and never-ceasing power of sin, but to find ourselves in constant conversation with our Lord. God is always available! He invites you to bring your cares and burdens and to place them at the foot of the cross. Through Jesus Christ He assures us: "The prayer of a good person has a powerful effect" (Jas 5:16).

I praise You, Lord, for hearing my supplications. You are always ready to help in times of distress. I will shelter in your love and cease to fear.

March 5 John 8:31-47

KNOW YOURSELF
If you obey my teaching, you are really my disciples; you will know the truth, and the truth will set you free (Jn 8:31-32)

It is amazing to discover how many people are strangers to themselves. They act without being able to justify the reason why they do certain things. They say things which they do not really mean; they despise themselves for their attitude towards people who live and care for them.

Unless one is absolutely honest with oneself, you will never discover the truth about yourself. To find the truth is not a simple exercise, because man is a master in self-delusion. Hard realities are often being glossed over, pretty names are given to bad characteristics and habits: thieving becomes lending and sin becomes weakness.

It is only in the light of the Holy Spirit that one sees oneself – not as you would have others see you, but as you truly are.

The clearer the image of your true self becomes, the more you will realize that your life is not simply darkness and depression. On the contrary, the Holy Spirit gives you an insight into what you are able to become through his power and wisdom.

As you grow in self-knowledge through the truth and wisdom of God, your imperfections and inferiorities will fall away and step by step you will develop the habit of approaching life with self-assurance. The truth will finally set you free. Praise be to God!

Holy God, grant that by your wisdom and truth I may become what You intended me to be. This I pray through the power of the living Christ and the work of the Holy Spirit.

March 6 Deuteronomy 33:24-29

LONELY – BUT NEVER ALONE
God has always been your defence; his eternal arms are your support (Deut 33:27)

We all experience times of loneliness when we feel that nobody understands or cares what happens to us.

When this kind of despondency settles in your life, it often feels as if even God does not care about you. It now becomes extremely easy to start wallowing in the marsh of self-pity.

When loneliness drives you to despair and threatens your spiritual stability, recall and cling to the encouraging words of Joshua 1:5: "I will always be with you; I will never abandon you."

Place your hope and expectations in the loving and omnipotent God and always assure yourself of his presence. Gradually your confidence will grow and you will be aware that God is with you, everywhere you go and in everything you do.

Even though it may seem at times as if you have lost God, He will never let you go. His love for you is steadfast and eternal and He loves you just the way you are. He believes in you, even when you have lost confidence in yourself. His eternal arms are there to support you.

Do you fear the uncharted road ahead? Rest assured that God will never abandon you. He will carry you through every crisis of your life.

My heavenly Father, through Jesus Christ my Saviour, I praise your holy Name in the joyful knowledge that neither my feelings nor my emotions determine your presence in my life, and that your eternal arms carry me lovingly from day to day.

March 7   Psalm 139:1-12

SOMETHING OR SOMEBODY
... You would be there to lead me, You would be there to help me (Ps 139:10)
When people threaten to crack due to situations of extreme stress or strain, they are often encouraged to reach out to something which can stabilize their lives, something which will help them relax and give meaning and purpose to an otherwise dreary existence.

Maybe you have personally experienced such a situation: a radical change in your life, or an emotional shock which left you in despair in the wilderness, seeking for something which would alleviate your stress and improve your outlook.

There is no profit in searching anywhere else for something or somebody to hold on to – the only One who can provide genuine relief is Jesus Christ. His peace is available at all times, however great the strain. He is there, waiting for you. He tenderly calls you to come to Him with your burdens and cares. He will bring calm and peace of mind into your life.

Nothing in this world can be compared to his love. His power is unlimited: He stills the storm by commanding the winds and the waves. In his presence, peace reigns.

Allow Him to hold your hand and you can rest assured that He will lead you to still waters and green pastures.

Thank you, Lord Jesus, for enfolding me with your love when the strains and burdens of this life become unbearable. Without You there is no calm or peace in my existence.

March 8 Psalm 4:1-8

A KNOCK-OUT BLOW TO FEAR
When I lie down, I go to sleep in peace; You alone, O Lord, keep me perfectly safe (Ps 4:8)

It is impossible to have implicit faith in God and yet live in fear. If you allow anxiety to control your life, your faith will eventually disappear entirely. The choice is yours!

Absolute confidence in God is more than paying idle lip-service, a vague feeling of piety, or even a loose connection with the church. It demands of you an unfailing knowledge of the presence of the living God in your life. Only then will you be able to deliver the final blow to fear and begin to understand what genuine peace is. It is also impossible to keep this peace to yourself. You will inevitably touch the lives of other people and bring a blessing to all with whom you come into contact.

What an overwhelming thought! God's perfect peace can actually flow through you to other people in order to combat and conquer fear. "Courage is not the absence of fear: courage is the conquest of fear" (R L Stevenson).

By his divine love the Spirit of God will equip you for this service. Perfect love will ultimately defeat fear and once you have grown in this love, fear will never again have dominion over you. Thus you can finally claim the inheritance which Jesus left you: "Peace is what I leave with you; it is my own peace that I give you" (Jn 14:27).

Merciful God of love and peace, thank you that your Son, Jesus Christ, removed the cause of my crippling fear. Grant that my love for You will drive all fear from my life.

March 9 Psalm 55:17-23

A STOUT HEART THROUGH THE DAY
But I call to the Lord God for help, and He will save me. Morning, noon,

and night my complaints and groans go up to Him, and He will hear my voice (Ps 55:16-17)

The camel-drivers of the Sinai desert follow a fascinating and unchanging daily routine.

Every morning each camel is allotted the pack he has to carry for the day. This load can only be placed properly in position if the camel kneels. His master gives the order and when the camel bends down the load is placed on its back. Now the day's journey can begin. As the desert-day advances and the sun grows hotter, the load will often start to chafe if it was not correctly balanced. The poor camel's grumbles, protests and complaints soon inform his driver of his discomfort.

Therefore the master orders his camel at midday to kneel again so that the load can be evenly balanced and the ropes tightened. Now the camel can proceed in comfort.

At sunset the animal starts to grumble, protest and complain again. Once more it is ordered to kneel. This time the burden is removed and the camel can rest after the day's arduous labour. He also receives a ration of food to renew his strength.

In his upper-room Daniel knelt three times a day before his heavenly Master. This was the secret of his strength which enabled him to perform his responsibilities – David called to God in the "morning", at "noon" and during the "night".

God does not necessarily free you of your burdens, but in answer to your prayers He gives you the strength to bear them nobly.

Thank you, dear Father, that You hear my prayers and grant me the strength to bear my burdens joyfully and without fear.

March 10 Romans 8:1-16

BLESSED ASSURANCE ... I BELIEVE
God's Spirit joins Himself to our spirits to declare that we are God's children (Rom 8:16)

It is not because we are virtuous that God saved us and called us to his service. On the contrary! He saved us in spite of our waywardness and incompetence. God does not call the competent, but He equips those whom He calls to perform his will.

God found in us only sin and digression; but it is against this backdrop that his power and love are fully viewed. "He will not break off a bent reed or put out a flickering lamp" (Is 42:3). If you think of yourself as a towering oak, there is hardly place for you in the garden of God's mercy.

When we confess our weaknesses and shortcomings to God, we are actually taking the first step towards power: If we rely on his power, He will strengthen us: "'My grace is all you need, for my power is strongest when you are weak.' I am most happy, then, to be proud of my weaknesses, in order to feel the protection of Christ's power over me" (2 Cor 12:9).

By virtue of your faith, allow the Holy Spirit to take control of your life, and the living Christ will become an inspiring reality to you. Uphold unbroken communication with Him right through the day; allow Him to reach you through his Spirit. Then you will experience the blessed assurance that you are inalienably his child, heir to his power and love.

Lord Jesus, Master of my life, by the power of the Holy Spirit I rejoice in my being a child of God. I praise and thank You for this privilege.

March 11 Ephesians 4:9-16

PREVENT RETARDED GROWTH
And so we shall all come together to that oneness in our faith and in our knowledge of the Son of God; we shall become mature people, reaching to the very height of Christ's full stature (Eph 4:13)

To be as perfect and mature as Christ . . . that should be the purpose of every Christian-disciple, the ideal of each congregation, the church of Jesus Christ on earth.

One has no control over one's physical growth. It takes its natural course: from infant to teenager; from teenager to adult, and then old age.

Over one's mental growth, however, one has control to a certain extent. It is therefore your own decision whether you are going to develop your intellect to the optimum. By reading the right books, by doing mental exercises and by extending your frame of reference it is possible to widen your mental horizons.

Spiritual maturity, on the other hand, according to Paul, is possible only if "we shall all come together to that oneness in our faith and in our knowledge of the Son of God". In other words, our relationship with God and our fellow-men must be right. This can only be done by the power and work of the Holy Spirit. It is He who awakens the desire for growth in your heart and who enables you daily to grow to perfection and maturity in Jesus Christ.

Through your power and love, o Holy Spirit, I have come to know the joy of a conquering faith and a firm desire to reach the very height of Christ's full stature.

March 12　　　　　　　　　　　　　　　　　　　　　Job 19:1-12

IRRITATIONS – HANDLE THEM MATURELY
Why do you keep tormenting me with words? Time after time you insult me and show no shame for the way you abuse me (Job 19:1-2)

Nobody can escape the irritations of life. But there are those who get more easily annoyed than others. It seems as if these people enjoy and flourish on these little vexations of life. They are discontented, easily upset, impatient and intolerant by nature. They are known as difficult people and they pride themselves on it.

However, it is foolish and childish to allow people and circumstances to irritate you. In order to conquer this negative attitude, you will have to work at it positively and learn to handle your annoyances immediately and in a mature manner.

Irritations don't disappear simply because you say you are not going to allow them to affect you. You have to tune your heart and mind to God's will for your life and become conscious of all the positive and uplifting things around you. In this way a spirit of peace and harmony becomes an integral part of your personality.

If your concept of God is limited and inadequate, you will meet with irritations in practically every sphere of your life. If you consider God majestic and sublime, worthy of his being, you will gain the ability to cope with any irritation or obstruction.

View your life and existence in the light of the greatness of God, and you will realize that nothing is important or provoking enough to make you forget the omnipotence of God. In this way you gain equilibrium and peace.

I stand in speechless wonder before your greatness, o God, therefore I cannot allow petty irritations to rob me of my peace of mind. By the power of your Holy Spirit, release me from impatience and narrow-mindedness.

March 13   Luke 12:13-21

THERE IS MORE TO LIFE THAN POSSESSIONS
Watch out and guard yourselves from every kind of greed; because a person's true life is not made up of the things he owns, no matter how rich he may be (Lk 12:15)

It is only human to look for a scapegoat when things start to go wrong. Adverse circumstances, an unreliable business partner, unfulfilled expectations, and many unpleasant factors seem to join forces to make your life unbearable.

Whatever the circumstances, you may never try to side-step your responsibilities. Even if everything around you falls to pieces, you will only be considered a failure the moment you declare yourself a lame duck and acknowledge defeat. It is usually in life's darkest moments that true courage and character are revealed.

Achievement is not the result of a change in physical conditions, but of a purposeful resolution to reach your goal in life and to become what God intended you to be. This is only possible if each area of your life is subjected to the dominion of Jesus Christ. Problems prompt you to seek God's help. In his power you find the grace to meet and cope with the complicated issues of life.

Not to rely on yourself and your possessions, but to draw your strength from the power of God, leads to a creative and victorious life. This is abundantly more than all the riches the world can offer you.

I thank You, gracious Lord, that in You I have more than all the wealth the world can offer me, and that I can live purposefully and trusting in your bounty.

March 14   Acts 7:54-60

FAITH AND CHARACTER
But Stephen, full of the Holy Spirit, looked up to heaven and saw God's glory and Jesus standing at the right-hand side of God (Acts 7:55)

It is possible for God's children to reveal their faith even in facing the most trying circumstances. Consider the young man Stephen. The early church of Christ was growing, but so was the opposition against the church. Because Stephen was blameless in doctrine and conduct, men were bribed to witness falsely against him, and he was brought before the Council. "All those sitting in the Council fixed their eyes on Stephen and saw that his face looked like the face of an angel" (Acts 6:15).

When Stephen was stoned, he prayed according to the example of his Master: "Lord! Do not remember this sin against them" (Acts 7:60).

He had the inner conviction that he belonged to God. No persecution or affliction could deprive him of this belief. His faith was the determining factor of his life. He knew without a shadow of a doubt that everything that was happening to him, was part of God's perfect plan for his life.

What Stephen experienced, is also the share of all those who love the Lord with a sincere heart. Whatever your circumstances may be, seek to know the will of God for you. Even though the pressure is unbearable and the enemy overpowering, your faith will carry you to victory. One faithful and obedient disciple on God's side, is a majority.

Lord Jesus, on You my faith depends from beginning to end. With my hand in Yours I shall face life courageously. Keep me close to You so that your power can strengthen me. I thank You for this and praise your holy Name.

March 15 Exodus 4:1-17

EXCUSES LEAD TO IMPOVERISHMENT
But Moses said, "No, Lord, don't send me. I have never been a good speaker, and I haven't become one since You began to speak to me. I am a poor speaker, slow and hesitant" (Ex 4:10)

When God calls you to his service, you should never evade it by offering excuses. If God did not consider you capable for the task, He would not have called you. The problem is that most people underestimate their own potential and are quick to simply say: "I can't!"

Humans are also inclined to pass God's commissions on to somebody else. Because you continuously refuse to obey his demands, the voice of God eventually fades and his assignments diminish. God then starts to look for others who are willing to do his will obediently.

A sure way of losing your usefulness to the Lord and of becoming spiritually impoverished, is to refuse to commit yourself unconditionally to his service.

It is highly probable that the tasks which God gives you may seem difficult and even impossible. Do not let this cause you to fear or drive you to seek excuses. When God calls you, He also equips you for the task. Rather say: "With the help of God I will try!" In moments of weakness He will strengthen you. Don't look for shallow excuses, but accomplish his instructions in faith and joy.

Help me, gracious Master, not to seek excuses when You call on me. Grant me the wisdom and the courage to be obedient to your holy will.

March 16　　　　　　　　　　　　　　　　　Philippians 4:1-9

OUR MINDS INFLUENCE OUR DEEDS
. . . fill your minds with those things that are good and that deserve praise: things that are true, noble, right, pure, lovely, and honourable (Phil 4:8)
The disposition and thoughts of many people are determined and coloured by public opinion of events of the day. If the world news is depressing, they feel gloomy and discouraged. But as soon as circumstances improve, they feel cheerful and light-hearted. The thoughts and actions of these people are regulated by the situations in which they find themselves.

By allowing circumstances around you to influence you adversely, you are inevitably cultivating a feeling of impotence and helplessness. There is absolutely no stability in such an attitude, and you have no sound foundation on which to build. You are tossed back and forth like a small boat on a stormy ocean.

However, if the living Christ stands in the centre of your life and you focus your mind upon Him at all times, He will guide you on his glorious road. Should circumstances threaten to influence your peace of mind, try to experience the presence of Jesus in a very positive manner. Ask Him for the power to conquer anxiety, doubt and fear. Seek his will and you will find peace and calm in your heart and mind. Positive thinking produces positive results, especially when Christ is in control of your life.

O Spirit of God, blot out my negative thoughts and deeds and fill me with Jesus Christ and a sincere desire to obey Him. I praise You for your peace.

March 17 — Ezekiel 37:1-14

SPIRITUAL BANKRUPTCY

He said to me, "Mortal man, can these bones come back to life?" I replied, "Sovereign Lord, only You can answer that!" (Ezek 37:3)

One of the greatest tragedies of Christianity is that the religious life of a great number of good and sincere people has become insipid and powerless. They have retained an outward form of religion, but their grip on everlasting matters is weakening. They no longer enjoy that faith which once was the hallmark of their spiritual lives.

This spiritual bankruptcy can have many causes. It may be that you have neglected your prayer life or Bible study, that you no longer have time to go to church, or that you no longer spend every day as if in the presence of the living Christ.

If your faith has cooled or even died, it can never by any stretch of the imagination be God's fault. He is the origin and the source of life, and it is his desire to grant you the fullness of that life.

The gospel is a message of rebirth and new life. That which is dead, can be born again by the power of God. A faith which is burning low, can be fanned into flame by the breath of the Holy Spirit, and Christ will be glorified once more as renewed purpose, joy and satisfaction strengthen your spiritual life.

The indwelling Spirit of the living Christ then renews your faith and it becomes a glorious reality.

I confess, holy Master, that my spiritual life is often lukewarm and even cold. Purify my soul by the fire of your Spirit and fill my life with your abundant grace and mercy.

March 18 — Proverbs 16:1-11

DO IT GOD'S WAY

Ask the Lord to bless your plans, and you will be successful in carrying them out (Prov 16:3)

A popular song tells the story of a self-sufficient man who claims that the success he had reached in life, can be attributed to this one fact: "I did it my way."

These so-called self-made men are found in all walks of life. They boast that they have achieved success because of their own capabilities, resourcefulness and talents. The assumption that you can conquer the world in your own power, can have far-reaching consequences. Life's road holds many hazards and dangers, and these have ruined the career of many a promising person and consequently left his loved-ones and dependants facing terrible crises.

There is, however, a safer and surer road – God's road – where you do things his way! Ask the Lord to bless your plans and you will be successful in carrying them out.

You can place your trust in the Lord because you have his unfailing promise that He will always be with you. Why then try to do it all by yourself – your way?

Start today. Invite Him into your life and make Him part of your plans. Do everything according to his will, and you will not only taste success, but also find joy and peace of mind.

O Lord my God, I place my life in your hand and wait upon your guidance. Lead, Kindly Light, and make me willing and obedient to follow.

March 19 — 1 Corinthians 13:1-13

THE GREAT ESSENTIAL

I may give away everything I have, and even give up my body to be burnt – but if I have no love, this does me no good (1 Cor 13:3)

There is no substitute for love. There is nothing else that can take its place. Paul states this clearly in 1 Corinthians 13, the eternal hymn to love. One may be able to speak in the languages of men or angels; one may have the gift of inspired preaching; or all the knowledge a person can accumulate; or even all the faith to move mountains – but if you have no love, you are nothing at all. Nothing, but nothing, can compensate for the lack of love.

Love is the most dynamic power in the world. You can give it away to others, but nobody can take it away from you. And the more you share love with others, the stronger its influence becomes in your life.

Love curbs hatred and bitterness. Without the sacrifice of love, Christianity loses its deepest meaning. Without love, the spiritual life becomes cold and lifeless and one is incapable of reaching the heart of God or one's fellow-men.

The most outstanding example of practical love is Jesus Christ on the cross on Calvary. Even throughout indescribable suffering, his love shone truimphantly. Neither physical pain nor spiritual brutalizing could erase his love for us.

You can also rise above your suffering, disappointment and afflictions by allowing the love of Christ to flow through you to the world around you. It is only by committing yourself totally to the Lord that love, a gift of the Holy Spirit, bears fruit abundantly in your life.

O Source of all true love, when I consider the frailty of my love, I am forced to take my refuge in You. Teach me the true meaning of the conquering power of pure love.

March 20 Romans 15:1-13

VICTORY OVER SLEEPLESSNESS
May God, the source of hope, fill you with all joy and peace by means of your faith in Him, so that your hope will continue to grow by the power of the Holy Spirit (Rom 15:13)

How many hours do you spend in anxiety because you seek your peace elsewhere but in God? How often do you chastise yourself unnecessarily because you obstinately seek your peace and calm anywhere but in God? Your reward will inevitably be ulcers, stress and insomnia. Peace of mind is the quiet but deep-rooted assurance that you are safe and secure in God's care, and that therefore the opportunities of this world are far greater than the stumbling-blocks.

The moment you accept God as the source of your peace and joy, and acknowledge that you are irrevocably tied to Him by faith, you have given the first important step on the road to inward peace.

Because your spirit is in harmony with God, you can also live in harmony with your fellow-men. However, if your relationship with God is unsteady, it is impossible to retain good relationships with those around you. Few things have the ability to shatter one's peace of mind quite as much as living in discord with God and man. To correct this state of mind, a positive attempt is necessary to rectify one's relationship with the living Christ.

Once you have given your life to God, a wondrous thing happens: God Himself leads you to green pastures and quiet waters. All you have to do is believe in the redeeming power of our Saviour, Jesus Christ.

Teach me, o Lord, to let your peace live in my heart, and to share it with those around me.

March 21 Ephesians 3:14-21

A BALANCED SPIRITUAL LIFE
To Him who by means of his power working in us is able to do so much more than we can ever ask for, or even think of: to God be the glory ... (Eph 3:20-21)

Spiritual life covers many aspects, and to develop one facet to the detriment of the others, can cause a serious imbalance in your attitude and actions.

Many Christians develop an intense social awareness and spend most of their spiritual energy in communal and political activity. The result is that very little time is left for meditation and personal communication with God.

Others again avoid the social and political implications of Christ's instructions and concentrate only on their own spiritual development. They isolate themselves entirely from the world and what is happening around them. Their spiritual life simply remains on a theoretical basis and never becomes practical discipleship.

Both these attitudes eventually lead to spiritual instability. To have a social and political faith, with prayer as an insignificant appendix, or to live a spiritual life in which the application of Christ's love is renounced, is to fail as his disciple.

Because Christ expects it of you, you should become aware of the distress and suffering around you, and try to alleviate it where you can. Out of gratitude for what God has granted you, you should partake in the social and political issues of the day, gaining your strength and wisdom from Jesus Christ.

Lord, teach me to live according to your will. Grant that my example will lead others to You.

March 22   Mark 7:31-37

GOD'S PERFECT MODUS OPERANDI
And all who heard were completely amazed. "How well He does everything!" they exclaimed (Mk 7:37)

One needs tender fingers to touch painful wounds. If the wounds are still fresh, any touch at all is practically unbearable. Only the loving, pierced hands of Jesus Christ are tender enough to touch your wounds with healing power.

He never reproaches you. He does not forbid you to think about your sorrow. He simply calls you to view it against the greater wisdom of an all-knowing and loving God.

When you experience times of painful distress and it leaves you with little or no faith, it becomes so easy to rebel against God and shake your fists at heaven. At such times it is impossible to look up at Him and say: "How well He does everything!"

Everything? you ask. Even by allowing my suffering? Is it possible? Is this the tender touch of the loving Christ?

Yes, it is. And you dare not succumb to the blows that cut your back or the losses you suffer. Faith sees God's holy purpose in each bitter cup – and also sees the greatness of his love behind it: God is purifying you to truly become his child.

We know that in all things God works for good with those who love Him – even if it feels as though your pain is being sharpened on the whetstone of sorrow. Seek God's holy purpose in your painful experience and the light will break through and you will move out of the dark shadows into the brilliant light of his mercy and love. Only then will you be able to look back in peace and admit: "How well He does everything".

God of comfort, I sometimes question your love in moments of suffering. Thank you for your Holy Spirit who always leads me back to your love as revealed in Jesus Christ.

March 23   Matthew 6:25-34

THE CANCER OF ANXIETY
Can any of you live a bit longer by worrying about it? (Mt 6:27)

There are people who become extremely anxious just because they have nothing to worry about. Anxiety has become an inseparable part of their lives. Even when everything goes perfectly well, they soon find something which causes them to worry.

People are not born this way. It is a habit one gradually acquires. It is, however, not to one's advantage, because it robs life of its sparkle and warmth, it influences one's mind negatively if you persevere with it, and eventually one will be unable to think constructively.

However, the want to sincerely care for others, should inspire you to pray and act positively.

Any other form of anxiety does not befit a Christian. A follower of Jesus Christ has a positive faith at his disposal which can conquer all negative powers. Without this your life will crumble under the onslaught of negative forces. If you are suffering as a result of the damaging habit of petty worrying, when you imagine each situation laden with disaster, you should commit your life to Christ anew. Then once again, you will be able to see an opportunity in everything, instead of imminent disaster.

Heavenly Father, I praise your holy Name that through the finished work of Jesus Christ and the Holy Spirit, I can conquer anxiety.

March 24 Matthew 7:1-14

A SIGNIFICANT CHOICE
But the gate to life is narrow and the way that leads to it is hard, and there are few people who find it (Mt 7:14)
There are many churches who accept people as members without challenging them to a life of consecration and commitment to Christ. Such a church may proclaim an all-inclusive gospel, but it certainly lacks the fire of the Holy Spirit who makes us aware of sin, righteousness and judgement.

Many people profess that they are Christians, yet they do not live accordingly. They still hate; cause strife; live selfishly, and in many other ways deny the faith they have solemnly confessed. Surely they will feel safe and at home in such an accommodating church.

Christ warned that the gate to life is narrow and the way that leads to it is hard. Paul emphasised the same truth when he said: "Your hearts and minds must be made completely new, and you must put on the new self, which is created in God's likeness and reveals itself in the true life that is upright and holy" (Eph 4:23-24).

To be able to choose the narrow way and live by faith, demands acceptance of the sovereignty of Jesus Christ; the rejection of a comfortable and accommodating religion, and strict obedience as to the will of God. The reward of this choice is that heaven becomes part of your life even here on earth.

Protect me, dear God, from the danger of going along with a religion which makes no demands on my life. Give me the courage to meet the challenges of my faith.

March 25 Proverbs 22:1-12

THE GLORY OF SHARING

Be generous and share your food with the poor. You will be blessed for it (Prov 22:9)

The objective of millions of people is to amass material possessions and to gain social prestige. They believe that it is better to receive than to give. Their philosophy in life is that the more they can pile up, the happier they will be. It is true that great riches and prestige do leave one with a sense of satisfaction and a feeling of security. However, there are countless numbers of people who have these things in abundance and yet are unsure of themselves and deeply unhappy.

Every person who has found the true source of happiness, is firmly convinced that one is only truly happy when one is able to give. Businessmen are tuned in on profit, but only by supplying honest and reliable services, can they really be successful.

If you want to form lasting friendships, you will have to learn to give yourself. Scripture teaches us that he who gives generously, will receive generously. By giving, you are liberated from selfishness and greed.

Kahlil Gibran says in *The Prophet:* "You give but little if you give of your possessions. It is when you give of yourself that you truly give."

When you commit yourself to Jesus Christ, all things are seen in perspective and it becomes easy to share. With this new outlook on life you will soon learn how glorious and lasting happiness really can be.

Lord Jesus, I commit myself to You once again so as to learn the secret of true love.

March 26   Deuteronomy 33:24-29

GOD OF COMFORT

God has always been your defence; his eternal arms are your support (Deut 33:27)

Nobody can escape the sorrow death brings. We live in a world full of pain and suffering, disasters and death. However, there is One who can change darkness into light; who can heal the broken heart, and touch a wounded spirit with peace and calm.

"Let us give thanks to the God and Father of our Lord Jesus Christ, the merciful Father, the God from whom all help comes! He helps us in all our troubles, so that we are able to help others who have all kinds of troubles, using the same help that we ourselves have received from God" (2 Cor 1:3-4).

God does not guarantee that his followers will be free from sorrow, but He does guarantee his loving presence and power to comfort us in our struggles.

Faith is not a remedy for all troubles, but it offers us the grace so that we can strengthen ourselves in order to meet the challenges of life nobly. It does not remove the burden, but it gives us the ability to bear it. The thorn remains in our flesh, but his grace is sufficient.

Through the cross on Calvary we know that even the innocent in this world suffer, but also that God's comfort helps us to triumph over all our losses. This knowledge enables us to be worthy bearers of our crosses and strengthens us to take them up joyfully and follow the great Cross-bearer without complaints or self-pity.

Holy heavenly Father, You, who by your power can change the shadows of night into glorious dawn, comfort those who at this moment are passing through the valley of darkness.

March 27   John 6:60-71

DISAPPOINTED DISCIPLES

Because of this, many of Jesus' followers turned back and would not go with Him any more (Jn 6:66)

It seems incredible that someone can meet Jesus Christ, walk with Him for some time, and then turn away from Him – back to the old life without Christ. How is this possible?

To find an answer to this question, we will have to know why people started to follow Him in the first place. It is well known that there was a strong national movement in Palestine at that time. The inhabitants of the country were preparing themselves for the time when God would hand the country back to Israel. They lived in anticipation of that day. When they thus heard Christ speaking of the Kingdom of God, they were under the impression that Christ was going to establish an earthly kingdom.

When, however, Jesus started speaking of spiritual matters, the enthusiasm of his disillusioned followers started to wane. They did not understand the mission and message of Jesus at all.

There are unfortunately, even in our times, many disappointed disciples. They had initially sworn an oath of allegiance to the living Christ, and then waited for Him to work miracles for them. Their expectations were based on their selfish desires. When these were not fulfilled, they felt that the Lord had failed them.

In order to become a loyal disciple, the will of God must be considered as more important than your personal desires. It is only by being unfailingly obedient that you start to understand the depth and riches of true discipleship.

I praise your Name, Lord, as the Holy Spirit leads me deeper into the sacred truth of your kingdom. Make me willing to follow You obediently at all times.

March 28   Acts 17:16-34

CHRIST: THE CENTRAL TRUTH
Yet God is actually not far from any one of us; as someone has said, "In Him we live and move and exist" (Acts 17:27-28)

Should modern man want to question the gospel of Jesus Christ, he will find ample reason to do so. Two thousand years ago Jesus' followers mostly came from rural areas and He had to explain his message in terms of parables and stories which were well known to them. Today his servants live in an entirely new world – a world of computers and technology, and many people question the accuracy of the scientific and historical facts mentioned in the Bible.

But even though society has changed, the sinful nature of man remained the same. Emotions such as greed, lust, jealousy, hatred and anger are still as much part of modern society as they were in the days of Jesus' sojourn on earth. The spiritual demands Jesus made so long ago, are just as valid today as they were then.

Whatever your interpretation of the gospel may be, you should always remember this important fact: It is the living Christ who saves, and it is only through Him, and by God's grace, that you can receive eternal life. A personal relationship with Christ is more important than precise historical facts. The moment He becomes the central truth of your faith, you will no longer find it necessary to agonize over less important facts. This relationship necessitates a personal experience with Him; an experience of his love and power. You should move beyond theories and dogmas, historical and scientific facts, and proceed into the kingdom of personal experience and the practice of love. This is where Christ will meet you, and become a living reality in your life. Only then can you truly believe.

Lord, I thank You that You have come into my life, and for the knowledge that I am eternally anchored in your love.

March 29 Matthew 15:1-9

TRADITION AND RENEWAL
And why do you disobey God's command and follow your own teaching? (Mt 15:3)
Tradition is important for man. It colours and stabilises his daily existence and strengthens the moral foundation of many things which would otherwise have fallen to pieces in this permissive age.

Tradition can also be an asset in our worship. But we must guard against the danger of tradition becoming a purpose in itself. It should always remain a means to an end. If our thoughts can no longer rise above the traditions which bind us to the past, tradition can become an obstacle and hinder our growth.

Traditional Christianness can easily be confused with a true Christian experience. You may have inherited an outward form or structure, but you are only truly a Christian when, by the grace of God, you start living in a personal relationship with Christ.

However rich and inspiring Christian traditions may be, they can never replace real, purposeful commitment to Jesus Christ. And never should you allow the influences of the past to obstruct the work of the Holy Spirit in your life. By all means, enrich your spirit by upholding your traditions, but make very sure that God's will always has priority in your life.

I praise and thank You, eternal God, for my spiritual heritage. I worship You in appreciation for my new life in Jesus Christ through the Holy Spirit.

March 30 Matthew 18:21-35

CAN YOU FORGIVE . . . AND FORGET?
"Lord, if my brother keeps on sinning against me, how many times do I have to forgive him? Seven times?" "No, not seven times . . . but seventy times seven . . ." (Mt 18:21-22)

To say that you will forgive but never forget, is to keep old wounds bleeding and to allow your whole system to be poisoned by bitterness and hatred.

It is a pity people don't realize how much they harm themselves by keeping old ill-feelings alive, when they could have let go of them long ago. Smouldering hate or increasing bitterness have a destructive effect on the person who harbours them.

All you really achieve is to make yourself extremely unhappy, and inevitably you'll lose the battle against yourself. When Christ implores us to forgive seventy times seven, it is not an unrealistic or impractical order – He is simply protecting us against ourselves.

If you acknowledge Christ's point of view, but yet find it impossible to forgive, it would be good to remind yourself that Christ does not only call on you to forgive, but that He will also grant you the strength and grace to do so. To this end He placed the indwelling power of the Holy Spirit at your disposal.

Christ Himself demonstrated this vital truth to us when He prayed for those who nailed Him to the cross. As his disciples, we are compelled to do likewise.

Almighty Lord and Master, by the grace of the Holy Spirit I am able to forgive and to forget. I praise your holy Name.

March 31   Nehemiah 1:4-11

PRAYER IN TIMES OF DISTRESS

Lord God of Heaven! You are great, and we stand in fear of You. You faithfully keep your covenant with those who love You and do what You command. Look at me, Lord, and hear my prayer, as I pray day and night for your servants, the people of Israel (Neh 1:5-6)

Sometimes one finds oneself in a situation where an immediate answer is required in order to solve a problem. The best one can do is to follow the example of Nehemiah and seek refuge with God in prayer. Indeed, nobody else has as much wisdom as our Lord Almighty.

The way in which God answers the prayers of those who are distressed but trust in Him completely, is simply amazing. Prayer is the life-line which puts us into direct contact with God. He hears even before you make your thoughts known to Him, and He answers if you subject yourself entirely to his will. In this way He is honoured by your faith in prayer.

Prayers of distress, however, may never replace your otherwise calm and regular conversations with God. It is only when a crisis cannot be delayed that you may call to God in this manner – and then only because you know how to communicate with Him in normal times.

God is always willing to listen to the prayers which are wrenched from the hearts of his children. In such instances He is already lovingly waiting to answer. Sometimes one is surprised by the sudden and simple outcome of one's prayers. And very often one sets it down to chance, thus denying God's intervention. Therefore, the miracles of God often pass unnoticed while you suffer real spiritual loss.

Almighty God, I praise You for the assurance that my humble prayers reach You; and that You answer them according to your holy will, and that You always have my spiritual growth at heart.

APRIL

PRAYER

Oh Lord, our Lord, your greatness is seen in all the world. We worship You during this month as "Christ Triumphant"!
You have conquered death on Calvary!
You have broken the power of Satan!
The tomb is empty!
The Lord has truly risen!
Let the heavens proclaim his glory!
Thank you, Lord, that You obediently walked the path which ended in death, and that You were raised to life and sit at the right-hand side of God pleading with Him for us!
I thank You that I can join your triumphant march through the ages.
I know that, because You have risen from the grave, You have made it possible for me to rise above the damnation of sin to a new life with You.
Grant that I shall never forget your living presence; that I shall cling to the assurance that there is nothing in time or eternity that can separate me from your love.
Forgive me, merciful Lord, if sometimes I live as though You were dead.
I want to dedicate my life to You so that I can live each day of this month and every moment thereafter in the comfort of your promise: "I will be with you always."
Amen.

April 1   Luke 24:13-35

A CLOSER WALK WITH THEE
As they talked and discussed, Jesus Himself drew near and walked along with them (Lk 24:15)

After the crucifixion of their Master, Cleopas and his disciple-friend were left facing the sunset of their dreams and ideals, the dark night of despair. In their sorrow they had forgotten all the Master's promises. For them the road to Emmaus was a road of grief, disappointment and heartache.

When Jesus joined them they did not recognise Him. He was a stranger to them. And when Jesus started to explain what had been said about Him in all the Scriptures, He became the Prophet to whom they eagerly listened. However, it was only when He stayed over with them and enjoyed their humble hospitality, that they recognised Him as the Master whom they loved. This caused them to step out joyfully towards a new dawn.

For many Christians the Emmaus-road is a well-known track – they walk along with Jesus without recognising Him. Maybe they have so often listened to the explanation of Scripture throughout the years, that they do not realize the astounding impact thereof. The joy and happiness of total commitment have evaded them for many years, and is still not theirs.

But even while you consider Him a stranger in your confusion and distress, He remains your loving and understanding Friend. He is waiting for your invitation, and when you ask Him into your life, He brings with Him unparalleled gladness and blessings.

Lord and Master, I praise your holy Name because You have revealed Yourself to me. You have come into my life as Saviour and Redeemer, and You overwhelm me with your abundant blessings.

April 2   Romans 1:1-17

IN THE WORLD, BUT NOT OF THE WORLD
And so I write to all of you in Rome whom God loves and has called to be his own people (Rom 1:7)

Scientists tell of an insect which is surrounded by its own "atmosphere" so that, when placed in water, it never gets wet. If we are truly Christians, an unique atmosphere becomes part of our lives – it keeps us undefiled even though we are surrounded by a world saturated with sin.

We are "called" by the Lord. Amidst all the voices calling us to the world, there is also another summons – the call of God. Moses heard the Lord's voice as He called to him from a bush; David heard it while he was taking care of his sheep. Paul heard it on the road to Damascus, the prophets heard it – and so does every servant of Christ.

We are "his own people" – which means that we should be holy. Holiness is to strive against temptation and conquer it – all through your life, up to the very end. It is to allow God from day to day to control your life and to renew you by his Holy Spirit. This requires unremitting spiritual growth and progress.

We are "in Rome", the universal city, set up in battle-array against Jerusalem the holy city of God. It abounds of idols and pagan temples which distract our attention from God. Earthly honour and fame are elevated to the highest good in Rome. It is of vital importance to conform, and perilous to be "different": Rome, where Christ was crucified and the blood of the martyrs flowed. It is in this Rome – this city of the world – that we have to be Christians, even at a price, and we should never become one with the world.

God of grace and mercy, keep me close to You so that in spite of this sinful world, I shall remain your faithful child.

April 3 Matthew 25:31-45

FAITH, LOVE AND ACTION
The King will reply, "I tell you, whenever you did this for one of the least important of these brothers of mine, you did it for Me!" (Mt 25:40)
There is a type of religion which is based on theological speculation and wishful thinking, but has no significance in practice whatsoever. It never produces acts of faith and is therefore unfruitful and useless. Paul says in Galatians 5:6: ". . . what matters is faith that works through love".

If my faith in God does not lead to a deeper experience with Him, it is simply a pretended faith. God is the source of all true love, and if we believe in Him, his love will generate a practical faith in us which will result in deeds of faith and hope.

If Jesus Christ becomes a living reality in your life, you will do his will unconditionally.

Faith can only be alive and meaningful if it is born out of love and finds its expression in Christian actions. Without love, faith is superficial.

Faith must be inspired by and dwell in love. If your faith finds expression in love, your religion becomes a living reality. It enables you to forget about yourself and your own problems and to recognise a world in distress. Faith also becomes the source of your faithful acts – deeds of love toward the weak and the poor.

Then your faith will no longer be a theoretical speculation, or pious but meaningless words, but your actions will speak of love and gratitude for what God has done for you.

Holy Lord Jesus, through my love for You I have learnt how to serve my fellow-men. Grant that my faith will be of such a quality that your love will be reflected in my actions.

April 4 Jeremiah 23:33-40

ARE YOU READY FOR ANSWERS TO PRAYERS?
What answer did the Lord give you? What did the Lord say? (Jer 23:37)
After you have prayed, you should live in a spirit of joyful expectation. Many people receive nothing because that is exactly what they expect. Their spiritual life becomes routine, a humdrum existence laced with frustration and disappointment. And when their prayers are answered, they don't even notice it.

When you sincerely believe that your heavenly Father will answer your prayer, looking forward to his reply becomes a joyful experience. From this point of view an answered prayer can never be attributed to chance.

You cannot dictate God's answer to your prayer. It will only lead to disappointment and blind you to the miracles He wants to work in your life.

When God answers prayers, He does it in his own perfect way. He is not subject to your view as to how He should act. In his supreme wisdom He knows what is best for you. Thus, when you move into his holy presence with a worshipping heart, you have to wait patiently and obediently for his answer.

Filled with expectation you become a joyful and willing fellow-worker of the Almighty, and the answers to your prayers become an exciting part of your spiritual experience. In this way daily prayer becomes the gymnasium where you develop muscular strength for your Christian life.

Faithful Saviour, help me to be able to confess: Not my will, but your will be done, o Father.

April 5 1 Peter 5:5-11

CAN YOU COPE WITH ANXIETY?
Leave all your worries with Him, because He cares for you (1 Pet 5:7)
Each one of us has his quota of worries – it may be because of financial obligations; a loved one who has gone astray on the dark road of sin; an unsure future, or a physical ailment.

You can never side-step anxiety, and to be faced with it does not signify a lack of faith. On the contrary, a person who proclaims that he never has a worry, is either dishonest or insensitive.

It is, however, of major importance how you react when you experience anxiety. Worry can easily force you to panic, and most probably you will react impulsively and without thinking. This can lead to disaster and remorse.

Clearly identify the cause of your worry, so as to be able to approach it constructively. Do something about it. Ascertain whether you have a legitimate reason for anxiety or whether it is simply a figment of your imagination. Sometimes we are so afraid of the shadows even though there is no ghost.

Remember, as a Christian you never walk alone. The Lord has promised to be with you at all times. Share the cause of your anxiety with Him. Not simply in passing, but explain your fears to Him in detail. He will give you the strength and the wisdom to cope with your anxiety. Trust Him. He cares for you, and He is capable of helping in all circumstances.

Praise be to You, Almighty God, for holding me up and securing my faith in the darkest night of anxiety. Lead me through your Holy Spirit.

April 6   2 Corinthians 12:1-10

YOU ARE STRONGER THAN YOUR WEAKNESSES

My grace is all you need, for my power is strongest when you are weak (2 Cor 12:9)

The moment you admit that your weaknesses are stronger than your ability to contend with them, you subject yourself to the tyranny of your failings. All too often one surrenders oneself to the crippling influence of one's failures, while you should triumphantly be aware of the positive and powerful potential you possess because you are a child of God.

If you harbour such negative thoughts, you deny the love of God as well as his power and wisdom. He faithfully supports you from day to day so that you can grow in spiritual, physical and moral strength. If you don't grow you will never be able to overcome your weaknesses.

Never use your failings as an excuse. Try diligently to overcome them in the power of the living Christ. Prayer, Bible study and meditation play a very important part in this process. But the greatest power, which enables you to overcome your weaknesses, is a genuine experience with our Saviour and Redeemer, Jesus Christ.

When you regularly and faithfully admit that the Spirit of Christ lives within you, you will gradually begin to conquer your failings one by one. Eventually the power of God will be revealed in every sphere of your life. Through Him you can finally triumph over your weaknesses. "I am most happy, then, to be proud of my weaknesses, in order to feel the protection of Christ's power over me" (2 Cor 12:9).

I want to conquer my weaknesses, Lord, not in my own strength, but in your almighty power. Help me do so by the work of the Holy Spirit in me.

April 7   Isaiah 40:27-31

SOLACE IN THE GREAT LONELY ONE

He strengthens those who are weak and tired. Even those who are young grow weak . . . But those who trust the Lord for help will find their strength renewed (Is 40:29-31)

Loneliness, despondency, depression, despair and a feeling of God-forsakenness are some of the most effective weapons in the arsenal of Satan. He uses them to victimize us, to make us doubt whether God knows about us and – if He knows – whether He cares.

To counter this subtle functioning of the Evil One in our spiritual lives, we must faithfully trust in God. In Jesus Christ He comes to our rescue when we are being sorely tried. Through his holy World He strengthens us and gives us all the help we need.

There are many kinds of loneliness and it is highly probable that you have already contended with one of them: loneliness in marriage, loneliness in old age; loneliness due to a sudden change; the loneliness of being "different" – and then that final loneliness through death.

However, Jesus grants comfort, whatever the reason for our loneliness. He is the great lonely One who once had to cry out his loneliness and God-forsakenness in order to assure us: "I will always be with you; I will never abandon you." Strengthened by this assurance, we know that we will still suffer loneliness at times, but that we will never be left alone. With the living Christ as our Redeemer we are not only released from our loneliness, but we also enjoy his fellowship.

I praise You, heavenly Father, for your promise that You will never abandon me; that You remain the same, yesterday, today and forever. Thank you for the blessed assurance that You know everything about me and that You care.

April 8   2 Corinthians 4:7-15

OPPRESSED BUT NOT DEPRESSED
We are often troubled, but not crushed; sometimes in doubt, but never in despair; there are many enemies; but we are never without a friend; and though badly hurt at times, we are not destroyed (2 Cor 4:8-9)

There are no instant explanations for the tragic events in life. We cannot judge them superficially. Problems arise without our being responsible for them, and we often become confused and rebellious. At such times we demand an explanation as to why something happened to us. In our confusion we even hold God responsible.

If we are honest and sincere in our search for a solution, we usually gain a new understanding of our problems. Through our trials and tribulations we come to grasp something of his love, mercy and forgiveness.

Then, together with Paul, we utter the language that speaks of a mighty faith: faith in an omnipotent God and loving Father; faith which is not based on our changing circumstances; a faith which knows without the shadow of a doubt: "His angel guards those who obey the Lord and rescues them from danger" (Ps 34:7).

Therefore we have to identify our problems and see them for what they really are, and in sincere prayer place them before our heavenly Father. Formulate your needs and requests clearly and honestly and then live in the conviction that God is greater than any problem we can possibly experience. If we express our willingness to obey Him and do his will, He will comfort us. Even amidst severe oppression, we shall never be depressed.

Heavenly Father, when my problems threaten to overwhelm me, when my view of the future is limited, teach me the truth about myself through your Holy Spirit. Strengthen my faith by the knowledge that, in Jesus Christ, You already have a solution to my problem.

April 9   Psalm 8:1-9

DISCOVER YOUR DEEPEST SELF
. . . what is man, that You think of him; mere man, that You care for him? Yet You made him inferior only to Yourself; You crowned him with glory and honour (Ps 8:4-5)

The view one has of oneself is of fundamental importance. It affects your attitude towards life as well as whether you will be successful or not. The same rule also applies to one's spiritual life.

There comes a time in the life of every Christian disciple that he is greatly burdened by guilt and remorse. Before you commit your life to the living Christ, you usually live according to your own imperfect standards, without ever considering the devastating effects of sin.

However, as soon as you accept the sovereignty of Christ, a new relationship with your heavenly Father starts to develop and gradually you become aware of the wonderful fact that you are his child. Sin now no longer reigns supreme in your life and you start to experience a spiritual freedom, which up to now you have never known.

Unfortunately many Christians – in spite of this newly found freedom – stubbornly keep recalling the sins of the past. Even though they rejoice in their new relationship with God, past sins are still given an undeserved place in their lives.

As child of God you have been delivered from sin and you have become a new being, striving for that which is good and noble through the Spirit and grace of God. You are a chosen one of God and with Jesus Christ, co-heir to his Kingdom.

O Holy Spirit, help me reach spiritual maturity to reflect the image of Jesus Christ more and more in my daily life.

April 10 1 John 1:1-10

HEALING THROUGH CONFESSION
But if we confess our sins to God, He will keep his promise and do what is right: He will forgive us our sins and purify us from all our wrongdoing (1 Jn 1:9)
It is impossible to grow spiritually if you persevere in building on the ruins of failures. One simply cannot wish away sin and sins cannot be conquered by pretending that they do not exist.

Sin is a terrible and destructive reality and you have to accept the challenge to destroy it root and branch.

When you acknowledge your sins, you have already taken the first step in gaining victory over them. Possibly you feel overwhelmed by the magnitude of your guilt and consider yourself unable to bear the burden. You are absolutely right. The perfect God is the only One who can forgive your imperfections and sins – if you honestly confess them to Him.

The good news is that God forgives sinners by the grace of Jesus Christ. He restores us to be his children. He sets us free from feelings of guilt and establishes his joy in our hearts. Thus happiness and meaning enter our daily existence.

Most Christians believe that God can forgive sins, and He verily does. However, they find it difficult to forgive themselves – and are surprised that sin remains such a terrifying reality in their lives. As God has forgiven you, you should learn to forgive yourself.

Dear Saviour, support me through your Holy Spirit, so that in the darkest hour of remorse, I will be able to accept your forgiveness and live a life of victory.

April 11   John 1:1-18

WHO AM I?
Some, however, did receive Him and believed in Him; so He gave them the right to become God's children (Jn 1:12)

Feelings of depression and dejection – when everything seems hopeless, aimless and cheerless – lead to emotional crises and confusion. It is at such times that you usually have reservations about your identity and purpose in life. Even the value of life itself is questioned.

Changes in your circumstances of life, disappointment, ill health, the death of a loved one – these and many other experiences can throw you off balance and drive you to the depths of wretchedness.

When a situation arises where you begin to question the meaning of your very existence, you need only consider the glorious heritage which is yours: you are an heir of God and co-heir of Jesus Christ. This knowledge deepens the meaning of your existence and life itself becomes a wonderful experience. You will no longer assiduously seek for an own identity. The Lord offers you the only genuine identity – you are a child of the living God. Life itself can hold no greater meaning than just that.

Gentle Lord and Master, strengthen me through your Holy Spirit so that I will know without a doubt to whom I belong – and who I am. I praise You for making it possible for me to be a child of God.

April 12   Luke 6:12-16

CHRIST OUR EXAMPLE IN PRAYER
At that time Jesus went up a hill to pray and spent the whole night there praying to God (Lk 6:12)

Many Christians run the risk of underestimating the importance of prayer. It is not that they don't believe in prayer any longer – only that other matters are of greater importance. Prayer, to them, is an uncomfortable, inconvenient formality amidst a bustling existence, while it should actually be the dynamic force behind such a life.

Time and time again Christ emphasises the importance of prayer. Apart from his usual fellowship with God in prayer, He also spent entire nights in prayer prior to each crisis or important decision. This restorative seclusion filled Him with inner calm and self-assurance. He understood the perfect will of God for Him beyond a doubt.

If it was imperative for Christ to maintain such a devoted relationship with his Father, how much more is it not necessary for us! Prayer is the source of power in your spiritual life and work. Faith cannot be undermined if you are constantly strengthening your prayer life. You cannot stumble when you are on your knees. By praying at all times, the will of God becomes clear to you.

Ask God and He will grant you the wisdom and ability to cope with everyday life and to maintain healthy human relationships.

You may follow Christ also in your prayer life, because as in all things, He is the perfect example.

Holy Lord Jesus, help me give the same priority to my prayer life as You have given Yours, so that your will may always be revealed in my life.

April 13   Psalm 40:1-17

YOU ARE PRECIOUS TO GOD

I am weak and poor, O Lord, but You have not forgotten me. You are my Saviour and my God – hurry to my aid! (Ps 40:17)

You have probably experienced those moments in life when you feel so insignificant that you are truly convinced that it does not matter to God or man whether you exist or not. Perhaps this is exactly how you feel right now.

Then immediately say with David: "The Lord is thinking of me." Remember that He is your Creator. He granted you the gift of life. He cares for you and gives you a purpose in life. He is interested in who you are and what you do – and He loves you. Therefore you never dare give in to a feeling of inferiority.

The Holy Spirit will reveal the gifts and talents which God has given to you and He will teach you how to utilise them.

In Jesus Christ you have become one of God's children. He expects you to act like the King's child. To this end you have his love to support you when your strength becomes insufficient.

Allow his Spirit to guide you on the road to faith and trust in God. If Christ has dominion over your life, you will testify and work for Him with confidence.

You are a unique creature of God and He has a divine purpose with you. Therefore you dare not defame yourself. By committing yourself to Jesus Christ and by following the guidance of the Holy Spirit, it becomes possible for you to conquer your weaknesses and truly live a full life.

Heavenly Father, You have redeemed me through your Son, Jesus Christ, and therefore I do not want to think and act pitiably. Encourage me by your Holy Spirit to live a victorious life.

April 14   Isaiah 30:8-18

THE DYNAMIC POWER OF SILENCE

Come back and quietly trust in Me. Then you will be strong and secure (Is 30:15)

Mother Theresa of Calcutta wrote: "It is very difficult to pray when you do not know how. We must teach ourselves. The most important thing that we must learn is silence. People who pray are people who are silent. We cannot come into the presence of God before we have subjected ourselves to outward and inner peace. Therefore we must practise to be silent: with our tongues, our eyes and our spirit."

We have to find God, but we cannot reach Him amidst noise or clamour. View his glorious creation and see how the trees, the flowers, and the grass grow in absolute silence. We have to learn to withdraw ourselves from the everyday bustle and the noise of the world. We cannot reach out to God with the sound of cash-registers, the city traffic, and the battle-ground of the stock-exchange in our ears and hearts.

The more we absorb during the quiet moments spent in prayer, the more can be put back into life. After a quiet conversation with God, we are able to view the world anew. If we want to reach the souls of people, we certainly need silence. What we say to God, is not as important as what God says to us, and what He says to the world through us.

It is only when we have become completely humble, that God is able to hear that we can wait on Him in silence. Then He becomes more and I become less important.

If we cannot understand God's silence, we won't be able to understand his words either.

Merciful Lord, I thank You sincerely for moments of silence and privacy with You, and for your blessings.

April 15   Isaiah 60:17-22

PERFECT TIMING
When the right time comes, I will make this happen quickly. I am the Lord! (Is 60:22)
God's timing is always perfect. For this reason we must never become impatient. The more your life is committed to God, the clearer the perfection of his timing becomes to you.

Never in your impatience and haste try to force God to comply with your time-table. You simply see your problems in the light of the limitations of time, while God sees them from the perspective of eternity. God is perfect wisdom and He knows what is best for you at any given moment.

It is not always easy to accept God's timing. Often you become so impatient that you rush into his holy presence and demand an immediate explanation for his actions. You urge immediate action to, in your opinion, avoid disaster. At such times you become prey to the temptation of acting in your own strength and supposed wisdom. The consequence will be nothing but failure and sorrow. To synchronise one's timing with that of God, is a lesson each Christian has to learn. This is only possible if you remain in close contact with God and develop a living relationship with Jesus Christ. If his will becomes the major issue of your life and you allow his Spirit to guide you, you will see God's perfect blueprint for your life unfolding and you will find peace of mind and heart.

Eternal God and Father, I am so grateful that You remain the same yester-

day, today, and forever. Help me to be patient and not to try and rush your timing according to my desires. I prayerfully bow to your perfect will.

April 16   Revelation 3:14-22

THERAPY FOR LUKEWARMNESS
I know what you have done; I know that you are neither cold nor hot. How I wish you were either one or the other! (Rev 3:15)

Many people are over-familiar with the Christian faith. They were instructed in it from mother's knee and grew up with it. They utter impressive vows, but these vows never become a blessed experience.

Perhaps people are afraid of becoming involved and therefore they shy away from total commitment. They don't deliberately choose to be lukewarm or cold, it is simply that they don't allow the Holy Spirit to work unrestrictedly in their lives. At closer examination a short-circuit is revealed in their relationship with the living Christ, and they miss the power and inspiration of his Spirit.

A regular and meaningful prayer life brings you into close contact with God, and in this way you will be able to discover the will of God for your spiritual life. With the Bible as your guide, you will experience the excitement and wonder of travelling God's road. This inexhaustible source of power is available to you, and will regularly rekindle your life and actions in the service of the living Christ.

Communion with fellow-Christians whose hearts have been touched by the fire of the Holy Spirit, will also have an inspiring influence on the coldness or lukewarmness of your spiritual life. The closer you live to the fire of the Holy Spirit, the more heat you will radiate.

May the fire of the Holy Spirit set my heart alight for your service, dear Lord. Protect me from spiritual indolence and lukewarmness.

April 17   Psalm 13:1-6

FOR DARK AND DISMAL DAYS
How long must I endure trouble? How long will sorrow fill my heart day and night? (Ps 13:2)

Many of God's devoted children have experienced times when, in their despair, they have wondered whether God knows of them, and if He knows, whether He cares at all.

Such a dark period in your life may be followed by a revelation as to God's purpose with you. He compels you to come to a halt on your hurried way so that you can listen to his voice for a change.

If you feel isolated from God, you should place yourself under the spotlight of the Holy Spirit in order to become more sensitive to the guidance of God. You are also given the opportunity to consider how to serve Him best. Close to God one realizes one's total dependence upon his power and love, and He enables you to develop the talents He gave you. Eventually you will have to declare with David: "I rely on Your constant love; I will be glad, because You will rescue me" (Ps 13:5).

It is easy to have faith in times of sunshine and prosperity, when you are experiencing the presence of the living God in a very special manner. But the quality of your faith is determined when the sky above you is overcast with threatening storm-clouds and you feel entirely separated from God.

In order to grow spiritually you should continue to pray, even though you believe that God isn't caring or listening. When the world becomes a dark and lonesome place, remember: God is always there. He knows and He cares. Remain steadfast in your faith and you will receive unexpected blessings, even in the darkest days.

Lord Jesus, allow me to cling to God faithfully – according to your holy example – even in times of darkness and despair.

April 18 John 15:9-17

THE PRICE OF DISCIPLESHIP
And you are my friends if you do what I command you (Jn 15:14)
An innumerable number of people want to be friends and followers of Jesus – on their own conditions. They travel along the road their own blind hearts have planned, and do as they like, simply to satisfy their own desires. They even piously expect God to endorse and approve of their actions and to forgive their mistakes.

Such a faith is superficial and self-centred and falls apart when things become difficult. Christ is abused for one's own convenience, and therefore this type of faith can never lead to spiritual growth or a deeper insight into what it truly means to be a Christian disciple.

If you are sincere about becoming a regular follower of Jesus Christ, you will have to start living in total obedience to his revealed will. Your pride and selfishness may revolt against such a total commitment. If, however, you compare what you now possess with the fullness that can be yours when you become his devoted disciple, you will realize how utterly foolish it is not to be obedient to the will of God.

Obedience to Christ is not always easy. It goes against our sinful nature to be obedient. Neither is it always easy to know exactly what the will of God is. However, the more you grow in spiritual stature, the clearer his desires and will become. Strengthened by this knowledge you will be able to experience life in the fullest sense of the word and being a follower of Christ the Lord, will become the source of an indescribable joy in your life.

I praise your Name, Lord and Master, that obedience is the key to the treasury of God's blessings. I am able to commit myself to You and worship You, because You grant me the strength through your Holy Spirit.

April 19   Matthew 5:3-12

ASSETS BORN OF SORROW
Happy are those who mourn; God will comfort them! (Mt 5:4)
One is never simply delivered to the power of a blind fate. Everything that happens in your life eventually has a holy purpose and stands under the decree of God. He has an objective with your life, also with your sorrow.

> "I walked a mile with Pleasure; she chattered all the way;
> but left me none the wiser for all she had to say.
> I walked a mile with Sorrow and ne'er a word said she;
> But o, the things I learned from her, when Sorrow walked with me"
> (C E Elcot)

Death cannot be bribed; it cannot be prayed away. It empties your heart ... empties your home ... empties your entire world! The greatest loss life can hold, however, is that you may survive the hour of your sorrow without any permanent profit to your soul. There are certain fruits that can only be produced if it rains; there are certain experiences that only sorrow can produce.

Sorrow teaches you to understand and appreciate the love and comfort only God can provide. It makes you aware of the kindness and love which God works in the hearts of your fellow human beings. Thus, through sorrow you discover God and your fellow-men anew.

Sorrow teaches you that you are never alone in your pain and loss. You can always rely on God's consolation, and through his love He urges your fellow-men to support you.

Lord, I need your help, support and comfort in my sorrow. Take my hand and reassure me that this dark night will soon turn to dawn.

April 20   Philippians 2:12-18

MEETING YOUR SPIRITUAL RESPONSIBILITIES
Keep on working with fear and trembling to complete your salvation, because God is always at work in you to make you willing and able to obey his own purpose (Phil 2:12-13)
When, at first, you accepted the sovereignty of Christ in your life, you also accepted certain responsibilities.

God granted you redemption of sin through the finished work of Jesus Christ, but it is your duty to strive for spiritual growth, or else the peace and presence of the Master will constantly elude you. You cannot avoid or side-step this obligation.

To be able to meet your spiritual responsibilities, you will have to maintain a healthy and dynamic prayer life. The Lord is always available, but time must be taken to meet and communicate with Him. If your communion with Him is neglected, you are actually scorning the opportunity to serve Him best.

To belong to Christ and serve Him as your Master is a truly joyous experience. But you have to acknowledge his dominion over your life, and commit yourself by living and practising as a dedicated witness of his love. To profess that you love Him, and still live in enmity and hostility with your fellow-men, or to bear a grudge against someone, is a public denial of your love for God. A healthy relationship with the Lord demands a love which has no limitations or conditions. It is your responsibility to grow to Christian maturity and radiate his love in that part of the world you occupy. In your sincere efforts you will be strengthened and sustained by the Holy Spirit.

Heavenly Father, I worship You for the privilege of being your child, and I don't want to shirk my responsibilities. Grant that your Spirit lead me in faith and love.

April 21 Matthew 6:1-4

IN THE LIMELIGHT OR BEHIND THE CURTAINS?
Make certain you do not perform your religious duties in public so that people will see what you do. If you do these things publicly, you will not have any reward from your Father in heaven (Mt 6:1)

Some people thrive only in the limelight. Otherwise, in private, they perform no work of any quality. Against this attitude Christ directs a very clear admonition.

He prefers quiet and unobtrusive ministrations as regards our fellowmen, service without the fanfare. It is a simple truth that most of God's work is done by humble people whose names never reach the headlines – people who often work without any recognition or appreciation.

However, these very people serve God with a joy which is born of their love for their Master. They ask no more than the satisfaction of knowing that they are doing his will. Their strength lies in their quiet dedication. They don't live for the applause and honour of men, but only to please God and fulfil his purposes.

To these devoted people no task is too humble or insignificant if it is being done to his honour and glory, or if it contributes to the expansion of his Kingdom on earth.

The moment a price-tag is attached to your service concerning the Lord or your fellow-man, it becomes forced labour, because your compensation will be determined by human standards. It produces no inner satisfaction or joy, is short-lived and unproductive.

If you follow Jesus Christ as the perfect example in service, your joy and compensation will be unparalleled when you hear Him say: "Well done, good and faithful servant."

Heavenly Master, make me willing to go wherever You send me, and to serve You humbly with the sole aim of doing your will.

April 22 Mark 4:35-41

MASTER, DON'T YOU CARE?
Teacher, don't You care that we are about to die? (Mk 4:38)
You stand small, afraid and distressed against the elements, the storm which the death of a loved one unleashes in your life. Your fear and sorrow drives you to unbelief, rebellion and despair.

This is what happened on occasion with the disciples of Jesus. They were panic-stricken and anxiously thought that Jesus was unconcerned about their distress. Their whole situation seemed hopeless. Only Jesus did not react immediately, that is, according to their timing.

At one moment our lives seem so calm and peaceful and we experience blissful communion; everything progresses according to our human desires. Then suddenly the storm breaks loose with unexpected violence and our faith is being tested to the utmost. Our trust in God is placed under severe pressure. In confusion and doubt we query: "Teacher, don't You care that we are about to die?"

Is there someone who cares? Is there someone who understands our sorrow and heartache? Is there someone who can answer the tormenting questions of our distressed hearts? Is there?

Yes. A thousand times yes. There is Someone who cares. God hears our anguished cries. In Jesus Christ He is with us in the storm, to enfold us with his love and comfort, and to protect us against the elements.

He is "omnipotent God" – He can calm the storm in our lives. In his good time He will grant us his perfect peace and quiet our raging spirits. Trust Him – He cares.

Thank you, almighty God, that I know from experience that You also control the storms of life and that You will give me peace and calm through Jesus Christ.

April 23 1 Thessalonians 5:12-28

THE MINISTRY OF ENCOURAGEMENT
We urge you, our brothers, to . . . encourage the timid . . . (1 Thes 5:14)
You only need to open the daily newspaper to see how highly achievement is valued in the times in which we live. The newsmakers and achievers are used to hitting the headlines because of their important role in society.

But there are just as many people, if not more, with hidden talents, who never reach the news because they are naturally reticent when it comes to publicity.

To also win these humble people for his Kingdom, God has ordained a special ministry of encouragement. Without superficial songs of praise, one has to indicate their inherent value, help them strengthen their self-esteem and conquer their feelings of inferiority and inadequacy.

You have to inspire them to develop their full potential and to use it to the advantage of others. You must encourage them to use their God-given gifts and talents so as to enrich the world around them.

When you help one of these sincere but timid people, you might not make the front-page news, but you have the comforting assurance that you have played an important role in the life of someone who would otherwise not have survived or attained success without your encouragement. Being faithful in this ministry will also bring joy and blessing to your own existence.

O Lord, my loving Master, support me in my ideal to always have a word of encouragement for the timid person.

April 24   Psalm 118:19-29

A PRECIOUS GIFT FROM GOD
This is the day of the Lord's victory; let us be happy, let us celebrate! (Ps 118:24)

The way you start the day, the disposition and attitude with which you get up in the morning, determines how successful your day is going to be.

Too many of us start the new day with negative thoughts and consequently it becomes increasingly difficult to derive the highest good. All too often we harbour unworthy and foolish thoughts and unthinkingly accept evil. Yet, even then it is possible to change your thoughts and attitudes by acting positively and praying for guidance and help.

Before you start each day, adjust your thoughts to be only positive. Wake with a hymn of praise in your heart. Thank God for a new day, the great opportunities and allow his Holy Spirit to guide you in glorifying Him right through the day. This simple act of worship will sustain you all day long and fix your thoughts on pure and noble matters.

If you meet God joyfully and with gratitude early in the morning, you will convey your gladness to all those who cross your way. Robert Louis Stevenson said: "When a joyful person enters a room, it is as if another candle is lighted." Christ did indeed say that we are like light for the whole world.

With the joyous songs in honour of God's Name in your heart, the most difficult task becomes easy, and your life starts to reflect Christ and his love. You will find yourself in harmony with your Creator and your fellow-men and your joy will carry you through the most trying day.

God of mercy, I praise and thank You for each new day. Let your Spirit control my thoughts and deeds. Grant that I may experience the joy which Jesus Christ has achieved for me.

April 25 2 Corinthians 5:11-21

GOD'S RECONCILING LOVE
Our message is that God was making all mankind his friends through Christ (2 Cor 5:19)

It is an amazing fact, but God sincerely wished to be reconciled with his estranged creation. Man was made perfect and good, according to the very image of God, but due to disobedience and rebellion, he drifted away from God, and the image of his Creator was marred beyond recognition.

It also seemed as if man was unaware of the catastrophe he had brought upon himself. He moved further and further away from God and the divine plan He had for man's life. Chaos, disobedience, hatred, licence and fear increased the rift between God and man to a seemingly unbridgeable chasm.

However, God still longs to restore his glory in man. He desires that his love, power, joy, peace and regenerative mercy will be evident in each person who accepts his salvation.

To reveal to man what he is able to become, God came and presented Himself to us through Jesus Christ. The King arrived in all his glory – Man without a flaw. Through his death on the cross God grants salvation and redemption of sin to all those who repent and accept Christ as their Saviour.

By an act of faith and total commitment, you can allow the life-giving love and strength of God to transform you into the image of his Son. Then life will take on a new meaning. Through the Holy Spirit you will come to know the joy of reconciliation with God, and the image of Christ will increasingly be reflected in your life.

Creator-God, I praise your holy Name for your redeeming mercy through Jesus and the Holy Spirit, and that I am privileged to benefit so abundantly from it.

April 26   Psalm 91:1-16

WHEN FACING SORROW
God will put his angels in charge of you to protect you wherever you go (Ps 91:11)
It is just possible that you are experiencing an emotional crisis right now: a loved one has forsaken you without any apparent reason; or death has tragically touched your family and left an empty place which can never be filled again; or your doctor has told you that you are suffering from an incurable disease. Whatever the circumstances, it remains difficult to accept that this is actually happening to you.

At such times one is inclined to become depressed. Nothing seems to make sense. Even when sympathetic friends try to comfort you with words of hope, it is all of no avail. Your prayers seem to be without purpose and you even start to question the value of prayer. In fact, you start to doubt the very existence of God.

In times of deep sorrow one must guard against the danger of becoming enveloped in self-pity. It will only contribute to the undermining of your faith and your estrangement from God.

Your behaviour in times of sorrow either accentuates your less noble characteristics or it brings you closer to God and strengthens your faith. If you sincerely believe that your heavenly Father is protecting you at all times, and will grant you all the love, comfort and courage you need, you will be satisfied to leave tomorrow, and the future, in his hands. He will take care of you. He will commission his angels to level the road for you. This knowledge will strengthen you so that you will be able to cope with your sorrow or distress.

Merciful Master, I am sincerely grateful that I can place my trust in You, whatever the circumstances.

April 27 Luke 23:33-43

CHRIST IN THE MIDDLE
When they came to the place called "The Skull," they crucified Jesus there, and the two criminals, one on his right and the other on his left (Lk 23:33) In the history of mankind the cross of Jesus Christ occupies the central position. We cannot ignore or pass it without becoming involved. Since that dark day that marks his cruel crucifixion, people have meditated upon the mystery of his suffering: What was its purpose and meaning?

To be able to understand Calvary does not so much demand an academic knowledge, however important that may be. When one has not yet entered into a personal relationship with Christ, his suffering and death seem like nothing but foolishness. But when Christ gains dominion over your life, you begin to understand the meaning of Calvary, and what it holds for you personally and for mankind as a whole.

Then you realize that the righteous do suffer and that the good die as a result of the power of Evil. In this mighty drama one sees how perfection seemingly falls prey to imperfection.

But you know that history does not end here. Because you are committed to Christ, you know by experience that you have discovered the redeeming power of love in the cross; the final victory when righteousness shall conquer all evil. Therefore, you bear witness to God's might to transform tragedy into triumphant victory.

Conquering and living Lord Jesus, grant that I will increasingly gain knowledge of your power and love, and that I will be a faithful witness for You.

April 28 Mark 14:22-31

A SONG IN MY HEART
Then they sang a hymn and went out to the Mount of Olives (Mk 14:26) A person who sings is a happy person. God ordained that song should enhance his creation. There is song in nature; the angels sang at the birth of Christ, and there will be song in heaven. Before Jesus went up to Gethsemane and Calvary, his disciples joined Him in a song of praise to God.

He could sing because his heart was in harmony with God and because He had meticulously carried out God's assignment. However, this does not mean that He found it easy, but the song of praise bears its own comfort, even in the darkest night. He could sing because his conscience was pure before God and because He believed that righteousness would prevail.

The song of Jesus testified to his obedience and subjection to the divine will of his Father. It bore witness to his willing self-sacrifice for the sake of others. By faith He was already visualising the victory over evil, and He could praise God for it in anticipation.

By his example Christ teaches us to rejoice in times of difficulties or distress. Our afflictions will not disappear, but we will receive the strength to bear them. When, by grace and trust, we have learnt to sing, we will carry a triumphant song of praise on our lips, even in the face of death. Jesus' life proved that this is possible if we live in obedience and consecration to God.

Lord Jesus, You know that circumstances often threaten to stifle the song in my heart. Thank you for your inspiring example and the power of the Holy Spirit which strenghens me.

April 29   Luke 23:33-49

THREE CROSSES
Two other men, both of them criminals, were also led out to be put to death with Jesus (Lk 23:32)
There were three crosses on Calvary that Friday afternoon – each bearing its own special meaning and message.

There was the cross that represents rebellion. It was that of the criminal who scorned Jesus and said: "Aren't You the Messiah? Save Yourself and us." He is the forerunner of all people who resist the cross; all those who are too proud to plead for mercy; people who reject Jesus Christ. This rebel died in sin, not because Christ could not save him, but because he chose not to be saved. He chose eternal death instead of eternal life through Christ. Through him we are divinely taught that one can be in close proximity to the Saviour, and yet be lost because of our stubborness and perseverence in sin.

There was also the cross of repentance and humiliation – the criminal on that cross found a new life in Jesus. He felt no bitterness and demanded no miracles. He asked no questions, but simply prayed for forgiveness. He only wanted Jesus to remember him. Jesus touched his life and purged him of sin and he became the first-fruit of Jesus' sacrifice and entered heaven joyfully.

The central cross bears the message of salvation. Jesus suffered on it and died for our sins. He saved the criminal, and He can save all who confess their sins and accept Him as Redeemer.

Crucified Christ Jesus, I come to You in faith and confess my sins. Grant me the pardon You earned on the cross for all people. I thank You and praise your holy Name.

April 30 James 4:1-10

OBSTRUCTIONS IN PRAYER
You do not have what you want because you do not ask God for it. And when you ask, you do not receive it, because your motives are bad (Jas 4:2-3)

There are so many stumbling-blocks which can render our prayers ineffective. When we are able to identify these obstacles and, as far as it is in our power, eliminate them, we will be able to practise a meaningful and blessed prayer life.

Sin can obstruct fruitful communion with God. Adam and Eve disobeyed God and because of their guilty feelings, they no longer had the courage or desire to face Him. When He came to them in the evening breeze, they fled and hid themselves from Him. Because Saul strayed from God, he no longer felt at liberty to talk to Him and rather consulted the medium at Endor.

Disbelief can nip prayer in the bud. Faith are the feathers in the arrow of prayer. Faith establishes the confidence which allows God's children to believe all his glorious promises.

Worldliness can be another obstacle in prayer. As soon as the world becomes too important to us, we lose our desire to pray.

Selfishness is yet another stumbling-block. We should utilize the Lord's gifts in his service. We should not always seek compensation or demand preferential treatment. A prayer based on selfishness is a sinful prayer.

Riches can also endanger our prayer life. It is possible that our material possessions can become so important the we forget God. All our earthly goods are rightfully God's, and should be entrusted to Him through prayer.

The only method to conquer these obstacles, is to persevere in prayer, asking for the help and guidance of the Holy Spirit.

Loving Father, You hear and answer my prayers. Help me to taste the joy of prayer through the Holy Spirit, who teaches me to pray.

MAY

PRAYER

Heavenly Father, during this month we joyfully recall the day of Pentecost when your Holy Spirit was poured out on all your children.
As always, Lord, You honoured your promises: You sent us the Great Comforter:
to be with us in our deepest sorrow and despair;
to be our Leader and Guide when we are unsure of the road we should travel;
to be our Teacher, who reveals to us your will for our lives;
to educate us in the love of You and our fellow-men;
to enable us to serve You in sincerity and humility;
to teach us to pray when we are at a loss for something to say.
Send your Spirit as a Flame, to purify me
of all selfish motives, all jealousy, bitterness, hatred, pride and my haughty self-esteem.
Send your Spirit as a Wind, to blow new life and growth into my stagnating and blacksliding spiritual lives;
Send your Spirit as Water, to cleanse me and wash me whiter than snow; to make me grow to maturity and holiness;
Send your Spirit like Dew, to refresh and to restore my strength and to enable me to live according to your will.
Renew us, oh Spirit of God, remould the lives of all Christian people, so that your will shall be done, your Kingdom shall come and your glory be proclaimed in all the world.
Amen.

May 1
Luke 24:1-12

HE LIVES! THE SAVIOUR LIVES!
Why are you looking among the dead for One who is alive? He is not here; He has been raised (Lk 24:5-6)

The Lord has truly risen and He lives. This truth is valid even in this age. The Lord who appeared to the two grieving women in the garden on the morning of the resurrection, is still a living Reality today – even though human eyes cannot see Him and hands cannot touch Him.

Perhaps you have a fervent desire to become aware of his presence. You may have spent long hours silently hoping that, in some mystic way, the Lord would reveal Himself to you. But your hope was not realized and now you feel deeply disappointed.

Nevertheless, it is true that He comes to you. He reveals Himself to his children in the most unexpected circumstances. Some may, for instance, become aware of his presence during moments of praise and worship.

It may also happen that, while struggling to resist a temptation which threatens to overwhelm you, you suddenly become aware of a power which takes hold of you and carries you to victory.

Or you may pass through a period of intense sorrow, and unexpectedly experience a comforting peace in your heart and mind.

The Lord reveals Himself to you when you need Him most: when you struggle with problems on the battlefield of life. He is waiting at this very moment to make you aware of his divine presence.

Heavenly Lord, I thank You for the privilege and the ability to call upon You in my desperate need, and that I know beyond any shadow of a doubt, that You are alive!

May 2
Colossians 1:9-14

GROWING TO THE FULL KNOWLEDGE OF GOD
Your lives will produce all kinds of good deeds, and you will grow in your knowledge of God (Col 1:10)

Are you also at times impatient with yourself because of your sluggish spiritual growth? Do you feel guilty and pained when Paul speaks of the wisdom and insight granted by the Holy Spirit to lead you to the full knowledge of the will of God? (v 9). Does it sometimes seem impossible to set sail for the deep spiritual waters? You know without a doubt that God saved you to live a life of power and love to the glory of his Name. And yet, despite this knowledge, you feel that your spiritual life has stagnated. Your relationship with God does not deepen, and you feel you have reached a spiritual *cul de sac*.

Perhaps you incorrectly expect to remain on the same emotional level as on the day of your conversion. Perhaps you are constantly seeking the extraordinary and because it does not happen every day, you start feeling spiritually inferior.

The deepening of your Christian life is a continuous process of growth, a gradual but steady progress – from day to day, year in and year out. Decide, especially in moments of depression, not to discontinue your growth in the knowledge of God and his mercy and love. Then your faith will elevate you above your feelings and you will be joyfully surprised by the growth He allows in your life. But then you must obediently follow the guidance of the Holy Spirit.

I worship You, Lord, as the Source of all true growth. I want to remain in You, so as to bear the fruits which will fit my redemption.

May 3   Lamentations 3:18-33

LIVE IN PEACE WITH YOURSELF
When we suffer, we should sit alone in silent patience . . . The Lord is merciful and will not reject us for ever (Lam 3:28, 31)
Some people cannot tolerate being alone for a single moment. They always have to be busy with some or other task, or be in the company of others. They never contemplate the mysteries and deeper meaning of their existence. If they suddenly find themselves alone, they fervently seek company or keep themselves busy with petty things, just as long as they can prevent being alone.

One thing is certain: you cannot escape from yourself. You carry your imperfections and fears, your feelings of inferiority and depression with you. Only when you have learnt to cope with them, do you find inner peace. Escape is no solution.

You can either enjoy inner peace and calm, or you can restlessly wander everywhere, forever searching. Do you live your life according to

God's prescriptions, or do you try living as others prescribe to you? Your choice will decide the quality of your inner peace.

Even then you can only live in peace with yourself if you can live in peace with God. You should never be self-satisfied and proud, because all your capabilities are a gift of God. When you live in harmony with God and obey his will, you will be able to make peace with yourself.

Then Christ will be your constant companion and loneliness will not scare you. You will derive great strength from your moments alone with Him.

Heavenly Father, protect me from the restlessness which will rob me of precious moments with You.

May 4   Romans 7:7-25

A HEALTHY SPIRITUAL SELF-IMAGE

What an unhappy man I am! Who will rescue me from this body that is taking me to death? Thanks be to God, who does this through our Lord Jesus Christ! (Rom 7:24-25)

God does not create any duplicates. You are a unique creation of God. Nobody is exactly like you are. It is this very variety in God's creation that makes life so challenging and exiting.

If you are suffering from a low self-esteem, you are in danger of trying to emulate someone else and then the following well-known words may become true of you: "Be yourself, I said to someone. But he couldn't, because he was no one."

It is a gift, by the grace of God, simply to be yourself. This does, however, not imply that you should be proud or arrogant. You should live positively, with the deep-rooted assurance that, within your limitations, you can make the most of what God has provided.

True self discovery leads to the conviction that it is futile to copy the life-style or personality of somebody else. Through the power of the Holy Spirit, you can realize your God-given potential.

Faith in Jesus Christ bears the fruit of joyous self-discovery. Only by faith can you conquer the feeling of false, foolish pride and inferiority.

Christ sets you free from sin so that you can enjoy the exciting adventure of self-discovery and live in the blessed assurance that, through his Holy Spirit, Christ lives in you.

I confess my sins and limitations, holy and merciful God, but I learn through the Holy Spirit and the merit of Jesus my Lord, to be what You intended me to be.

May 5 Matthew 7:24-29

THE TEACHER WITH AUTHORITY

He wasn't like the teachers of the Law; instead, He taught with authority (Mt 7:29)

Jesus was an influential teacher. Thousands followed Him, not only to see Him perform miracles, but to listen to his teachings. He must have had a clear, carrying voice, because He often spoke to large crowds in the open air. They could understand his parables, and his messages were full of hope and inspiration.

It is an irreparable loss to humanity that many of his messages were never recorded. Shorthand typists and tape recorders were unknown at that time. As a result, Christianity is so much poorer.

What Jesus said was of prime importance, but the spirit and style in which He taught, his attitude towards life and people, was of even greater importance. Through all his messages we can trace the golden thread of the gospel of joy: the unfathomable love of God; the need to forgive and love your fellow-men; the duty to live to the honour and glory of God. Love to God and man was the central theme of his teachings.

But to have high esteem and appreciation for the lectures of Christ is not enough by far. Truth is powerless until it is revealed in a person's life.

You may have an understanding of what the Master taught, but if what you have learnt does not become part of your practical everyday life, it is of little value. By the regenerating power of the Holy Spirit, God enables you to live according to Christ's example in word and deed. Then you are truly a Christian scholar and a witness to Christ.

Help me, dear Lord, to be a witness of your truth in my daily life, through the power of your Holy Spirit.

May 6
Philippians 3:1-10

SPIRITUAL PRIDE
If anyone thinks he can trust in external ceremonies, I have even more reason to feel that way (Phil 3:4)

As a confessed Christian you have the responsibility to live out your witness in a practical manner, so as to reflect the image of Christ to the world. If you hold a position of authority in a home, a community, an institution of education, or wherever, you have a responsibility which can only be met if you are aware of your total dependence upon God.

Spiritual pride is a very real danger against which we must constantly be on our guard. It is a subtle and destructive power which can render your service to the Master worthless. When God calls you to perform a specific task which demands leadership, you have a responsibility towards the Christian community, who trust you and look up to you for inspiration and guidance.

It is imperative to grow spiritually, in order to back up your increased responsibility. A breakdown in your communication with Christ, will force you to rely on your own resources of wisdom, inspiration and leadership. Remember the words of our Lord and Master: ". . . you can do nothing without Me" (Jn 15:5).

The greater the responsibility Christ delegates to you, the more important it is for you to develop a practical and meaningful prayer life. It is prayer, and not status or authority, which should be the driving force behind your service and witness.

If at times your responsibilities become an unbearable burden, remember that He who called you, is faithful and will equip you for the task He allocated to you.

I praise You, Lord, that You do not only call the qualified, but also qualify those whom You call. I trust in You to protect me from spiritual pride and to make me true to my Christian calling.

May 7
1 Corinthians 12:1-11

JESUS IS LORD
. . . and no one can confess "Jesus is Lord," unless he is guided by the Holy Spirit (1 Cor 12:3)

To confess that Jesus Christ is Lord of your life, is to commit yourself to a Christian way of living. It means, in essence, that you have totally consecrated your life to Christ, that you trust Him unconditionally, obey Him without question, and steadfastly believe in Him.

To live under the sovereignty of Christ does not guarantee immunity against temptation, failure, or sin. At one moment you may rejoice in your alliance with Christ, and the next be filled with dismay and alarm when you discover that you are threatened by severe temptation.

Yet it remains an overwhelming thought that Christ has dominion over your life and that He not only accepts you as you are, but also promises his support. He elevates you to a new relationship with Him and assures you that He will always be with you. He changes your life so that the world will be able to see Him through you.

He is your Lord, but He is also your Friend and through the work of the Holy Spirit in you, you become his co-heir.

This divine acceptance, after you have committed and dedicated yourself to Him, is the guarantee of God's love and presence in your life. Now you can confess: Jesus is Lord. I am His and He is mine.

If you accept this truth, you will experience the glorious results of a life committed to God.

Lord Jesus, I place my total life under your divine dominion. I worship You as Lord of the universe, but also of my life.

May 8 1 Corinthians 3:9-23

DWELLING OF THE SPIRIT
Surely you know that you are God's temple and that God's Spirit lives in you! (1 Cor 3:16)
The divine purpose of the creation is the glorification of God. We contribute to this purpose by allowing God to rule supreme in our lives and to proclaim his greatness together with all creation.

Although this divine purpose was apparently obstructed by sin, God refused to neglect the work of his hands. The earthly temple would be but a feeble reflection of what God could make of the life of redeemed man: "He is the one who holds the whole building together and makes it grow into a sacred temple dedicated to the Lord. In union with Him you too are being built together with all the others into a place where God lives through his Spirit" (Eph 2:21-22).

With the advent of the Holy Spirit, God renewed and cleansed each heart dedicated to his service, making it a dwelling fit for the King. For this reason we must listen intently and responsibly when this statement is made: "Surely you know that you are God's temple . . ." This is true because the Holy Spirit moved into our hearts and changed it into a worthy dwelling for God. This is why Paul could testify: ". . . so that it is no longer I who live, but it is Christ who lives in me" (Gal 2:20).

In this way Christ's promise, that He and the Father would come and dwell with us, is fulfilled. It is such a gift of grace that you can only kneel in absolute amazement and worship before God. The Holy Spirit changes you into a temple for God by his cleansing power, on condition that you hand over the keys of every room of your life to Him. There is no doubt that He will enter: "And because of the Spirit that God has given us we know that God lives in union with us" (1 Jn 3:24).

I pray fervently, Lord Jesus, to be a worthy temple for your Spirit.

May 9 Philippians 2:12-18

THE SPIRIT OF GOD GRANTS CAPABILITY

Keep on working with fear and trembling to complete your salvation, because God is always at work in you to make you willing and able to obey his own purpose (Phil 2:12-13)

Possibly you have on occasion felt overwhelmed by the thought of the great responsibility a Christian has to bear. Perhaps you have experienced feelings of hopeless inefficiency, when you consider what God expects of you. He demands nothing less than total commitment and as all human beings are mere sinners, this seems totally impossible. Like Paul, we sometimes feel like saying: "What an unhappy man I am . . ."

But you must never lose courage or yield to the temptation of giving up your discipleship because you feel incapable of meeting Christ's high demands. Even God's most devoted followers felt this way.

Turn to God; seek the presence of Jesus in prayer; open your heart to the Holy Spirit. Make Him part of your daily life; consecrate yourself to Him unconditionally and serve Him enthusiastically.

Ask the Lord to make you sensitive to the guidance of the Spirit. Soon you will experience an overwhelming desire to serve Him with your whole life. The power of the Holy Spirit will be working in you. He will take over your life. He will lead you and give direction and purpose to your entire being.

Heavenly Father, through the Holy Spirit I will honour You, and in obedience to Jesus Christ I will seek your will for my life and try to do what You expect of me.

May 10 1 Corinthians 3:9-23

GOD PROTECTS HIS PROPERTY
Surely you know that you are God's temple and that God's Spirit lives in you! (1 Cor 3:16)
Many people crack under the strain and pressure of modern life. They lose their self-respect, withdraw into their own dark world of self-deprecation and fall prey to negative feelings of inferiority.

These people often seek refuge in excessive drinking, drug abuse, and many other forms of escape.

We should never forget that we were created by God for Himself. He never promised that we would not experience pressure or strain. He did, however, promise to support us in our every need; to help us cope with whatever confusing situation we are called upon to handle. He promised to be our refuge and strength. "Why then do you complain that the Lord doesn't know your troubles or care if you suffer injustice? . . . He strengthens those who are weak and tired" (Is 40:27, 29).

Through his Holy Spirit He supports us and assures us of his eternal love and faithfulness. Therefore we should – rather than destroying ourselves through the abuse of alcohol, drugs and sedatives – once again become the temple of God. God protects his property.

Lord and Master of my life, in your power I will meet the challenges of each day in the knowledge that, through the work of the Holy Spirit, I can live a victorious life.

May 11 Matthew 12:43-45

WHO OCCUPIES THIS HOUSE?
When an evil spirit goes out of a person, it travels over dry country looking

for a place to rest. If it can't find one, it says to itself, "I will go back to my house" (Mt 12:43-44)

It is impossible to fully live out your commitment to Christ if you have not completely renounced your "old life". It will only lead to failure, as it is impossible to build a structure of faith on a foundation of unconfessed and unforgiven sin.

When first you accepted Christ as your Saviour and Redeemer, you were so filled with joy that everybody around you noticed it. After a while, however, the feeling of elation wore off. You experienced disappointments and the indescribable moments of your conversion became a vague memory. When your faith was put to the test you started questioning the sincerity of your conversion.

The reason for this is that you relied upon yourself and your fleeting emotions, without committing yourself to Christ in absolute faith. You never allowed the Holy Spirit to take control of your feelings, your mind and your thoughts.

Complete surrender to Christ does not only bring great joy, but added responsibilities. When you are purified by the Spirit, you must proceed in faith and grow in the living Christ. Trust in Him steadfastly and obey Him unconditionally. Do not become like one of those who proclaim: "Christianity does not work", while it is in fact they who have failed, because they were unwilling to live according to the example of Jesus Christ. Allow Him to occupy your spiritual home and fill it with his Holy Spirit.

I commit my life to You, good Lord. Dwell in me through your Spirit and strengthen my faith while I follow You obediently.

May 12   John 16:1-15

CHRIST WITH US THROUGH HIS SPIRIT

. . . it is better for you that I go away, because if I do not go, the Helper will not come to you. But if I do go away, then I will send Him to you (Jn 16:7)

The knowledge that they would lose their Lord and Master, saddened the disciples. For this reason Jesus wanted to comfort them.

There were many limitations to Christ's physical presence with them: they would not be able to go everywhere with Him; they would continuously be saying farewell to Him; in his human body He could not reach the heart, mind and conscience of all people. If He went away time and place would no longer be determining factors. The Spirit, on the other hand, would not be limited. The Spirit would be moving the hearts of people the world over.

Through the Spirit we can live in unceasing communion with God. By the work of the Spirit the Word of God would now address all men and lead them to repentance and conviction of sin, and to conversion.

The Spirit convinces us that we are truly children of God, that Christ is the Son of God and our Brother. He makes us aware of the judgement of God. We dare not live as we choose, because we will have to account to God for our deeds.

The Spirit convinces us that we will not be condemned, but saved by the grace of God and the achievement of Christ on the cross of Calvary.

Christ promised to be with us always. Through the Holy Spirit He gloriously fulfills this promise.

Praise be to You, Lord Jesus, that You have not left us behind as orphans, but sent us a wonderful Helper who is with us for ever.

May 13   1 Peter 1:13-25

THE CHALLENGE TO SANCTITY
The scripture says, "Be holy because I am holy" (1 Pet 1:16)
The word "holiness' is not very popular. It conjures up thoughts of hypocrisy and spiritual pride. To call someone a "saint" is not a compliment in our day. Yet, even if subconsciously, we are all striving after perfection.

The call to sanctity is a loving demand to conform to the image of our Lord, Jesus Christ. As you grow in your knowledge of Christ, you will discover truths about yourself that you have never been aware of. You will find that you are capable of more noble deeds than you have ever thought possible. Your interest in and understanding of people increase and become more meaningful. The horizons of your existence expand to include areas which you did not know existed.

Christ, who is perfect and holy, calls you to absolute consecration. By doing this, you will lose nothing but will actually gain in integrity and obedience. You will become sensitive to the guidance of the Holy Spirit. You will no longer live, but Christ will live in you. You will become less and He will become more and more important.

Christ was completely and perfectly human. He promised you this "holiness" if you allow his Spirit to fill your life. Do not be afraid or reticent of being made completely whole. It is the Master-sculptor chiselling away at your life. Eventually He will reach his divine purpose with you.

I accept the grace You grant, holy and perfect Master. Mould me according to your perfect example.

May 14   John 14:15-31

PROMISE OF COMFORT
I will ask the Father, and He will give you another Helper, who will stay with you for ever. He is the Spirit who reveals the truth about God (Jn 14:16-17)

Jesus was aware of the sorrow and heartache of his disciples. In his deep understanding of the needs of man, the Lord promised them a Helper – Someone who would be able to translate their desires into words.

Do you know this Helper? This Comforter? Not only with your intellect, but by personal experience? Do you have the conviction that Christ sent Him into your life as a living reality?

Jesus was human, just as we are, and He knows how desperately we sometimes need comfort, especially in times of parting and sorrow. Hence this rich promise of a Helper, a Comforter.

He heals the broken heart; He strengthens the distressed spirit; He calms the storm. He leads us to victory in every situation; He strengthens us in the hour of temptation; He teaches us to control our passions and desires.

All of us know sorrow and pain. But the Lord promises comfort, even in times of confusion and depression. He tenderly treats the wounds of our mind and spirit. He offers the promise of a new day in the night of sorrow and suffering. Praise the Lord, oh my soul!

Saviour, Lord Jesus, thank you for not only promising us a Comforter but for doing what You have promised. May He be our Helper and lead us to overcome our sorrow.

May 15 John 14:15-31

GOD-GIVEN TEACHER
The Helper, the Holy Spirit, whom the Father will send in my Name, will teach you everything and make you remember all that I have told you (Jn 14:26)

All through our lives the Holy Spirit wants to guide us deeper and deeper into the unfathomable truths of God. At no point in time can any Christian claim that he possesses the whole truth. Therefore he must continuously make himself accessible to renewal by the Holy Spirit.

It is the Holy Spirit who, like a sympathetic teacher, guides the weak hand of the scholar with his mighty hand to form the letters which will eventually enable the child to write beautifully.

Many subjects are taught in the school of the Holy Spirit: He teaches us to cope with sorrow – although it is a difficult subject, we can pass *cum laude* if we rely on God. He teaches us to handle life itself, and instructs us to grow spiritually. He teaches us the truth about ourselves, and reveals to us how sinful we really are. He also teaches us about the grace and love of God, who sent his only Son, Jesus Christ, to redeem us from sin.

Thus the Holy Spirit leads and instructs us in the knowledge of Jesus Christ as a living reality in our lives, by whose merit we are reconciled to God and through whom we are taught to travel the road of sanctification.

Heavenly Father, I thank You for enlightening our minds, renewing our hearts and leading us on the path of spiritual growth.

May 16 Acts 19:1-10

RECEIVE THE HOLY SPIRIT
Did you receive the Holy Spirit when you became believers? (Acts 19:2)

How does one receive the Holy Spirit? How does it happen in your life?

Firstly: Place your life at the disposal of God. You must totally commit your body, mind and soul to Him: your thoughts, your personality, your love, your ambitions – everything which is precious and important to you. It is so simple, and yet so difficult and demanding.

Secondly: You must pray to God to let the Holy Spirit descend upon you. Although the almighty God can allow this to happen even if you have not asked Him, He has decreed that you should ask. Why are you so slow to do so? Man has become so independent and self-sufficient that he considers it such a disgrace to ask, that he would rather live a life of spiritual poverty.

Thirdly: God grants his Spirit to those who obey his will. Are you willing to obey Him without question and to do what He expects of you? What does He ask? That you will live according to the requirements of his Holy Word. Simple – not so? But at the same time so exceedingly difficult.

Lastly: You must have faith. You receive the Holy Spirit through faith, as you receive salvation through Jesus Christ by faith. The Spirit comes to you in the power of God and if you are willing to accept this incomparable gift of God, the quality of your Christian life will change beyond recognition.

Almighty God, I have accepted the Holy Spirit as your gift of love to me. Let me live through the Spirit to your honour and glory.

May 17 1 John 4:7-21

DWELLING FOR CHRIST
We are sure that we live in union with God and that He lives in union with us, because He has given us his Spirit (1 Jn 4:13)

One of the glorious truths of the Christian faith is that Christ dwells in the hearts of his followers. This is not something we deserve. Neither can we achieve it. From the moment we accept Him as our Saviour, He makes our hearts his dwelling, simply by his love and mercy.

This holy occupation of our lives can be a very disturbing experience. The more Christ gains domination in your life, the more He refuses to share it with other loyalties and emotions. If you are truly dedicated you will allow Him to take precedence over all departments of your existence, instead of allowing Him a limited part of your life.

Christ grants his Spirit to his children as a gift of mercy, but this does not relieve us of our personal responsibilities. When we receive the Spirit of the living Christ, it will be revealed in our life and actions. Our thoughts will be pure and positive; we will be observant and sensitive to his desires; we will be eager to constantly seek his presence and learn the art of life from Him.

You may think that as a sinful human being, you will never be able to comply with his demands. But once again the grace of God grants you the assurance that his presence in your life is very real. By his wisdom and strength you don't simply exist – you "live" in the true sense of the word, because Christ lives in you.

Living Lord Jesus, I praise and honour your Name for the gift of the Holy Spirit. Through Him I can know your will and live with the knowledge of your holy presence in my life.

May 18 Psalm 127:1-5

A CURE FOR INSOMNIA
It is useless to work so hard for a living, getting up early and going to bed late. For the Lord provides for those He loves, while they are asleep (Ps 127:2)

To many people the night is a time of fear. Sleep constantly eludes them and they relive each unpleasantness of the day during the night. They fear to think of all the disasters that may befall them the following day and their self-reproach because of lost opportunities are magnified beyond all proportion.

The more you think of your personal problems and the morbid world in which we live, the less you are able to fall asleep. It is of little comfort to know that others are also suffering from the curse of insomnia, because of exactly the same reasons.

The only cure for this unfortunate ailment is to ban all negative and destructive thoughts from your mind. It is within your power to decide which thoughts you will harbour in your mind. If you are convinced that perhaps it could work for others but not for you, you are already accommodating negative thoughts. However, the human mind can never be a vacuum. Each waking and conscious moment is spent thinking. The most inspiring and advantageous thoughts you can have while awake, is to think of Jesus Christ – your Saviour and Redeemer.

Pray for his peace, trust in his love, and believe that you have already received his gift of sleep. Then you will blissfully fall asleep without effort.

I thank You, Loving Lord, that You grant peaceful sleep to those who trust You unconditionally.

May 19 Psalm 27:1-14

LIGHT IN THE DARKNESS
The Lord is my light and my salvation; I will fear no one (Ps 27:1)
When we think of God, we involuntarily think of a bright light which dispels all darkness. Christ declares that He is the Light of the World, and Scripture tells us that heaven is the place where God Himself is the light.

It is therefore a grave mistake to think that God is not present in the darkness of our lives. The shepherd's psalm confirms it: "Even if I go through the deepest darkness, I will not be afraid, Lord, for You are with me" (Ps 23:4). However dark the road may become, God is there. In his own good time He will transform the darkness into light. It can never become so dark in your life that God will not be there.

That is why we may never yield to the powers of darkness: this is still God's world and He will never disappoint those who place their trust in Him.

We can cling to the encouraging truth that God visits and supports us in our darkest moments: in our realization and confession of sin; in physical sickness and suffering; in marriage strain and disintegration; in the suffering of children; in economic or financial stress. In each dark moment of life God accompanies us, and where we can't walk, He carries us.

God wants to take your hand and lead you out of the darkness of despair into his glorious light of hope and inspiration.

God of light and love, I glory in the knowledge that it can never become so dark in my life that You will not be present. Your light brings hope in my darkest moments.

May 20 1 Kings 19:1-18

A HERO OF FAITH UNDER THE TREE OF DESPONDENCY
"It's too much, Lord," he prayed. "Take away my life; I might as well be dead!" (1 Kgs 19:4)
Human "breaking-point", where despondency and despair take over probably differs from person to person, but it will mainly be determined by the quality of your faith in God. Elijah reached this point

when he fled into the desert in fear of Jezebel. There he sat in the shade of a tree and wished to die. It is inconceivable that this prophet who, when confronted with the Baal priests at Mount Carmel, revealed himself as a hero of faith, could become such a despondent and despairing creature.

There are, however, times when the pressures and demands of life become too much for us. Relationships go awry; everything you start, goes wrong; hurried and injudicious decisions take their toll. Nothing goes according to plan.

Suddenly your faith is under pressure. Prayer is no longer a motivating power in your life. You question the meaning of life and seek an easy escape – even if it means death.

For each human frame of mind, there is a deep-seated cause. Physical and spiritual exertion demands a period of rest. Sometimes we try to do too many things in quick succession and never taste the satisfaction of one task well done. Take time off for self-examination under the guidance of the Holy Spirit. This time is never wasted. Rediscover the power of Christ. Read his promises in Scripture and make them your own. In his presence, peace and calm will flood your soul. In his Name you will be able to face the challenges of life without fearing the Jezebels of this world. By faith you will conquer your "breaking-point" and transform it into a "departure point" to victory.

Lord, I glorify your Name because I need no longer fear, even though I am sometimes desperate. Under your protection I am safe.

May 21 Ezekiel 34:11-31

RAINS OF MERCY AT THE RIGHT TIME
I will bless them and let them live round my sacred hill. There I will bless them with showers of rain when they need it (Ezek 34:26)
Don't always expect the worst of life. If you are experiencing an exceptionally difficult period, don't despair and convince yourself that the future can only be worse. If you are a pessimist by nature, you will never know the joy which is generated by a living faith.

Faith doesn't blind you to your problems, but it helps to prevent them from overwhelming you. If you steadfastly trust in God, you can meet life with confidence and a quiet mind.

When your faith in the living Christ is the central truth in your life, you can look beyond the tribulations and heartaches of the present, to a future full of promise – because the future is in the loving hand of Christ. He blesses your life and allows the rain of his benevolence to fall at the right time.

God plans only the best for your life. You may pass through a trying period, and it may seem as if you have reason to doubt God's kindness, but He loves you, and therefore wants to bless and lead you.

Always be aware of the many blessings of God which can be yours through Jesus Christ. Apart from material blessings, God has granted you the privilege of prayer. Why not make use of it more often? It makes you aware of his presence. Thank Him for his love which makes life worthwhile. Always rejoice in the Lord. Showers of blessing will descend on you – if you don't hold an umbrella of disbelief over your head.

Merciful God, forgive me my moments of doubt and despair. I accept your abundant blessings and thank You for them. Help me to use them to your honour and glory.

May 22 John 13:30-38

A NEW COMMANDMENT
And now I give you a new commandment: love one another. As I have loved you, so you must love one another (Jn 13:34)

In the household of God love is not an idle, empty word, but a way of life.

If you are disappointed, bitter, or angry because of what somebody said or did to you, you can only be healed if the love of Christ cleanses your life.

The love of Christ is perfect and He demonstrated it in a very practical manner. He prayed for those who harmed Him, even when they nailed Him to the cross. Only this type of sanctified love can expel revenge and bitterness. It is the acid test of true Christianity.

If the love of Christ is in you, you will be patient, friendly and tolerant, regardless of how provocative the situation may be.

You will be able to see the good in every person; to discover the image of God in each human being; to become aware of your unity in Jesus.

This sort of love is the fruit of the Holy Spirit in your life. As you are led deeper into the knowledge of the Holy Spirit, your lack of love will be overcome and it will be easier for you to reflect the love of Jesus.

Then you will have no choice as to whom you will love. You will feel one with all God's children all over the world and you will live according to the law of love. The world will notice this love and will know that you are a disciple of Jesus Christ.

Lord, I worship You as the source of all true and genuine love. Teach me, through your Spirit, how to love all people and thus bring glory to your Name.

May 23 — Micah 7:1-13

VICTORY OVER DEPRESSION

But I will watch for the Lord; I will wait confidently for God, who will save me. My God will hear me (Mic 7:7)

One of the most upsetting experiences a depressed person can have is to hear someone declare: "Cheer up!" As though you yourself have chosen to be depressed and are enjoying it.

Unfortunately this is partly true – you can do something to alleviate your feelings of depression. Identify the origin or cause of your feelings. This is not always an easy task and perhaps you will need medical or psychiatric help to do so. To most of us, however, a session of absolute honesty with God may reveal the cause. Through the work of his Holy Spirit He will focus on that dark area in your life and indicate to you what is wrong. Perhaps someone has deeply hurt or ignored you. Perhaps you have not received the recognition you think you deserve. There are so many things which can cause a person to become dejected or unhappy.

Develop a broad outlook on life and cultivate an attitude of understanding and acceptance. Accept the people around you as they are; make peace with yourself; accept the love of God as a personal gift. Your spirit and mind must be stronger than the things which upset you. All this will depend upon the quality of your relationship with the living Christ.

If Jesus is your Saviour and Redeemer and you live according to his will, you will experience that He equips you to cope with your depression so constructively that you will eventually taste victory.

O Holy Spirit of God, thank you for helping me to conquer my depression. Thank you for leading me out of the depths of my dark moments into the light of Christ's love.

May 24   John 20:19-29

FAITH IN THE UNSEEN
Do you believe because you see Me? How happy are those who believe without seeing Me! (Jn 20:29)

When you try to explain who Christ really is and what He does, you will find that you are trying to express the unfathomable. It is beyond human power to explain the arrival of God in the flesh through his Son, Jesus Christ.

There is more to life than the limited seventy odd years we are granted to live. Eternal abstractions such as love, purity, unselfishness, and sacrifice, reveal a minute part of what eternity holds in store for us: "What no one ever saw or heard, what no one ever thought could happen, is the very thing God prepared for those who love Him" (1 Cor 2:9).

It is the Christian's privilege to see beyond this temporary existence. While you lose yourself in the living Christ, you become more and more aware of your union with the eternal.

Many people will consider this an emotional, mystic experience. Yet it has very real and practical implications for your life. You notice anew, as with new-found sight, the wonder and greatness of God's deeds around you. Your view on life expands and you develop a perspective of eternity.

When you live in awareness of the unseen, you realise that your greatest asset on earth is not the gifts which you receive by God's hand, but God Himself – his grace and your increasing growth in the knowledge of God through his Spirit.

Eternal and Almighty God, grant me a true realization of your greatness, so that I will be able to grasp the eternal things. Help me, by the grace of Jesus Christ, to see the unseen and so to grow in my faith.

May 25 2 Thessalonians 3:1-15

A LOVE WHICH DEMANDS RESPONSIBILITY
May the Lord lead you into a greater understanding of God's love and the endurance that is given by Christ (2 Thess 3:5)
You receive the love of God free and undeserved. Nothing you can do, or promise to do, can earn it. God loves you because his nature is love. This is an astonishing truth for which you should be eternally grateful.

Because God's love is without end, you must guard against the assumption that it is a love which will allow you to live in sin, without being punished. The moment you discover that you can share in the privilege of this divine love, you should also realize that there are certain responsibilities attached to it, which will have to be met if you want to grow spiritually.

God ignites the flame of love in your heart. Your duty is to see that nothing will extinguish it. This can only happen if you reciprocate God's love. You must allow the Holy Spirit to command your thoughts and enable you to practise this love. The fruit of the Spirit is indeed love. To this end you receive your daily inspiration by way of your communion with Him. Then each act of your life will be founded on the love of Christ. Everything you do and say will be in honour of his Name, because you love Him.

God loves you with an undying love, which you will never be able to fathom. As his disciple it is your responsibility to make that love a practical reality in your life and in that part of the world which you occupy for Him. If you are unwilling to do this, you are an obstacle to his work and his Kingdom.

Lord, my God, grant me the full experience of your divine love, so that I will be a flame in the fire of your cause and that I will convey that love to others.

May 26 Leviticus 20:1-8

TRUE SANCTITY
Keep yourselves holy, because I am the Lord your God. Obey my laws, because I am the Lord and I make you holy (Lev 20:7-8)
It is generally assumed that a "holy" life implies a sad farewell to all forms of joy and happiness. Many people cannot associate holiness with a full, joyous and compensating life. The pursuit of holiness can, in fact, become the most dynamic and creative power in your life.

This power, however, cannot be obtained unless you are in the right relationship with God – the Source of holiness. If this is the case, your life will not only be enriched, but you will gain a better understanding of others and your relationships will improve.

Sanctification brings about a sincere desire to grow in the likeness of Jesus Christ and to convey his attitude to others.

Hypocrisy can never be part of holiness. The power of the Holy Spirit enables us to live sincerely and honestly, and to approach life in a positive and balanced way.

To strive after holiness is an exciting challenge which allows no time for boredom or depression. Living according to God's values is indeed the only way to obtain true happiness and success.

Holy Master, sanctify my every thought and act.

May 27 Psalm 102:1-17

PRAYER IN THE DARK VALLEY
He will hear his forsaken people and listen to their prayer (Ps 102:17)
There are times in the life of every Christian when it is difficult to pray. In such times one feels as if you are losing your grip on the only permanent anchor in your life – a living awareness of the abiding presence of God. In such times of spiritual barrenness and drought, the God who was always a living presence seems aloof and in hiding. Many disciples of Christ think of these times as "seasons of drought" and simply dismiss them as minor sins. They don't recognize the significance of these times. They incorrectly assume that God has turned his face from them and no longer cares.

It demands an act of faith to keep on believing that God is present in your life – faith does not depend on your emotions. Just as an earthly father must sometimes let go of his beloved child's hand to teach him how to walk, God wants you to walk with Him, not only in the light, but also in the darkness – even though sometimes you do not feel his guiding hand.

When you learn not to rely on your emotions, the presence of God becomes a living reality to you. The darkness will pass. Don't revolt against your inability to pray, but rather try to discover what God wants to convey to you. Your emotions may change, but God's love for you will never change.

Gracious Guide and Father, help me to look away from myself and my problems when I am in the dark valley of desolation, and to trust in your love until You change the darkness to light.

May 28 Ephesians 4:1-16

WHERE IS GOD? LOOK INWARD
There is one Lord, one faith, one baptism; there is one God and Father of all mankind, who is Lord of all, works through all, and is in all (Eph 4:5-6)
Through the ages man has sought God. They saw his majesty in the heavens; they studied his handiwork in nature; they observed the perfect order He created and the regularity of seasons and times. But He remained a "distant" God, separated from man in his distress, a Father-figure, quick to judge and slow to forgive. In times of dire affliction they pleaded for help and comfort, but He was always far removed from the human race.

The advent of Jesus Christ changed this impression of God. The living Christ came to teach us that the eternal God is not a distant Holy One. Jesus, who is in perfect harmony with God, invites ordinary people to share in this elevating and enriching experience.

Christ opened a new world of relationships and untold riches of the spirit to us. However, this world can only be entered through total commitment to Him. This happens when we are born again (Jn 3). It is simply the point of departure into a whole new world in the company of Jesus.

If you want to experience God's presence, you must look inward into your own mind and spirit. You cannot find the eternal God unless you have become aware of Him in your own life. Confirm his reality in your life and you will be able to joyfully witness to his divine presence.

Dear Lord Jesus, by your Holy Spirit I know with assurance that God dwells within me.

May 29 Isaiah 26:1-19

THE SECRET OF PEACE OF MIND
You, Lord, give perfect peace to those who keep their purpose firm and put their trust in You (Is 26:3)

There are people with a "house-fly approach" to life. They touch a great variety of things in their flight, but do nothing with enough purpose as to make a positive success of it. What is more: such people never find peace of mind because of these opposing interests which rob them of their inner calm.

Inner peace is born out of constructive purposefulness. If you know what you desire of life and strive for it with enthusiasm, you acquire inner stability and you are liberated from restlessness.

It is never easy to strive after and to reach high ideals. If, however, you ask for the help of the Holy Spirit and ask Him to decide upon the course of your life, He will never disappoint you. He may reveal his guidance in a very dramatic way to you. Or you may simply quietly become aware of a deficiency in your life. Out of this awareness the Spirit often gives birth to new idealism and enthusiasm.

If you sincerely ask God to give you a purpose in life – a cause which will motivate you and to which you can dedicate all the powers of your body, mind and soul – the joy of fulfilment will flood your heart and the peace of God will enter your life like sunshine and fresh air. Where others will know restlessness and never taste fulfilment, you will draw inner peace from the Holy Spirit and your divine calling, and you will come to experience peace of mind.

Loving Father, I thank You that I can have a clear ideal in this confused world. Thank you for Jesus, my Lord, who gives me his peace, through the Holy Spirit.

May 30 Galatians 5:16-26

THE HOLY SPIRIT SANCTIFIES MY SERVICE
The Spirit has given us life; He must also control our lives (Gal 5:25)

There are many people who profess that they are totally committed to God and are in his service. They do a great deal for their fellow-men and naturally their sincerity is beyond reproach and above suspicion. Service to society is their watchword.

But these are all virtually deeds about which man decides for himself. When anything, even social welfare, takes the place of the worship which God deserves and destroys our communion with Him, it becomes powerless and futile.

The busier you become in serving your community, the more you need to spend time with God. If you neglect this duty, your service will be denegrated to a worthless waste of time.

The Lord grants us his Holy Spirit to guide us from day to day to where He needs us most. The world wants us to digress from God and does so by the very work we do for Him. Our most urgent need is to meet with God every hour of every day and to plead in prayer to be filled with the Holy Spirit. Only then do we understand the will of God for our lives and in our work. Then we don't serve outside his will but in obedience to his desires.

Let us continuously thank God for this loyal Helper who constantly renews us and sanctifies our service. When we – inspired by the Holy Spirit – sacrifice, give, love, share, work or do intercession through prayer, our service is purified and ennobled. Thus it truly becomes a service of love to his honour and glory.

God Almighty, fill me with the Holy Spirit by the grace of Jesus Christ and make me your priest and prophet in this world.

May 31 — Joshua 1:1-9

TO FIGHT OR TO FLEE?

Remember that I have commanded you to be determined and confident! Don't be afraid or discouraged, for I, the Lord your God, am with you wherever you go (Josh 1:9)

A difficult situation may be a nightmare to one person, while to another it is a God-given opportunity and challenge. One person succumbs and is trodden down and he refuses to get up again; another is inspired to call upon all his faculties to battle until the victory is won.

It is of no avail to try and escape from your problems: "It will be like a man who runs from a lion and meets a bear. Or like a man who comes home and puts his hand on the wall – only to be bitten by a snake" (Amos 5:19)

The Christian faces his problems and wrestles with them in faith, in the knowledge that God also gives strength for victory. Then we can joyously proclaim: "I have the strength to face all conditions by the power that Christ gives me" (Phil 4:13)

The Christian soldier is not ignorant of the dangers, and there is often fear and trembling in his heart. But courage is not the absence of fear, it is the conquest of fear; it is victory by faith and in the strong Name of Jesus Christ.

For this reason we can look up to God and know that He will support and help us to see our problems for what they are, to wrestle with them and conquer them. By our association with Christ we no longer fear the powers of evil, but we live with victory in sight.

Lord Jesus, You triumphed over all your problems and troubles because You steadfastly trusted your Father. Help me to face my tribulations in the same manner and reverse them into opportunities through the power You grant me.

JUNE

PRAYER

Holy God and divine Creator,
winter carries its own enchantment and
its own anxieties.
Thank you for blossoms in winter – even tough
they be freak blossoms – yet,
they remind us how nearly impossible your love
for us, sinners, seems to be.
Thank you, Lord, for rain and cold and time to read; for
slumbering nature, expectantly waiting for new growth.
Let winter teach me to make time for You, Master, and
to find peace and quiet in your holy presence: to slow
down my pace so as to meditate the essential things of
life, and to gather strength for a new period of growth.
The cold of winter brings with it many anxieties:
to the aged and the poor who die of privation
while we are cosy and warm at our firesides;
to the unemployed who don't know where
tomorrow's bread will come from;
to the hungry, whose eyes plead as I pass by;
to the homeless, out there in the cold, who feel the frost
of human indifference most of all.
Help me to give freely and to stretch out
a helping hand.
Warm the stark, unfeeling coldness of this
winter-world by the warmth of
Christmas in June.
Amen.

June 1   2 Timothy 1:1-14

THAT ONE TALENT

For this reason I remind you to keep alive the gift that God gave you when I laid my hands on you (2 Tim 1:6)

There are many people who live out a colourless and biased existance, because they deny the special gifts which God has granted them. They are overwhelmed when they see the achievements of others and convince themselves that they will never be capable of doing anything worthwhile.

They refuse to start any new venture and they become inactive spectators instead of creative and dynamic instruments in the hands of God.

Every person has at least one talent and if that gift is developed, others are soon revealed. Unfortunately, many people never discover the concealed talents they bear within their deepest self, and this happens purely out of ignorance or laziness. Unfortunately there is little which can be done for people who are totally convinced that they have no talents. Through unbelief their talents will remain hidden.

The sluggard will always be complaining about lost opportunities and pretend that failure does not effect him. Only the Holy Spirit can reveal this weakness to them and rejuvenate them to new life and activity.

To discover your gifts from God, you must first seek God's guidance and be willing to commit yourself to a life of creativity and obedience. This demands courage and daring, but the Lord never dissappoints those who trust and obey Him.

Grant me, o Lord, the desire and the courage to discover my gifts from You, and to be unconditionally obedient in using them to your greater glory.

June 2   Ephesians 4:1-16

RESPONSIBLE DISCIPLESHIP

Instead, by speaking the truth in a spirit of love, we must grow up in every way to Christ, who is the head (Eph 4:15)

When you have accepted Christ as your Saviour, you also accept certain definite responsibilities. If you refuse these, there is a weakness in your spiritual life and your relationship with Christ is at fault.

To be a Christian means to enter an entirely new life with new values, standards and aims. You no longer live for yourself, but you glorify your Master by self-denying service to others and in the ministry of love and caring for your neighbour.

Your "new life" in Christ carries with it certain demands and you are compelled to spiritual growth. The only way to grow spiritually is by honouring God by unconditional obedience to Him in your daily life. When this is your life-style there will be no place for pride and self-assertion at all. His will becomes your will; his road your road; his commands your joy.

You must open your heart to the Holy Spirit to dwell in you and to work out your salvation and growth to maturity. In this way you become a servant of truth and a loyal witness of his love and mercy. This is only possible if you have had a firsthand experience with Christ as your Redeemer.

When you meet these requirements, you grow like a healthy branch obtaining its strength from the tree. Each day you become more aware of his living presence and increasingly desire to be filled with the Spirit of God. Eventually the image of Christ is reflected in your life, to the glory of the triune God.

Heavenly Father, because I found new life in Jesus Christ, I accept full responsibility as your disciple, by the help of the Holy Spirit. Grant me courage to persevere from day to day.

June 3   Isaiah 26:1-11

A BALANCED SPIRITUAL LIFE
You, Lord, give perfect peace to those who keep their purpose firm and put their trust in You (Is 26:3)
We will never be able to grow to spiritual maturity if we rely entirely on our emotions. A positive and living faith exists independant of "feeling" or "atmosphere". Many people think that if they constantly live in a state of spiritual high tension, or continuously can remain on the mountaintop of glorification, they will grow spiritually strong and muscular. They place their trust on their emotions and as a result their spiritual experiences vary according to their state of mind.

When the inspiration of the emotional moment has passed, they experience a period of spiritual recession or even paralysis. To be able to live victoriously we must not live by our emotions only. This is a too inconstant and deceptive foundation to build upon. Our worship and witness dare never be void of emotion, but neither dare we exclusively trust upon it.

A life of victory does not depend on external circumstances, but upon a heart and spirit which has found peace in God, which fully trusts Him and permanently lives by his grace and mercy.

We can do this only if we allow the Holy Spirit into our lives. He makes us capable of total trust, even in the most desperate circumstances. Then emotions and practical faith bring a perfect balance to your spiritual life.

I glorify and laud your Name, dear Lord, that I may be your child, and that I can trust in You under every circumstance of life. Help me to stay close to You at all times.

June 4   Psalm 27:1-14

FAITH TEMPERS SORROW
I know that I will live to see the Lord's goodness in this present life. Trust in the Lord. Have faith, do not despair. Trust in the Lord (Ps 27:13-14)
No human being is entirely safeguarded from sorrow. And it comes upon you unexpectedly. You are taken by surprize. Sometimes for a short while, at other times for months or years on end. There are very few people who can survive this experience without their whole life being thrown out of gear.

Whether it is by death or any other tragic experience which has enveloped you, this very real sorrow has a greater influence on your life than you would like to admit. But if you succumb to your sorrow, you allow it to dominate your life. This can cause a detrimental and dangerous situation.

A strong and living faith is the only weapon against sorrow. When one has faith, one can withstand the destructive power of grief and affliction.

If you believe in the eternal goodness of God, you will accept sorrow as a natural part of life, without becoming bitter or giving yourself over to self-pity.

If you believe in the resurrection to eternal life, the death of a loved one becomes bearable. When your dreams and ideals lay shattered at your feet, a living faith will give you strength to rise again to a life of victory, by the grace of Him who makes all things new. Eventually you see in your sorrow a glorious challenge to trust God without question, and this brings comfort and peace to your grief-stricken heart.

Lord Jesus, I praise your holy Name for the strength to conquer my grief by the power of the Holy Spirit.

June 5 1 Peter 5:1-11

THE GRAVEYARD OF WORRY
Leave all your worries with Him, because He cares for you (1 Pet 5:7)
Sometimes your life's course does not unfold according to plan at all. Everything you touch ends in failure and disappointment. Then it is so easy to become depressed and discouraged, and for you to despair of ever living a life of victory.

When you try to conquer your setbacks and problems in your own strength, and when you seek a solution by your own wisdom, you become physically and spiritually exhausted and you easily reach your breaking point.

It may sound pious to profess that you will accept everything life deals to you, but when you are physically and spiritually too tired to even try to get your life into gear, you need a very real experience with God. Then only do you learn to place your life entirely in his hands and allow Him to organize your life according to his holy will.

When you consciously share your worries and cares with Him, He gives you the power to remain standing unshakeably, even when it seems as if the foundations of your life are crumbling.

It is comforting to know that God has full knowledge of your circumstances, that He cares and that He is mighty to help. If you know Him intimately, also during the dark times of your life, every worry and care becomes an opportunity to see the omnipotent God at work. You learn to know and to trust Him as at no other time of your life.

It is a comfort to know, dear Lord, that You are aware of my cares and that I can leave them with You. Let this assurance be my daily inspiration. Give me your peace, even in the midst of the storms of life.

June 6 2 Corinthians 7:2-16

THE MINISTRY OF ENCOURAGEMENT
But God, who encourages the downhearted, encouraged us with the coming of Titus. It was not only his coming that cheered us, but also his report of how you encouraged him (2 Cor 7:6-7)

Paul discovered that encouragement means so much to the faithful that, being encouraged, he in turn encourages others. So it happened in the congregation which encouraged Titus, and he in turn could encourage Paul in his struggle.

Paul needed encouragement at this moment. He was wrestling with all the problems of the early church – either people persecuting the church, or members who deliberately tried to lead believers astray. No wonder that Paul knew times of deep depression.

With the arrival of Titus, Paul received the encouragement he so dearly needed. God made use of Titus and the congregation to lighten his burden and to encourage him.

There are very few of the Lord's followers who never become discouraged. Every one of us, at some time or other, feels that things become uncontrolable and very easily we lose our faith and our grip on life. Or perhaps you are fighting a lonely and losing battle against overwhelming evil and your courage is very low.

Possibly there is a discouraged person near you, who is desperately seeking for spiritual support. If you know about him and do nothing to encourage him, you are disappointing God and denying a fellow disciple. Perhaps you feel there is nothing you can do. But through prayer and by allowing the Holy Spirit to work through you, God will show you how to help. By offering sincere friendship, by simply listening sympathetically, God could possibly heal his wounds. God blesses you by making you a blessing to others through the ministry of encouragement.

Use me, Lord, to encourage the discouraged, through your Son and the Holy Spirit.

June 7 1 Corinthians 1:1-17

UNITY IN CHRIST
One says, "I follow Paul"; another, "I follow Apollos"; another, "I follow

Peter"; and another, "I follow Christ." Christ has been divided into groups! Was it Paul who died on the cross for you? Were you baptized as Paul's disciples? (1 Cor 1:12-13)

Satan often succeeds in sidetracking Christians by convincing them that they have come to the Lord by the wrong road. However, how you came to Christ is not important. What is of prime importance is that He is now the sovereign ruler of your life. One person is converted in a sudden and dramatic manner. Another simply grows quietly and steadily into a new life in Christ.

Therefore you can rejoice in the knowledge that you are saved by grace, because Jesus died for you on the Cross of Calvary.

To you the way in which Christ brought you to faith, will be of special significance. You will feel attracted to people who had a similar experience and who consider the same things of importance in their spiritual lives. It is important to be encouraged by people who believe as you do and experience their religion in a similar way.

But you may never look down upon people who have had a different experience on their way to faith. You may not withhold yourself from the community of the faithful just because people belong to a different denomination.

If you allow this to happen, you are depriving yourself of sharing in the rich variety of discipleship over limiting boundaries. It leaves you so much the poorer. Our love for and faith in Christ, should create common ground where people of different traditions and denominations could reach out to each other and demonstrate their unity in Jesus Christ. Through his love, in spite of our differences, we can be one in Christ.

Spirit of God, give us love in our hearts and make us one in Jesus Christ, so that the world will know we are disciples of Christ.

June 8   Psalm 42:1-11

THERAPY FOR DESPAIR

Why am I so sad? Why am I so troubled? I will put my hope in God, and once again I will praise Him, my Saviour and my God (Ps 42:11)

If you feel depressed you must never consider yourself a lost sinner. Some of God's most dedicated followers knew depression and despair and were often prey to it. If you handle this experience correctly, it may lead you to a fuller knowledge of the way God works in your life. Then you realize that times of desolation and desperation can be indications of spiritual deepening and growth.

One has just to remember that there is always a human cause for depression and despair; possibly Christ is no longer at the centre of your life but your own person; perhaps you have allowed a spirit of negative cynicism to control your acts and relationships; possibly jealousy is poisoning your attitude towards your fellow-men. There can be many reasons for your unhappy state, but if you sincerely pray for the guidance of the Holy Spirit, He will reveal the cause to you. When the cause becomes clear to you, you have to do something constructively about it. Don't nurse your depression. Confess it to your heavenly Father in prayer; share it with Him without shame. From Him you will receive the strength to renew your thoughts and life through the power of the Holy Spirit. Then you are emancipated from this darkness of your soul and you start acting positively. Soon you will be singing hymns of praise from a joyful heart and your depression and despair disappear like mist before the morning sunshine.

My Lord and my Saviour, I praise your holy Name for making it possible to rise above my despair and depression. Thank you for letting the dark night pass and sending a new day of sunshine and song.

June 9 Ephesians 2:11-22

CHRIST THE GREAT BRIDGEBUILDER
But now, in union with Christ Jesus, you who used to be far away have been brought near by the sacrificial death of Christ (Eph 2:13)

It remains a wonder through all the ages that the Son of God became man and lived amongst us on earth. We celebrate this occasion with songs of joy every time Christmas comes around.

The Light of the world, stripped of the glory of paradise, became human. But He was without sin. In our case our humanity reminds us of our sinful nature. By the Word – and by our life – we know that the flesh is constantly in conflict with the Spirit. Paul says in Romans 8:7: "And so a person becomes an enemy of God when he is controlled by his human nature; for he does not obey God's law, and in fact he cannot obey it." And those who obey their human nature, become enemies of God.

But the humanity of Christ was entirely different. He was without blemish or sin. Yet He was here on earth in the figure of a humble servant. He was equal to us in everything, barring sin.

This is the glory of which Christmas reminds us: Immanuel – God with us. The God who was enthroned high above us, and since the fall of man was separated from us, came down from heaven in the person of his Son to dwell with us. He did so to make it possible for man to enjoy his mercy and grace; so that they who were "far" away could be brought "near".

He became man to bridge the gap between God and ourselves; to become the Mediator who would reconcile us to God. To become the Saviour of a lost world. God above us; God far from us, but – praise be to God – through Jesus Christ, He became: God with us!

Heavenly Father, I marvel at the amazing wonder of your Son becoming human, Jesus Immanuel. I accept it by faith and rejoice in the blessed assurance that He did it also for me.

June 10   Matthew 9:27-31

DARE I BELIEVE IT?
"Do you believe that I can heal you?" "Yes, sir!" they answered. Then Jesus touched their eyes and said, "Let it happen, then, just as you believe!" – and their sight was restored (Mt 9:28-30)

When we consider what Jesus teaches and what He claims to do, an ordinary person is inclined to ask with Nicodemus: "How can this be?" (Jn 3:9)

And yet if we look around us we see how that which Jesus promised, was fulfilled. We see how the lives of sinful people are regenerated and they become good; we see how weaklings suddenly gain power and act accordingly; we see how grief-stricken people regain hope; we see how addicts are eventually released of their captivity. Homes which were previously dwelling places of the Evil One, become places of love where God is served; selfishness changes to sharing; hatred becomes love. They who feared life, suddenly find confidence and courage. People who recently sought for a meaning in life, find life a noble and elevated calling.

Relationships which were hopeless, are suddenly made healthy. It is indeed so that everything that was made sinful and imperfect, received an inner healing through God, by the love and mercy of his Son Jesus Christ.

When you steadfastly believe that Christ can rectify all the wrongs in your life, He will fulfull his promises to you. Many express their need to Him, but they do not sincerely believe that He can help. And because they do not believe, no miracles happen in their lives.

It is human to doubt, but you can start by trusting God in the minor things of life. Dare to trust God and great things will happen in your life.

Lord, I want to grow in faith and commit my whole life to You. Thank you that this is possible because You love me.

June 11 Luke 12:13-21

CONTROL YOUR AMBITIONS
Watch out and guard yourselves from every kind of greed; because a person's true life is not made up of the things he owns, no matter how rich he may be (Lk 12:15)

A philosophy of life which is very popular in our time, is the conviction that anything is possible, and that you can obtain anything if you just pray sincerely enough and think positively. Of course this is only partially true, because prayer alone cannot solve all problems. Discipline, careful planning and hard work are important components of success.

Many people dream of things far beyond their potential. It is true wisdom to know your limitations and to aim for high but attainable ideals and to faithfully work towards them. To constantly dream of the impossible is an invitation to disappointment and frustration.

If you have decided upon an attainable ideal, you must ignore all other matters and concentrate on that which you can and want to reach. When you do this, you will find that your whole approach to life changes radically. Then you realize that true joy and satisfaction is not necessarily found in material possessions, prestige or the high esteem of people. A worthy cause to which you devote your dedication and labour, brings peace to your mind and acceptance of your limitations.

True happiness in life has very little to do with earthly possessions. It is something much greater than these fleeting things. True happiness is to have an attainable ideal and to work towards it to the glory of God and the advancement of your spiritual character. Then life becomes an adventure and you find your happiness by striving for ideals which God has placed within your reach. The greater your commitment is to Him, the less dominion earthly possessions will have over your life.

Praise and thanks to You, Lord Jesus, that You grant me sanctified ideals and desires through your Holy Spirit, and that I find my purest joy in reaching them.

June 12   Psalm 18:25-42

MAINTAIN HIGH SPIRITUAL STANDARDS
He is the God who makes me strong, who makes my pathway safe (Ps 18:32)

At times life can suddenly become very confused. For a time things run smoothly and you feel strong and full of confidence. Then the unexpected happens: friends disappoint you; problems overwhelm you; sorrow and grief darken your horizons – and suddenly your faith is losing its power and joy. Everything is disrupted and it seems as if life itself has no longer any purpose or meaning.

In your darkest moments you must remember that God has a perfect plan for your life, and He expects of you to comply to his wishes obediently.

Under no circumstances must you consider lowering your spiritual standards to comply to the world around you. If you do so, you will deny the power of God in your life. A life devoted to God does not suffer double standards.

You know instinctively that God expects you to walk in his way and live by his power, but because you think yourself incapable of doing this, you compromise with the world and become satisfied with a second-class faith.

You must allow God to reach his perfect purpose in your life. This demands absolute faith and total consecration. It demands of you a Damascus-road experience where you, blinded by the glory and sanctity of God, will ask: "What will you have me to do, Lord?" Then you experience his omnipotence and you find the power to travel your road with success and joy, to his honour and glory.

Heavenly Master, I attain to my highest fulfilment in You. Help me to live according to your will, through the power of the Holy Spirit.

June 13   Luke 18:9-14

SPIRITUAL PRIDE

Once there were two men who went up to the Temple to pray: one was a Pharisee, the other a tax collector (Lk 18:10)

There are few things which are more repugnant than spiritual pride. And at one time or another we are all guilty of it. The temptation is always there to tap yourself on the shoulder and to praise yourself for your pious living.

People so readily compare their spiritual condition with that of other people. People who do not attend church services are criticised; or people who never pray at a prayer meeting; or people who seem to be very disinterested in religion. It gives so much satisfaction to our sinful nature to condemn others, because then you can subtly give yourself a pious pat on the shoulder.

There is but one criterion for all Christians to measure their spiritual stature. It serves no purpose to compare ourselves with others, or to praise our own virtue. We can only attain to a rich spiritual life if we keep our eyes set on Jesus Christ, the Leader and Finisher of our faith.

To come to a stop and then look around with self-satisfaction and say to yourself: "I'm not doing too badly! In fact, I am doing much better than many of those around me . . ." is a dangerous habit. It proves beyond a shadow of a doubt that you are no longer growing, because you have taken your eyes off Jesus Christ and focussed them on yourself.

A Christian must not strive to be better than others. All we are, we are simply by the grace of God. Our aim must be to become more and more like Jesus, and to this purpose we must devote our prayers, our time, our strength and our talents.

Saviour Lord, help me by the power of the Holy Spirit, to keep my eyes fixed on You and live according to your holy example.

June 14 Genesis 29:15-30

YEARS SEEM LIKE DAYS
Jacob worked seven years so that he could have Rachel, and the time seemed like only a few days to him, because he loved her (Gen 29:20)
For Joshua the sun stood still in the Valley of Ajalon: it was a miracle of the power of God Almighty in answer to the prayer of his servant.

For Jacob the sun ran on its way, because love is timeless – like God Eternal! When a person truly loves, he is never in a hurry, because he knows that love must serve an apprenticeship. True love knows what patience is and is capable of waiting.

Because, according to Scripture, love is the greatest virtue of all, Satan makes it the target of his fierces and most violent attacks. He proclaims that love is solely "sex", and sex has become so "liberated" that a young man and woman can hardly love each other anymore.

True love has no substitute. Though I speak with the tongues of men and of angels, have all the knowledge and understand all the secrets, have the faith needed to move mountains, dole out all I possess and give up my body to be burnt – and I have no love, I am nothing.

Paul says in 1 Corinthians 13 that true love is patient and kind; not jealous, conceited or proud; not selfish or irritable. True love is absolutely honest and does not live behind a disguise. It is to protect your partner against temptation and stumbling.

Love knows its limits and never confuses freedom with licence. True love is a gift of God and the most ennobling priviledge in life. When temptation whispers: "If you love me, you will . . ." pure love answers: "If you love me, you will not . . ." That is why love can wait. Years seem like days. Then we follow in the footsteps of Jesus Christ – the Source of all true love.

God of love and mercy, there are so many pitfalls on the road of love. Hold my hand and grant me self-control, so that years may seem like days.

June 15 Philippians 2:12-18

YOU HAVE SPIRITUAL RESPONSIBILITIES
Keep on working with fear and trembling to complete your salvation, because God is always at work in you to make you willing and able to obey his own purpose (Phil 2:12-13)

One has to consider your spiritual responsibilities seriously. When you are converted and become a child of God, you commit your life to Him and strive to comply with his purpose for you. He demands a practical, lived out faith and absolute obedience to his will. Your surrender is not simply an emotional step, but it demands that you practise it in your life from day to day.

When your consecration is not simply a shallow confession of your mouth, but also becomes visible in your life, Christ can freely work in you. However, it remains your responsibility to meet the requirements of your confession. What you profess with your mouth and believe with your heart, must be reflected in your life.

You can only meet your responsibilities as a Christian, if you have surrendered to Christ and allow Him to control your entire being. Then your spiritual responsiblities are no longer a burden, but a joyful pleasure. You spend more time in prayer and Bible study and your worship is genuine and without hypocrisy.

Realizing your spiritual responsibilities, you open up your life to the person and work of the Holy Spirit. He now controls your thoughts – thoughts which lead to noble acts. To this end you must work diligently and faithfully: It is your responsibility, but also your great privilege as a child of God.

Merciful Lord, by your love, wisdom and power working in me, I accept my responsibilities with joy and gratitude.

June 16 John 6:1-15

LOOK FOR MIRACLES

A large crowd followed Him, because they had seen his miracles of healing those who were ill (Jn 6:2)

Never complain and assert that the days of miracles are past. Life is full of miracles, if we would but see them. The problem is that most of us are blind to the wonders which surround us. We are so inclined to look for the extraordinary – the sensational – that we don't see the miracles wrought in and around us in an ordinary manner every day. Because something happens with regular monotony, such as the coming and passing of seasons, it is no longer a miracle to us.

When you take time to notice it and open your mind to it, you become aware of the greatest miracles. Then you learn to appreciate them: a life converted and renewed by the love and mercy of Jesus Christ; the privilege of spending time in the presence of a living and loving God; the wonder of being able to honestly forgive a person who has trespassed against you; the blessed assurance that, through Jesus Christ, you are truly a child of God.

There are miracles of creation: the breaking out of new life in spring, the miracle of growth and ripening, the smell of rain on scorched and barren soil; of newly ploughed land; a breath-taking sunset; a moving piece of uplifting music; the shout of a sea-gull over a deserted beach; the smile in the eyes of an infant . . . these are all miracles for those who have eyes to see.

If you make a habit of searching for miracles in your daily life, you extend the horizons of your spirit and you will become more aware of the power of God. It is an enriching experience which fills you with amazement and lets you confess in adoration: "How great Thou art!"

Teach me, loving Father, to notice the miracles You send on my way every day and to appreciate them as gifts of your hand.

June 17 Isaiah 41:1-7

SUPPORT ONE ANOTHER
The craftsmen help and encourage one another (Is 41:6)
Life is not always easy: rising costs of living; strained personal relationships; fear of unemployment and the ghost of incurable diseases. Many people accept these things as part of life and believe that these tribulations should be borne, and that one must not try to evade them.

Being a Christian colours your attitude towards them. If you complain when confronted by them, if you feel that God has deserted you, you become part of the chorus of lamentators, who sing a sad but useless song of afflictions and injustices which life deals to them. This attitude simply increases your misery.

When the Spirit of God is at work in your life, He will prevent these negative attitudes. When you seek solutions for your problems and they constantly evade you, turn to your heavenly Father who will provide them. He has all the answers and nothing is beyond his power. This knowledge releases you of all the paralysing fears of your life, and you can really start living. Then you will also be able to comfort and encourage others. By sharing your faith and confidence with them, you support them in bearing their burdens of sorrow and distress; to look past their afflictions and see what God is willing and able to do for them. By helping others, you help yourself and strengthen your own faith.

I praise You, dear Lord, for each opportunity You grant me to encourage and comfort others. I cannot do otherwise, because You have touched me with your love.

June 18 Matthew 28:16-20

SOMETHING TO REMEMBER
And I will be with you always, to the end of the age (Mt 28:20)
Here we have one of the great promises to the children of God. It is one of the wonders of the mercy of Jesus Christ, that He promised always to be present in the lives of his followers. Wherever you may be, He is with you; whether you are surrounded by friends or absolutely alone, He is with you. His continuous presence does not depend upon circumstances, places or emotions. He promises to be with us "to the end"!

Life has not only good and beautiful days, but also bad and dark days. This is why it is imperative that you will not depend on your emotions for your spiritual development. You dare not measure the strength or quality of your religious life by how you feel at any given moment.

It is unwise and dangerous to use your feelings as a criterion to decide whether Christ is with you or not. His promise entails no qualification including your emotions. He promises simply and unconditionally that He will be with you as a comforting and strengthening Presence. "I have been given all authority in heaven and on earth." It doesn't matter whether you are in the valley of shadows and darkness, or in the warming sunshine of faith – He is a comforting presence in your life.

Hang on to this liberating promise, especially when circumstances place your faith under pressure. It is in times of depression and despair when you need his power; then you must have faith of a special quality. This will help you to move triumphantly out of the darkness towards the light of his love.

I kneel in gratitude and wonder, o Lord, that You are with me at this moment and at all times, to strengthen my faith and carry me through each crisis.

June 19 John 14:15-31

YOU HAVE A DIVINE INHERITANCE
Peace is what I leave with you; it is my own peace that I give you. I do not give it as the world does. Do not be worried and upset; do not be afraid (Jn 14:27)
Jesus left this glorious inheritance to his followers of all ages. He knew that the search for "peace" would be the passion of the hearts of all people of all times. But the peace the world offers is a feeble reflection of the deep inner peace Jesus offers freely to his children.

To be able to claim this inheritance, we must first rectify our relationship with the Testator. We must become children of God by accepting Him in faith. We must accept his forgiveness and become cleansed of all sin.

We must also allow Him to control our whole life. We must seek his perfect will for us, accept it unconditionally and obey his commands.

In his testament Christ grants us the highest peace possible – the peace of God. This peace is unique, different to the so-called peace of the world. It is a perfect peace. It spans our whole life, including every single area. It is a constant peace and does not change with our changing moods and emotions. It is authentic, and not a false peace which winks us into the desert of despair like an illusion. It is universal and not limited to one certain place or a few privileged people.

This peace becomes our gift through Jesus Christ when we honestly commit our lives to Him. It is the ultimate antidote for worry and fear.

I thank You, loving Father, that I can claim my inheritance, because Jesus Christ opened the way to your heart for me. Help me not to deny this peace through fear or alarm.

June 20 Romans 8:1-8

TWO LEVELS OF LIFE
Those who live as their human nature tells them to, have their minds con-

trolled by what human nature wants. Those who live as the Spirit tells them to, have their minds controlled by what the Spirit wants (Rom 8:5)
Many people have a materialistic outlook on life. This is understandable, because things which can be seen and touched, are constantly occupying our senses. Yet it is so that an incessant pre-occupation with tangible things tends to dull the intrinsic values of life and are spiritually detrimental.

If the Holy Spirit leads you into a deeper insight of spiritual values, you start to realize the excellence of the things of the spirit in contrast to the visible and temporary values. It is only when you outgrow material values, that you reach the full knowledge of what "life" really means.

To many people this philosophy of allowing spiritual values to gain preference above tangible assets, sounds like exaggerated piety. They have no desire to be classified as religious, but deep-down in their being they know that life must offer more than simply the demands of the material world.

It is only when your spiritual relationship with God is strong and healthy that you are released of the chains of selfishness and materialism. Then you do not exist, but you "live" in the presence of God and you enjoy the true freedom He offers. You are compelled to a choice between these two levels of life.

Father of love and mercy, grant me the insight and wisdom not to make the wrong choice in life. Let your Spirit teach me the art of true living, and let me live a life to your honour and glory.

June 21 John 14:15-31

PEACE RATHER THAN NARCOSIS
Peace is what I leave with you; it is my own peace that I give you (Jn 14:27)
Everybody yearns for release from the pressures of uncertainty; from nervous stress and the tremendous strains placed on you in your efforts to reach your ideals and ambitions.

Where do we get this relief in these times in which we live?

Many seek the answer in narcotics or opiates – sedatives, tranquilizers, calmatives or alcohol. Others again seek and find it in the finality of death – when the pressure becomes too great, they commit suicide.

There is only one solution, only One who can deliver you, and that person is Jesus Christ, our true Saviour. He is the only "way" to cope with life and to gain relief from the unbearable pressures which modern society places upon you. Absolute consecration of your life to Christ brings freedom and peace of mind.

It does not matter what the problem is you are confronted with, if you only open your heart and life to the love of Jesus Christ. This love will take control of your thinking and your emotions, and you will find peace and calm in green pastures and quiet waters of the Spirit.

Spend time in the calming presence of the Redeemer. Open your deepest self with all your problems and despair to Him and let Him communicate with you through his holy Word. The storms will be calmed and you will find perfect peace.

Lord of love and peace, I turn to You for the perfect peace which is only to be found in You.

June 22 Matthew 27:45-56

THE MYSTERY OF SUFFERING
My God, my God why did You abandon Me? (Mt 27:46)
Why must good people suffer?

They who have suffered themselves and emerged from this battle victoriously, know the answer to this question. The suffering of Calvary acquires a new meaning to those who experience suffering in their own person. Others can at best speculate about it.

Suffering brings us to the mystery of the meaning of life. Only when we have been in contact with death, we understand the life of the resurrection. With pain and anguish it is so much like with wilted flowers or overcast skies. It is impossible to expect that flowers will never wither or fade, or that the heavens will always remain cloudless.

Suffering and love are so entangled that we can hardly separate them. There is but a hair-breadth between great happiness and the deepest sorrow. The more we love, the greater our suffering is. However, who would elect never to suffer and thereby never come to understand the true meaning of love? As much as God expects us to love, He demands of us to be cleansed by the purifying power of suffering.

It takes light and shadow to produce a fine painting. We must guard against the danger of seeing only the dark sections of a work of art. The Man of Sorrows is with us in our suffering: He knows, He understands, and He can comfort as no other can. In our darkest moments of distress we come to understand the true meaning of the word "Love"!

Eternal Father, I lay my suffering and sorrow at the foot of the cross in confidence and faith, knowing that You are able to let it work together for my greatest good.

June 23 1 Samuel 3:1-21

LEARN TO LISTEN
Speak; your servant is listening (1 Sam 3:10)

To listen to God is not as easy as it sounds. He doesn't speak to us with an audible voice, as He spoke to Samuel. But there are different ways in which God speaks to his children in our time.

The most important requirement is to meet God in a quiet place, away from all other persons and things. Talk candidly and openly to your heavenly Father, remembering that He knows you better than you know yourself. Don't expect to obtain a feeling of sanctity and piety, of expectancy in prayer, immediately upon entering his presence. Trust in your faith and not in your emotions. Open up your life to Him and share every aspect – however insignificant – with Him. Do not expect a stunning revelation every time you enter the presence of God.

If you persevere faithfully in your prayers and meditation, you will be increasingly enriched. You will feel his love flowing through you as the branch receives its strength from the tree.

During these holy moments devoted to God, you will hear God speaking to you. You may suddenly experience a thought so clearly and genuine, that you can impossibly doubt that it is a message from God to you. When you have learnt to listen to God, it will have far-reaching results in your life.

You with God – and God with you, alone! There are rich blessings waiting for those who have learnt to listen to God with a sensitive ear and heart.

Lord, teach me to listen, so that I can say honestly: Speak, Lord, your servant is listening. I praise your Name, Jesus Christ, for making it possible for me.

June 24   1 John 4:7-21

LOVE . . . THE ROOT FROM WHICH FAITH GROWS

God is love, and whoever lives in love lives in union with God and God lives in union with him (1 Jn 4:16)

Love is a recreating and renewing power in the life of every Christian. It is not simply a superficial emotion. To confirm your love to God, you must commit your entire life to Him and allow his Spirit to renew you. You must also accept Christ's unquestioned dominion over your life.

Out of love to Christ, you subject yourself to his will, and you desire to know Him better and to follow Him more obediently. When you know this kind of love, you also know gratitude for all the blessings God showers upon you. Then you don't allow depression and despair into your life, because you know that He loves you and cares for you.

This is not a false or spurious love which goes hand in hand with your changing emotions – this would be a mockery of the eternal and constant love of God.

To obtain this love, we must open our hearts to the power and influence of the Holy Spirit. This is an act of faith: you must firmly believe that the God of love holds your life in his powerful hands.

In this manner your faith becomes an essential and living part of your everday existence, because the love of God is living in you and working through you.

Almighty God of love and mercy, may the love in my life never be simply a passing emotion, but a lasting experience carried by my faith. Let the Holy Spirit help me to love as Jesus Christ loved.

June 25   Isaiah 37:8-20

COPING WITH BAD NEWS

King Hezekiah took the letter from the messengers and read it. Then he went to the Temple, placed the letter there in the presence of the Lord, and prayed (Is 37:14-15)

We all experience bad news at one time or another.

Many people fall apart when they receive bad news. They are not capable of thinking clearly. As a result of this they sometimes make foolish utterances or act irresponsibly. Others again receive bad news in a fatalistic manner and desperately try to hide their true feelings – to the detriment of their spiritual health.

The Christian knows that he must share bad news with the Lord in prayer and meditation. It isn't, as many may think, an effort to escape from reality, but it is a productive way to consider and judge facts by the wisdom and power of God.

Only God is capable of enabling you to regain your equilibrium. You experience his comfort when your heart is breaking. He guides you when you have to make important decisions.

Follow Hezekiah's example when you receive bad news. Share it with your heavenly Father. You can do this only if you have a growing relationship of love and faith with Him. Learn to spend time in his holy presence, also in days when you are experiencing no problems whatsoever. It will serve as a shock-absorber when the storms of life ravage and harass you. With the power and love of God as allies, bad news can strike you but it will never destroy you.

Lord, because I am convinced of your love, I am never unsure as to what I have to do with bad news. I glorify and thank You for this comforting privilege.

June 26   Isaiah 53:1-12

THE TRIUMPH OF LOVE

But because of our sins he was wounded, beaten because of the evil we did. We are healed by the punishment he suffered, made whole by the blows he received (Is 53:5)

The outstanding quality of love, is that it always gives – only the best and the noblest.

There is nothing that love cannot do. Nobody can take it from you; you must give it willingly, and the more you give, the stronger the influence of love becomes in your life.

The ability to give yourself through love, was the triumph of the martyrs. They refused to fall prey to bitterness and hatred and rather suffered physical hardship. They were even capable of loving those who persecuted them. When actually, with broken bodies, they had nothing more to fall back upon, their love carried them through triumphantly.

Their shining example through all their suffering, was the Source of all true love – He who gave Himself out of love for humanity. The purest demonstration of Christian love, is Jesus Christ on the cross of Calvary. Through indescribable suffering and sorrow, his love shone victoriously and He could pray for them who nailed Him to the cross.

You can also obtain this love. Through your life the love of God will spread to the lives of the people in the world around you. Every consecrated and committed person, becomes a reflection of Christ and is willing to practise this love in that part of God's world which he occupies.

God of love, I praise your Name for the love which sent your Son, Jesus Christ to this world to reveal your love to us. May your love be demonstrated in my life at all times.

June 27   Hebrews 12:1-11

TRUE RELIGION IS PRACTICAL
. . . and let us run with determination the race that lies before us. Let us keep our eyes fixed on Jesus, on whom our faith depends from beginning to end (Heb 12:1-2)

Many people are under the misapprehension that their spiritual life stands entirely loose from their existence of every day. They believe that there are fixed times for worship and spiritual experience, but in general, life is a battle which has to be fought on the practical front.

One can never separate the spiritual from the practical, because the one is supplementary to the other. The spiritual must have its influence on the practical, and the practical needs the spiritual inspiration, guidance and elevation. When Christ enters our lives, we know true joy, happiness and satisfaction. But not if we try to exclude Christ from the non-spiritual areas of our lives. A life in Christ is a solid unity built up of both the spiritual and the practical.

There are people who believe that if you transfer a living, spiritual attitude into practical life, you rob life of its joy and sparkle, and so they avoid doing this. However, if your life is dedicated to Christ, you put back the joy and happiness into practical living.

When you focus your mind and spiritual energy upon Christ, He gives you the strength and inspiration for a full and compensating life. During his life on earth He demonstrated to us how to grow and enjoy spiritual abundance – also here on earth. In his presence our religion becomes a practical reality – and our practical life is ennobled to serve Him in our everyday existance.

Loving Master, I draw my inspiration for my daily life from You. Thank you, Lord, for a full and compensating life when I live according to your standards.

June 28   1 Corinthians 15:35-58

DEATH IS DEAD

So when this takes place, and the mortal has been changed into the immortal, then the scripture will come true: "Death is destroyed; victory is complete!" (1 Cor 15:54)

Jesus Christ vanquished death on Calvary. Death is buried there, and for this reason physical death can never again be final to the Christian believer. This is a fundamental truth of the Christian faith.

When one considers this fact from the perspective of eternity, the spiritual death of one's soul is far worse than the death of one's body. If you refuse to accept Jesus Christ as your Saviour and Redeemer, you will die the eternal death.

In Jesus Christ we have life – true life, even in death! He conquered death so that the corruptible takes on incorruption. The Christian dies, only to be raised to eternal life. He remains victorious, even though he dies. We will be ignorant of all the dimensions of true life, until we have died. For this reason we must stop fearing death, and rather guard against the evil powers which destroy the soul and so cause eternal death.

We aren't the only ones in conflict with the Evil One. The knowledge that death has no final dominion over us and our loved ones, renews our courage. We have the assurance of eternal life, through Jesus our Saviour.

Christ did indeed say: "A grain of wheat remains no more than a single grain unless it is dropped into the ground and dies. If it does die, then it produces many grains" (Jn 12:24). Only through death we have eternal life, because Christ transformed death into everlasting life!

God of life and love, grant me to live each day in the knowledge that death has no power over me and that I have received eternal life through the finished work of your Son, the living Christ.

June 29 Matthew 26:36-46

UNANSWERED PRAYERS
My Father, if it is possible, take this cup of suffering from Me! (Mt 26:39) Have you considered what an untold tragedy it would have been for humanity if God had granted this prayer? Then Jesus Christ would never have become the Saviour of the world, and we all would still have been groaning under our burden of sin.

God always knows what is best for us. Paul also had to learn this lesson when he prayed for the removal of the thorn in his flesh. God did not grant him his prayer, but Paul found comfort in God's enduring promise: "My grace is all you need, for my power is greatest when you are weak" (2 Cor 12:9). This enabled Paul to be proud of his weaknesses, in order to feel the protection of Christ's power over him.

There are times when the Lord does not grant you your prayers, because He has something much better in prospect for you. God did not answer the fervent prayer of Moses to be allowed to lead his people into the promised land, because Moses was disobedient to God at Kadesh. God granted him the heavenly Canaan, which was much more than he could ever hope or pray for (Deut 32:48-52).

David pleaded with God for the life of his child, but in vain. This was a spiritual turning point in David's life and only thereafter could he truly confess his guilt and sin (Ps 51).

God answers all petitions made in prayer. Not always as we would have it, because we are limited in our knowledge and do not know all the answers. But when we look back later on, we are extremely grateful that He answered our prayers according to his wisdom and not according to our desires.

Jesus of Gethsemane, teach me to pray after your holy example: Yet not what I want, but your will be done.

June 30 John 7:32-39

FILLED WITH THE HOLY SPIRIT

"Whoever believes in Me, streams of life-giving water will pour out from his heart." Jesus said this about the Spirit . . . (Jn 7:38-39)

If you want to be filled with the Holy Spirit, you must sincerely believe that this fulfilment is also intended for you. You must be convinced that it is God's will for you; that it is part of his inclusive plan for your life; that it is included in the benefits of Christ's saving work. Filling with the Spirit isn't simply a luxury-model of Christianity, but a divine prerequisite for every Christian.

You should not consider it as an abnormality. It is something singular, because there are few people who are totally filled with the Holy Spirit. In a world of sick people, health would be unusual, but not abnormal.

If you sincerely desire a Spirit-filled life, you must be willing to consecrate your life to Christ. Don't be half-hearted about it because you think that you live a fairly good spiritual life and don't really need to be filled with the Spirit. You pray, you read your Bible, you go to church, you contribute to missions, you don't drink or gamble and you enjoy singing the Lord's praises. Isn't that enough? you ask.

If you want to follow Christ to the utmost and desire a deeper and richer experience with Jesus Christ, you must ardently pray for God to fill your life with his Spirit. Then you will know what abundance really means and everybody around you will notice the difference. This is what the Lord offers his believing children when He promises that we can be filled by the Spirit.

Spirit of God, come into my life in all your abundance, now and forever.

JULY

PRAYER

Lord, it is time for the July holidays, when many of us will go on tour. Some will go hunting in the Lowveld. Others will go to the game reserve, the seaside, or to visit their families.
This is the time when death mercilessly takes its toll on our roads and causes irreparable loss and grief.
You gave us our most precious possession: life. Help us then to act with great responsibility, especially during these carefree days.
Thank you for a period of rest together with our families. Bind us anew to one another, and to You, our Saviour.
Thank you, Lord, for friends with whom we can share our holidays and for the beautiful memories we will be able to take home with us.
We pray for those who have to work while we are on holiday.
Thank you for the beauty of the winter wonderland.
Renew our spirits while our bodies rest.
Let us not forget You during this period. Help us to continue our regular Bible study, prayers and meditation – our communion with You, the Master of our lives.
Make us, your children, the salt of the earth and the light of the world.
In the powerful Name of Jesus Christ, our Lord and Redeemer.
Amen.

July 1   Psalm 27:1-14

A FAITH FOR LIVING
Trust in the Lord. Have faith, do not despair. Trust in the Lord (Ps 27:14)
We are so easily paralysed by fear. And there are so many things in life we fear.

Some dread a visit to the doctor and the anxious waiting for the results of the medical tests. They fear to be admitted to hospital where they will be alone amongst strangers and be wheeled into the operating theatre with nobody to hold their hands.

Others may stand beside the ruins of a once happy marriage with fear in their hearts for the future that lies ahead. There are those whose hearts may ache with longing for an estranged child.

Where do you go to with your distress, your anxiety, fear, sorrow, agony and dark depression? Who will listen? Who cares? Who is able to help?

When the psalmist says: "Trust in the Lord", he does not imply a passive or negative attitude, or that you should try to escape from the realities of life. No, he wants you to place your faith and trust in God, even in the most desperate circumstances; you can trust Him with your life, and He will never disappoint you.

Only then can you rejoice in the assurance given in Psalm 13:5-6: "I rely on your constant love; I will be glad, because You will rescue me. I will sing to You, o Lord, because You have been good to me."

What a privilege, loving Master, that I may come to You with all my fears; that I can trust You to change my fear to joy, my distress to worship, and my sorrow to happiness. In the powerful Name of Christ, the living Lord.

July 2   Job 23:1-17

SPIRITUAL DROUGHT
How I wish I knew where to find Him, and knew how to go where He is. I would state my case before Him and present all the arguments in my favour (Job 23:3-4)
However blessed your spiritual life may be, there will be times of spiritual drought when you may feel that God is neglecting you. You may even wonder why you ever set out on this spiritual journey.

You are not the only Christian pilgrim who has known depression of the spirit. However, many Christians have experienced that such times often precede periods of growth and maturity.

When you feel dejected or depressed you must cling to your faith and not allow your emotions to take control. Otherwise you may destroy everything you have gained over years of spiritual growth and depth.

Make sure that this spiritual drought is not caused by your own stubborn unwillingness to comply with God's blueprint for your life. If you persevere in executing your own will and desires, you are building a wall of separation between yourself and God.

It is possible that God might be using this difficult period to strengthen your relationship with Him. It might be his way of pointing out to you that you are starving yourself spiritually instead of nourishing yourself with the riches of his mercy. Whatever the case may be, you can be sure that He is busy working in your life and is eager to strengthen you, to forgive your weaknesses, and to lead you to a richer, fuller life. But then you must commit your life to Him by renewal and believe in Him unconditionally.

God of love and mercy, I sincerely want to believe and cling to my faith in You, even if at times I find it extremely difficult. Help me to triumph through my love for You and never to drift away from your love when my emotions take control of my spirit.

July 3   Isaiah 61:1-11

SCHOOLED BY SORROW
He has sent me to comfort all who mourn, to give to those who mourn in Zion joy and gladness instead of grief, a song of praise instead of sorrow (Is 61:2-3)

Fruit trees only bear abundant fruit if they are pruned regularly. Similarly there are certain fundamental truths of life which can only be taught in the school of sorrow. An old Persian proverb proclaims: If one is always in the sunshine, one is in the desert. It is only by experiencing sorrow that one can truly appreciate happiness.

In times of sorrow we realize how utterly dependent we are on God. This dependency brings us closer to God than ever before, and allows us to experience the incomparable riches of his comfort and mercy. Only then can we be freed from the destructive forces of sorrow.

Christ once said to his disciples: "Let us go off by ourselves to some place where we will be alone and you can rest for a while" (Mk 6:31). We also need such a place "alone" with God, where we can lay our burdens before Him: a broken marriage, addiction, estranged children, humiliation, disgrace, or the death of a loved one.

Remember that God is holding your hand in the dark moments of life to comfort you in your sorrow, to give you joy instead of grief; happiness instead of heartache (Is 61:1-3).

Lord my God, support me when sorrow strikes. I glorify your Name because life can never become so dark that your light will not shine through.

July 4   1 Corinthians 13:1-13

YOU GAIN LOVE BY GIVING IT

I may be able to speak the languages of men and even of angels . . . but if I have no love, this does me no good (1 Cor 13:1, 3)

When the Pharisees and Sadducees confronted Jesus with complicated theological and dogmatic problems, He reminded them that the foundation of the law was to love God and your neighbour. That is why Paul considered love the greatest of all spiritual gifts.

A love which has its origin in God is never selfish and is not limited to special people. You must love all the people who cross your way. Even though love is such a strong emotion, it will eventually lose its power if it does not become an act of practical commitment.

If you want your love to grow, you will constantly have to bestow it on others. The more you give, the greater the love of Jesus Christ will grow in your life.

The sea of Galilee has an inflow of pure, fresh water from the streams of Mount Hermon, but in turn this sea feeds the Jordan river. Because the water is always moving, it remains fresh and full of life. The Dead Sea receives its water from the Jordan, but it has no outflow. Because it never gives, it is "dead".

Christian love is incomprehensible to many people, because it gives without expecting to receive anything in return. To love in this manner, is humanly impossible. Only when your life is fully committed to the power of the Holy Spirit, does this become possible.

God of love, rule my life so completely that I will reflect your love. Teach me to give freely of my love, so as to be filled more and more with your divine love.

July 5   Galatians 5:1-15

STAGNATION BRINGS DECLINE AND DEATH

You were doing so well! Who made you stop obeying the truth? (Gal 5:7) Spiritual retrogression inevitably causes spiritual decline, which in turn can lead to spiritual death. So many Christians are satisfied with a lukewarm relationship with God. This attitude is strongly rebuked by Jesus (Rev 3:16). The road of spiritual pilgrimage is scattered with the idle dreams and unrequited yearnings of people who, at a time in their lives, were full of enthusiasm to walk with God.

Why are the initial fervour and enthusiasm of people so easily killed? Christ places his finger on the cause when He orders John to write the following to the congregation of Ephesus: "But this is what I have against you: you do not love Me now as you did at first. Think how far you have fallen!"

One reason why Christians cool down, is because something else becomes more important to them than Jesus Christ. Satan manages to shunt them onto a sideline where useless arguments cause a living faith to weaken.

Another reason may be that few Christians find it possible to accept the discipline which is necessary for spiritual growth.

Too much emphasis can also be placed on the emotions. The reading on the spiritual barometer then changes with the changing of the emotions. It is imperative to grow past the emotional, up to that point where God becomes a glorious reality in your daily life.

When you allow your faith to be subjected to these negative influences and you give in to temptation, you will never grow in faith – on the contrary, you will fall prey to spiritual stagnation and degeneration.

Lord, my God, I place You in the centre of my life and plead that You will discipline me through your Spirit so that I will have a positive and growing faith.

July 6 Genesis 1:26-31

LIVE LIKE A REPRESENTATIVE OF GOD
So God created human beings, making them to be like Himself (Gen 1:27)

Perhaps you have a low self-esteem. When people run you down, you may feel – even though it hurts – that they might possibly be right. You may even feel that, because you are not very clever, you will never accomplish anything important in life. It is also possible that you are often told by family or friends that your company is dull and your life lacks sparkle.

In this way you can add to the list of your imperfections until you reach the dangerous point where you not only agree, but submissively accept it. However, a truly mature person does not necessarily accept the judgement of others concerning his capabilities and potential. Seclude yourself with your heavenly Father and pray to see yourself as He sees you. He loves you dearly and holds your life in his hand – you are indeed his creation.

Through his Word you know that God created you with a divine intention. He gave you the precious gift of life. He expects of you to live in such a way that the world will know that you are of royal descent; child of the King! God expects nothing more, and nothing less from you.

If you live according to the demands of God and not according to the wishes of other people, you will never doubt your worth as a human being. If you execute your tasks – however humble they may be – to the glory of God, they will become important and worthy of your noble heritage. You are a unique, singular creation of God; his representative in this world.

Lord, I doubt myself so easily, and I doubt your love. Help me to live to your honour and according to your will. Make me your worthy representative in this world.

July 7 Isaiah 53:1-12

BEARABLE SORROW
But he endured the suffering that should have been ours, the pain that we should have borne (Is 53:4)

The mercy of our heavenly Father is so great, that He even makes our grief bearable by sharing it with us.

There is no indemnification against sorrow. Everybody has to pass through this dark valley at some time or another. That is why it is so important to know that, through Jesus Christ, we can triumph over our sorrows. When we go to Christ with our grief and sincerely believe that, through his help, we can conquer our sorrow, He will surely not disappoint us.

There are so many things that can cause sorrow: the death of a loved one; the deterioration of someone dear to you through serious illness; the waywardness of a child or member of the family on the dark road of sin . . . Like the psalmist you can then call to God in your distress: "I am exhausted by sorrow, and weeping has shortened my life. I am weak from all my troubles, even my bones are wasting away" (Ps 31:10).

When sorrow threatens to overwhelm you, you must guard against self-pity. Remember that life goes on and that you have a responsibility towards yourself, your family and life itself. You dare not blame God or call Him to account. God is filled with pity for you and wants to enfold you in his love. This is the promise of Psalm 34:18: "The Lord is near to those who are discouraged; He saves those who have lost all hope."

God is capable of handling any situation, no matter how serious it might be. Nothing is beyond his power. Don't think that because you are unable to cope, it is the same with God. He will support you to the end in your sorrow and distress.

Holy Spirit, sent by God to comfort and support us, I rejoice in the knowledge that You are with me in the dark days of desperation and grief.

July 8 — James 3:1-12

THE DRAGON BEHIND OUR TEETH
But no one has ever been able to tame the tongue. It is evil and uncontrollable, full of deadly poison (Jas 3:8)

Many people find it difficult to communicate. It often happens that you say something to somebody and then find out that it has been so distorted or misunderstood, that it no longer has the meaning which you had originally attached to it. On the other hand, one can make a hurting remark about a person and disguise the barb by making it sound like a joke. If somebody were to point out the implications of your words, you would vehemently deny that they were meant that way.

Careless and irresponsible words may have far-reaching effects. James says: "Just think how large a forest can be set on fire by a tiny flame" (Jas 3:5). We must think carefully before we talk or else be willing to bear the bitter consequences.

Misunderstanding between people always causes pain. It can sow spiritual destruction. Children of God often make ambiguous statements without thinking of the negative and unpleasant results.

Jesus Christ, our perfect example, chose his words very carefully and everything He said was acceptable to God. Paul said that we must adopt the disposition of Jesus – and this undoubtedly includes our words. Then others will not misunderstand us so easily and we will endeavour to be a mouthpiece of his grace.

The philosopher Zeno said: "A person has two ears and one mouth. Therefore we are called to listen twice as much as we speak." These wise words will prevent you from being devoured by the dragon behind your teeth.

Put a guard before my mouth, o Lord, and teach me to think before I say anything that might hurt someone else.

July 9　　　　　　　　　　　　　　　　　　　　　　　　　　　Jude :21

EXPONENTS OF HIS LOVE
. . . and keep yourselves in the love of God, as you wait for our Lord Jesus Christ in his mercy to give you eternal life (Jude :21)

God grants us salvation, free and undeserved. There is nothing we can do to deserve God's love, but He freely gives it to everyone who is willing to accept it in faith.

However, such is the quality of human nature that man has greater appreciation for that which he has to pay and labour for, than for that which is granted and which he obtains without effort. Nobody can buy or earn the love of God. His love, which is complete and perfect, is offered to you totally free of charge. The only obstacle which can prevent you from making this love your own, is your stubborn unwillingness to accept this divine gift.

The love of Christ is complete and nothing can reduce its quality. But how this love will be revealed in your life, depends entirely upon you.

If you want to maintain a meaningful relationship with your heavenly Father and desire to see the fruits of his love in your life, it is imperative that you strengthen and enrich your spiritual life. This can only be done by consistent prayer, Bible study, meditation and by living quietly and confidently in the presence of God. When you allow God to make his love an integral part of your life, you will be able to meet the challenges and demands of a world without love.

God is love and He lets you share in this love when you commit your life to Him. Then you become a worthy exponent of his love in that part of the world where He has placed you.

I thank You, loving Lord, for granting me your love. Make my whole life a reflection of that divine love.

July 10   Romans 12:1-8

SELF-EXAMINATION
Do not think of yourself more highly than you should. Instead, be modest in your thinking, and judge yourself according to the amount of faith that God has given you (Rom 12:3)

Many people have a very low self-esteem. When asked to perform a simple task, they refuse because they are convinced of their incapability. They avoid other people because they feel threatened by them. Such people lead unhappy and unfulfilled lives, because what a person believes of himself, is what he allows himself to be.

As a follower of Jesus Christ you will have to examine yourself honestly at some time or another. To do this you will need the enlightenment of the Holy Spirit. Such an examination could be both a disillusionment and a revelation. You might feel ashamed and humiliated when you meet your true self and discover how petty, deceitful and hypocritical you are. But if you accept God's pardon for you, just as you are, you will recognize your potential – that which you can become through his grace and mercy.

To derogate yourself and to believe that you will never be able to achieve anything, will only cause frustration and unhappiness. You should never forget that God created you after his own image and that you are precious to Him.

When this truth becomes part of your life, you will stop underestimating yourself. You will no longer expect failure, but will grow spiritually. You will gain new hope and the ability to live a life of true service and dedication to God despite your limitations.

Father in heaven, because I am your pardoned child, I can meet life with courage and perseverance. Lead me step by step through your Holy Spirit, to be what You intended me to be.

July 11   Acts 1:1-11

PROFESSION AND PRACTICE
But when the Holy Spirit comes upon you, you will be filled with power, and you will be witnesses for Me . . . (Acts 1:8)
You might think that as a witness for Christ you are of no great value. Or you might be of the opinion that you would be a more powerful witness for his cause if your circumstances were different. Perhaps you would even prefer to witness for Him in surroundings where you are not so well-known, because you are aware of the fact that you do not practise what you preach.

If this is the case, you will have to plead for God's help to rectify the situation and to enable you to do your duty as his witness. There is no room in the household of God for people who do not live according to their witness. Such people live out lies that cause frustration which robs them of their peace of mind and the assurance of their faith.

It is impossible to bear witness to something you have no knowledge about. If Christ is not a living presence in your life, you can impossibly lead others to Him.

Genuine witness does not simply mean to talk to others about Christ. Your life must also be an example of your lived-out commitment and love to God. You must also allow the Spirit of God to guide you in choosing the right time and place to speak to a person. The witness which glorifies God, always has its origin in the Holy Spirit. Without the Spirit your witness is futile, tainted with spiritual pride and self-glorification. A spirit-filled life is the launching pad of a powerful witness.

Gracious Lord, grant me the mercy never to profess that which I don't practise. Do this by the indwelling power of the Holy Spirit.

July 12   Romans 8:31-39

GOD'S ABIDING LOVE

For I am certain that nothing can separate us from his love . . . there is nothing in all creation that will ever be able to separate us from the love of God which is ours through Jesus Christ our Lord (Rom 8:38-39)

When you are stricken by pain, suffering, grief or sorrow, your first reaction is to isolate yourself from the rest of the world and find refuge in seclusion.

In this hopeless desolation you lose your grip on life until you are no longer in control. You seem unaware of the reality of God's presence in your life and convinced of the fact that He has deserted you. You might even believe that He is responsible for your pain.

We easily identify with poets and writers who blame God for the suffering of humanity.

This is possibly how you feel about God at times. However, this is not what God feels and thinks about you! God's love for you is permanent and unchanging. Your emotions and perceptions may change with changing circumstances, but God keeps on loving you, even when you reject Him.

To become conscious of God's love is more than an emotional experience – it requires a life of absolute consecration. God's love has a wonderful healing power. Even though you have turned your back on Him, He will come to meet you and embrace you in his love, the moment you return. He is waiting patiently for your love. Even in the times when you fled from Him and repudiated his love, you were constantly surrounded by his love.

Merciful Saviour, your unfathomable love for me, is the source of my joy and strength. I thank You for the support of your abiding love even in the darkest moments of my pilgrimage.

July 13   James 2:14-26

FAITH AND DEEDS IN PERSPECTIVE

. . . what good is it for someone to say that he has faith if his actions do not prove it? Can that faith save him? (Jas 2:14)

The writer expounds an irrefutable truth when he says: "So it is with faith: if it is alone and includes no actions, then it is dead" (Jas 2:17).

When you profess that you believe, you must demonstrate your faith by actions. True faith in the living Christ is an inspiration and a source of unlimited spiritual power. But faith which is not practised and demonstrated, is a useless ornament.

The practical application of the principles of our faith, makes a living reality of it, even in our earthly lives. Faith and deeds go hand in hand, and to neglect the one in favour of the other, leads to an unbalanced spiritual life.

If you desire a spiritually well-balanced life, and the love of God to become visible and flow to others, you must maintain a positive and creative prayer-life and make a thorough study of the will of God in his Word. From these two sources an inspiring and practical faith will originate. To claim that you believe in Jesus Christ and yet not allow Him to work through you, is actually a denial of your faith.

That is why it is so essential to withdraw from the rush of life from time to time to be alone with God. In this way your faith is renewed and you experience spiritual grace. During such times you learn to know God's will for your life and you discover what He expects from you in practising your faith. In this also, Jesus Christ is our perfect example.

I thank You, Lord Jesus, that You are the Vine, giving me strength to confirm my faith by deeds of love.

July 14 Psalm 37:1-11

MY ROAD AND HIS WILL

Give yourself to the Lord; trust in Him, and He will help you . . . (Ps 37:5)
The future is the great unknown. You might possibly have a vague idea of the road stretching ahead of you, and might even be planning your future. However, you have no guarantee that the future will unfold as you plan it.

Your plans can go wrong. For this eventuality you must develop an unshakeable faith and a positive attitude as shield against disappointment and failure. You must not allow your life to crumble because your plans are shattered. Learn to make adjustments, even though it might cause a radical change in the course of your life.

To be able to do this, you must have an open mind for the guidance of the Holy Spirit. If you are committed and obedient to Him, He will lead you and help you to overcome the obstacles and pitfalls on your way. This obedience demands consecration of such a quality that it will enable you to always place God first on your list of priorities. You will still make mistakes, or be unsure whether you are doing his will, but don't be discouraged.

If you faithfully trust the guidance of your heavenly Father, He will help you to overcome your faults and uncertainties and lead you to glorious victory.

Loving Leader, in gratitude I trust You with my future. Guide and enlighten me through your Holy Spirit.

July 15   1 Corinthians 10:11-22

DO NOT UNDERESTIMATE TEMPTATION
Whoever thinks he is standing firm had better be careful that he does not fall. But God keeps his promise, and He will not allow you to be tested beyond your power to remain firm . . . (1 Cor 10:12-13)

If all Christians were immune against temptation, this world would have been carefree and uncomplicated. Unfortunately we are all subjected to temptation in various forms and different degrees of intensity. The wise disciple arms himself against this danger.

We need the grace of God to detect the destructive power of temptation behind the friendly mask it wears. We dare never underestimate the power of temptation or play a naive game with it. Satan entices people with all kinds of mirages and fantasies of wonderful things they will experience. His victims live in a dream world where they constantly try to convince themselves that they are in full control of their actions and emotions. In a moment of weakness temptation becomes an awful reality and the dream world changes into a nightmare. You become a slave of your own passions and desires and an inmate of a prison erected by your own deeds.

The dedicated disciple of Jesus Christ rejects temptation before it lays hold of him. He prays for the wisdom to recognise it for what it really is, and the power and grace to conquer it in the Name of Christ. It is a blessed assurance to know that He will not allow us to be tempted beyond our strength.

Almighty Saviour, I praise your Name every time temptation comes my way, because it forces me to take shelter in your strength. Give me strength to remain steadfast in the hour of my testing and to gain victory through your power.

July 16 Psalm 146:1-10

FAITH WHICH SINGS IN THE DARK
Praise the Lord! Praise the Lord, my soul! I will praise Him as long as I live; I will sing to my God all my life (Ps 146:1-2)

We are often astounded by noble and elevating deeds of sacrifice and unselfishness, and surprised that people are capable of performing them. But the noblest and most uplifting deed humanly possible, is to praise the almighty God under all circumstances.

It is a pitiful fact that in our worship we often neglect to praise God, and this unavoidably affects our lives adversely. If we don't even sing in the sunshine, how will we ever be able to sing in the dark?

Singing the praise of God is much more than a religious duty. It is a life-style inspired by our faith in Jesus Christ. Praise to God cannot be limited to two or three hours per week. It must fill every minute of our lives!

Praise to God is the practical power of faith which sanctifies ordinary things. You can only glorify God if He is at the centre of your life and all other things are subjected to Him in praise and worship.

If you carefully think about this, you will realize how easy it actually is to praise God. He grants us so much. Everything we have was given to us by Him. Therefore it should give us joy to sing his praises in everything we do in his Name. Once we have learnt to glorify God, we will find courage to overcome even the most difficult circumstances.

I will praise You as long as I live, o Lord, my Redeemer. I will praise You in prosperity and adversity; in sunshine and in darkness.

July 17 Matthew 5:1-12

PEACEMAKERS FOR GOD
Happy are those who work for peace; God will call them his children! (Mt 5:9)

The search for peace is never-ending – just like the search for truth. Those who seek lasting peace, are doomed to disappointment.

Peace cannot be acquired by material possessions. It originates in the hearts of men. Boundaries and gold cannot wage wars – but people can. The sinful nature of man demands it. Peace is excellent, but if we seek it by force and not by open discussion, it will be unacceptable and of short duration. Peace without justice is but tyranny called by another name, however hard we may try to sugar the pill.

The task of the peacemaker is an extremely difficult one. It is not a passive state of rest, but a positive, dynamic action. Although it is often a thankless task, it remains a God-given mission.

The peacemakers of whom Jesus speaks, are not people who evade their responsibilities. They wrestle with the problem until they succeed. If we want to be makers of peace, we will have to do our duty painstakingly – even if it is by way of conflict.

Jesus wanted to teach us not to rely on our fickle emotions. Once we have found peace with God, we will be able to pray for our enemies. The Lord does not promise happiness to those who "have" peace, but to those who "make" peace. As co-workers of God we then reach our highest fulfilment and contribute to bringing peace to his world.

O Lord, reveal your love to me, so that I can be a peacemaker in a world full of hatred and distrust.

July 18   1 Kings 19:1-18

SELF-PITY
I am the only one left – and they are trying to kill me! (1 Kgs 19:10)
In the north-western part of England there is a small mining town with the name of "Pity Me". The town is of no great significance, except to those who live there. Figuratively speaking, however, this town has a population so large that it can hardly be calculated, because there are so many people living in a place called "Pity Me". These people constantly bewail themselves and thrive on the pity of others.

It is a good thing to show pity to others, but we must guard against harming people by our pity, by exploiting their moral or character weaknesses. If you pity a person but fail to speak the truth in love, you can do more harm than good.

If someone pities himself, it is unwise to be over-sympathetic. It would be better to help him forget about himself and teach him to become involved with people whose problems are more acute than his. To be able to help a person in this way, he must be approached with the honesty one can only obtain from the Holy Spirit. But honesty without love increases pain. Only honesty born of love can contribute to the destruction of the negative powers of self-pity. Then you have solved the problem at its source and a new beginning can be planned. To this end the recreating power of the Holy Spirit is needed.

Dear Lord, keep me safe from the harmful ailment of self-pity. Help me to grow in my service to You and to my fellow-men.

July 19   Exodus 33:7-23

PEACE DEMANDS COMMUNICATION
The Lord would speak with Moses face to face, just as a man speaks with a friend (Ex 33:11)
When we learn to speak to God and to listen to Him, we will find peace in our hearts. As long as the dialogue with God continues, we have hope, tranquility and peace – however dark circumstances may seem.

When Adam and Eve disobeyed God, they fled from God and would not speak to Him. The idyllic peace of Eden was shattered and fear took its place. When Cain refused to speak to his brother Abel, he became a murderer who had to flee before man and God. When God spoke to Moses as with a friend, he found peace of mind. How nobly Abraham persevered in talking to God and pleading with Him on behalf of Sodom and Gomorrah! (Gen 18:16-33). Even though these ungodly cities were destroyed by fire and brimstone, Lot and his family found peace and safety in Zoar.

Through his Son, Jesus Christ, God came to communicate with us in a perfect manner about everything that would contribute to our peace. His enemies thought that they had finally smothered his voice on Calvary, but on the day of Pentecost He started talking to all people – in all languages.

God still speaks to us through his Word. He has something to say to us in every situation, if only we would listen and open our hearts to his words. He speaks to us of redemption from sin; of joy born of sorrow; of happiness through tears; of love in spite of hate – of peace for all who persevere in speaking to God and listening to Him . . . and then carry his words to a world anxiously waiting for peace.

Loving Father, open my heart and my ears to catch up your words, which will convey your perfect peace to me and to the world.

July 20 Romans 12:1-8

AWAY WITH MASS MENTALITY

Do not conform yourselves to the standards of this world, but let God transform you inwardly by a complete change of your mind. Then you will be able to know the will of God – what is good and is pleasing to Him and is perfect (Rom 12:2)

Most people are only too willing and content to simply drift with the current. We develop a mass mentality and bow to the domination of the majority. In this manner we are reduced to a grey, colourless mass which simply exists to second the motions of the mass. Occasionally there is a sign of protest, but then we comfortably slip back into the protection offered by the mass. We become yes-men without any respect for the God-given individuality granted to us by the divine Creator.

When you commit your life to Christ, you obtain new values and standards, which bring along new responsibilities. You often find yourself out of step with popular opinion; selfishness is replaced by compassion; dishonesty makes place for unswerving truth; love grows to include even your enemies. No longer do you travel your own way and seek your own desires – now you seek the will of God and it is your greatest joy to obey Him in all things. The Holy Spirit is powerfully working in your life and you no longer resist Him. The Holy Spirit is allowed to control your mind and your thoughts, and He monitors each opinion and principle of your being. If this becomes the situation in your life, you will not easily fall prey to the mass mentality of the day.

Then you will discover with surprise and joy that public opinion is relative and that your greatest happiness is gained by obeying God and living according to his will. In your endeavour to serve and obey God, you will find peace of mind.

Recreate my thoughts and my spirit, o Lord, and reveal to me, through your

Holy Spirit, your will for my life. Make me willing and obedient to follow You in love and consecration.

July 21 John 14:1-14

VICTORY OVER THE LAST GREAT FEAR
"Do not be worried and upset," Jesus told them. "Believe in God and believe also in Me. There are many rooms in my Father's house, and I am going to prepare a place for you" (Jn 14:1-2)

In one of his essays Bacon said: "Men fear death as children fear to walk in the dark." It is the uncertainty of what lies beyond death, that fills our hearts with fear. Shakespeare calls it "that undiscovered country from whose bourne no traveller returns".

It is only through faith that you will be able to live with peace of mind, joy and without fear of death. If you have made your peace with death, this destructive fear will disappear. Your thoughts are widened to encompass eternity. The glorious life in your Father's house becomes a reality. You discover that Shakespeare was wrong: Christ conquered death and He came back triumphantly. You start living in the Spirit, denying the dominion over the flesh. The fear of damnation and a confused perception of heaven may be the conflicting emotions when you consider death. If, however, you are convinced by faith that you will be clothed with immortality when you lay off this mortal body; that you will praise and serve God to perfection when you are with Him for ever – then you have conquered the great last fear of mankind.

Damnation is to be separated from God. Heaven means to live in perfect harmony with Him for ever. That is why heaven and hell don't start when you die physically, but you experience one or the other while you live here on earth. Eventually death is but a sleep, a time of rest from which your Redeemer will come to wake you and lead you into that shining glory which we name heaven – with the Lord for all eternity!

Source of life and love, I praise You for the knowledge that my physical death is only one short episode of the great epic of eternal life, which becomes mine through the saving grace of Jesus my Lord.

July 22 1 John 3:11-24

THE THEORY AND PRACTICE OF LOVE
. . . our love should not be just words and talk; it must be true love, which shows itself in action (1 Jn 3:18)

Love is the most dynamic power in the world; therefore it is important to choose the object of your love very carefully. If all that matters to you is self-interest, your love will be crippled by selfishness. If your love is focussed on Christ, you will experience the joy and freedom which only He can grant.

However, this joy and freedom will never be yours if your love is purely emotional and stripped of all practical commitment to it. It is a privilege to live in communion with God through prayer, worship and meditation. Then your mind is flooded with pure thoughts and you are inspired with noble motives. By living in consecration to God, this indescribable love becomes an integral part of your very being.

It is, however, not enough simply to experience this love in your heart. If love must be perfect, it must be revealed in the practical life of everyday. If you want to keep this love in your heart to protect it against the garish realities of life, you are limiting God's love and making it weak and insufficient.

Jesus Christ demonstrated to us how great and strong love really can be in practice. The depth and quality of his love was confirmed on the cross of Calvary when He prayed: Forgive them! To love even when your mind is in revolt against it, is what Christ expects from his followers. Not only when it is a comforting emotion, but when the situation cries out for vengeance, then the true glory of the love of Christ is revealed!

Loving Saviour, help me by the power of the indwelling Spirit to demonstrate a love which is inspiring and practical.

July 23 Luke 11:1-13

THE COST OF AN UNFORGIVING SPIRIT
Forgive us our sins, for we forgive everyone who does us wrong (Lk 11:4)

The price which you have to pay when you refuse to forgive, is exorbitant: it simply means that God cannot forgive you. You are then carrying the germ of a deadly disease in your heart and life. Some wrongs are so outrageous that it could be accepted as a sign of weakness to forgive them. Your answer to this challenge will depend upon your principles and standards. If you reject the teachings of Christ, you will allow emotion to dominate your mind.

If you assert that Christ's standards do not take the demanding realities of this world into account, you will never know peace of mind.

The philosophy of an "eye for an eye and a tooth for a tooth" is not acceptable to the followers of Jesus Christ. His policy of love and forgiveness, even towards your enemies, is proof of a sober approach to life and lays the foundation of a healthy and peaceful spirit.

If you allow feelings of hatred and vengeance to control your life, you deny the healing power of forgiveness. Then you are building a wall of separation between yourself and God and you are eventually cut off from his rich blessings. To receive forgiveness and live a happy and liberated life, you must first learn to grant forgiveness freely.

It is not easy to forgive and to forget, but it is God's way and therefore it is the best way. Place your unforgiving spirit under the recreative power of the Holy Spirit and allow Christ to establish his disposition in your heart and mind.

Holy and loving Master, teach me to forgive as You forgive. Make me willing to be taught this important lesson by the Holy Spirit.

July 24   Psalm 94:1-11

WE WORSHIP A GOD WHO LISTENS
God made our ears – can't He hear? He made our eyes – can't He see? (Ps 94:9)

It is a great comfort to have the assurance that we worship a God who listens; a God who hears our prayers and who cares for us! The moment is never inopportune to God. It may be early or late – He is always there to listen. Unlike our mortal friends, our heavenly Father is always available. He never considers us to be troublesome. On the contrary, He waits longingly for us to share time in prayer with Him.

To Him nobody is too humble or too important. There is no class prejudice. Everybody has a free and unobstructed way to the throne of grace, because Jesus opened the way into the sanctuary with the sacrifice of his blood.

Age is of no importance to God. The old Victorian adage that children should be seen but not heard, is not applicable when we approach God. He commands that children should not be prevented to come to Him.

Some people have to travel a lonely road in old age and often long for somebody to speak to. God never forgets them – He is always available when they want to speak to Him.

God is aware of the fears of childhood, the storm and stress of youth, the fatigue of the adult years, the loneliness of old age. He is available for anybody to communicate with Him in prayer, worship or meditation. He does not want us to pray to Him only in times of crisis, but to open our hearts to Him at all times. The miracle is that God listens to each one as if he were the only person on earth. His hearing spans the world – but it narrows to hear your prayer! Praise be to God!

I confess, o Lord who hears, that I sometimes doubt whether my prayers are of any importance to You, or whether they even reach You. Thank you for the renewed assurance, through Jesus Christ, that You listen and care.

July 25 Genesis 42:25-38

A SHORT-SIGHTED MISTAKE
Do you want to make me lose all my children? Joseph is gone; Simeon is gone; and now you want to take away Benjamin. I am the one who suffers! (Gen 42:36)

The aged Jacob experienced an accumulation of affliction and tragedies. His beloved Rachel had died and with her all the romantic dreams of his youth. He believed Joseph was dead. Simeon was a prisoner in Egypt and now they wanted to take Benjamin away from him. The country was in the grip of a terrible drought. In these devastating circumstances Jacob felt that everybody and everything were against him.

We often experience times of similar crises, when all the promises which life held, lie shattered at our feet. Everything goes wrong: at home, at work; in our relationships. This is when we are easily inclined to self-pity.

In his sorrow and disappointment Jacob made an error of judgement. He forgot that God was still in control – also of his life. God is not only there when things go well; He is also present in times of drought, sorrow and distress. He is able to turn the bad to good.

Jacob made the short-sighted mistake of thinking that his separation from Benjamin could only lead to the worst to happen. Jacob was mourning Joseph's death, while God was using Joseph to feed the world. Jacob eventually would receive his three sons back and his joy would be indescribable.

We must not always expect the worst from life. We are often so attached to our Benjamins and our Josephs that God has difficulty in fulfilling his purpose with us. Instead of lamenting: "I am the one who suffers!" let us rejoice: "If God is for us, who can be against us?"

I thank You, heavenly Father, that even at times when it seems as if all hope is lost, You are still for me, through the redeeming work of your Son, Jesus Christ.

July 26 1 Kings 19:1-18

HOW MUCH DISCOURAGEMENT CAN YOU ENDURE?

"It's too much, Lord," he prayed. "Take away my life; I might as well be dead!" (1 Kgs 19:4)

Some people cannot come to terms with dejection. At such times they are inclined to cry out in despair: "I can go no further! I have reached breaking-point!" The prophet Elijah, the hero of faith on Mount Carmel, experienced this type of utter despondency.

We do indeed live in an age trademarked by stress and pressure. Human relationships become strained and problematic. It seems as though everything we attempt is doomed to failure. Nothing goes according to our prearranged plans. In such a time we are in dire danger of losing faith. Prayer is no longer an inspiring power and we even question the meaning of life: Is it all worth while?

Don't become entangled with the symptoms, but look for the cause. Are you not perhaps overburdening your physical powers? Are you not trying to undertake too many things simultaneously? Do you still have a living and healthy relationship with the Source of your power and love?

Introspection and soul-searching are of great importance. It may be a golden opportunity for a new, inspired experience with the Lord. Our prayer in this time of spiritual barrenness should be: "Examine me, oh God, and know my mind; test me and discover my thoughts. Find out if there is any evil in me and guide me in the everlasting way" (Ps 139:23-24).

Then you can make all his promises of a fulfilled and fruitful life your own. You will experience peace of mind and life will once more become meaningful.

Merciful Lord Jesus, allow your good Spirit to lead me to a new discovery of your renewing strength so that my life will glorify your holy Name.

July 27   **Psalm 130:1-8**

LEARN TO WAIT
I wait eagerly for the Lord's help, and in his word I trust. I wait for the Lord more eagerly than watchmen wait for the dawn . . . (Ps 130:5-6)
One of the most difficult things in life is to wait! It is much easier to be active than to discipline yourself to positive meditation and reflection.

To live creatively, we need to plan. Like the psalmist on his pilgrimage we must make time to wait upon the Lord in faith and trust. Times of forced waiting can be of great benefit and blessing in our lives.

During these times you have the opportunity to observe your fellowmen with compassion. This will prevent you from shirking involvement like the priest and the Levite. Perhaps you have fallen into the habit of only "taking" from life – now God gives you the grace to "give" of yourself. You can also use the time of waiting to search your soul. Prayerfully wait upon the Lord and be sensitive to what He has to say to you. Perhaps the Holy Spirit wants to make you aware of some dark or unproductive area in your spiritual life. What you discover there might not look good or flattering, but it will drive you to God; He who makes all things new and causes you to grow spiritually.

Do not neglect or reject the opportunity to wait upon the Lord. If you wait faithfully and trustingly, you will hear his loving word. These times will then not be not wasted, but will bring forth resounding deeds.

Slow me down, o Lord, so that I can hear what You have to say. Help me to see myself and the world around me through your eyes.

July 28 1 Peter 1:1-12

THE BLESSEDNESS OF BELIEVING WITHOUT SEEING!

You love Him, although you have not seen Him, and you believe in Him, although you do not now see Him. So you rejoice with great and glorious joy which words cannot express, because you are receiving the salvation of your souls, which is the purpose of your faith in Him (1 Pet 1:8-9)

Some of the most important things in life are invisible. We cannot see the air which we breathe, but without it we cannot live. The love of our dear ones cannot be measured, yet without it life would be much poorer. Peace, faith, trust, joy, patience, and compassion, are all enriching qualities that cannot be seen or measured.

A person who claims only to believe in what he sees and feels, inevitably leads a very limited life. Like Thomas, we must learn that our faith is not located in our fingertips or in our eyes. The greatest joys of life cannot be seen or analysed in a test-tube.

If you love and trust God, you prove that you believe without seeing. Even though God is invisible, you can see his work in the lives and circumstances of people. God is working in different areas of our existence and if we sincerely seek Him, we will surely find Him.

If you consider the wonder of creation and appreciate the amazing power of God, you will find joy and inspiration. It may at times seem as if evil is ruling the world, and that all that is good and noble is being threatened. But faith convinces us that this is still God's world and that He reigns over it. Place your trust in Him and you will have the quiet assurance that God is in control and that the final victory is His. Omnipotence is the essence of Him whom you cannot see.

Almighty and living Creator, I glory in your living presence, even though I cannot see You. Thank you for revealing Yourself to me in the person of your Son, Jesus Christ – my Saviour and Redeemer.

July 29 James 1:1-8

DON'T HIDE BEHIND A MASK

A person like that, unable to make up his mind and undecided in all he does, must not think that he will receive anything from the Lord (Jas 1:7-8)

There are very few people who reveal their true selves to their fellow-men. They wear masks to fit the occasion. In this way they conceal the truth about themselves. Everybody wants to be accepted by others, and therefore strives to present the best image. This often happens at the cost of one's principles.

Although it is natural to try to hide your true feelings from others, you must never try to conceal your true self or your deepest feelings from the living Christ.

You can't hide from Him behind a mask. If you are not absolutely honest with Him, you will never understand yourself, and your relationship with the Lord will suffer. When you are totally honest with Him, you will gain a deeper insight into yourself. You will grow spiritually and the presence of Christ will become a living reality to you, while you are gradually stripped of all hypocrisy and pretence. You will never again yield to bad influences or be persuaded to perform acts that are contradictory to your own beliefs.

If Christ controls your life and your emotions, you will no longer need to hide behind a mask. You will be able to be true to yourself, and the Holy Spirit will enable you to live an honest and faithful Christian life.

Make me absolutely honest with You, o Lord, so that I can be released of the stress of professing to be what I am not. Grant me spiritual honesty and integrity through your Holy Spirit.

July 30   Acts 17:16-34

IDLE DREAMS OR INSPIRED VISIONS?
He did this so that they would look for Him, and perhaps find Him as they felt about for Him. Yet God is actually not far from any one of us . . .
(Acts 17:27)

There are times when life is dreary, tedious and monotonous. Then the hours drag by, and as the weeks pass, your daily existence becomes a test of perseverance, instead of the joyful and inspiring experience God intended it to be.

In this unhappy situation you hang on to your dreams but you don't have the driving force to realize them. Your inspiring visions have been degraded to idle day-dreams.

This type of disappointment and frustration is not God's intention for your life. He created you with a divine purpose and until you declare yourself willing and obedient to discharge your divine calling and to consecrate yourself to Christ, you will live, but unfulfilled and disappointed.

It is when you sincerely strive to obey God's will to the best of your ability, that life gains meaning and becomes filled with deep satisfaction and joy. By living to the glory of God and doing his will unconditionally, you attach yourself to the greatest power on earth and in the universe. This Power is constantly seeking channels through which He can reveal Himself to humanity. By your dedication to Him you become such a channel and you experience the uplifting and inspiring support of the Holy Spirit.

Then life becomes exciting and challenging again. The humdrum routine is something of the past because you live in the presence of God from day to day. By the work of the Holy Spirit your idle dreams become inspired visions of what you can be and do for God.

Lord Jesus, I praise You in the knowledge that I have found meaning and purpose for my life in You. I thank You for the happiness and fulfilment I find in your service.

July 31   Romans 8:1-17

BLESSED ASSURANCE – I AM A CHILD OF GOD
Those who are led by God's Spirit are God's sons (Rom 8:14)
It is absolutely wrong to contend that man is "nothing"! Even though Scripture repeatedly reminds us that man is dust and that he withers like the flowers of the field. But the overriding theme of the New Testament is that God loved man so much, that He sent his Son into the world to reconcile man with Himself.

You are of great importance in the eyes of God. He even invited you to call Him "Father"! Therefore you may never speak disparagingly about yourself. The Spirit guides you to rejoice in humble thanks for the fact that you are redeemed through Jesus Christ and have become a child of God.

To accept that you are a child of God and yet dig up old sins which have been forgiven a long time ago, is a denial of your Father's love and mercy – of your very relationship with God.

The Holy Spirit leads you to the acceptance of God's forgiveness through the salvation wrought by Jesus Christ. You start on the road to victorious living. This is God's will for you and you dare not be satisfied with anything less.

A continuous awareness of God as Father never implies self-sufficiency or spiritual pride; it is not a form of self-hypnosis or fantasy – but it is a practical and concrete result of a constant relationship with the living Christ. No longer slave, but child and heir. An indescribable privilege and miracle of divine grace!

Merciful and loving Father, it is my eternal joy and my source of power to be your child. Thank you for your love and patience with me.

AUGUST

PRAYER

Heavenly Guide, lead me through this month.
I desperately want to believe unconditionally – like Abraham, Enoch and Moses, and each of the gallery of heroes mentioned in Hebrews 11.
But like Thomas, I also must see first and feel before I can believe. My faith is often limited to what I experience through my fingertips and my eyes.
I so much want to believe in the unseen, and be able to confess: "My Lord and my God!"
Lead me through your Spirit to an honest and practical faith, which will bind me to Jesus eternally.
I so much want to treasure hope in my heart – hope that all the noble, burning desires of my soul will become a glorious reality;
that my spirit will grow in optimism, knowledge and truth; that I will be able to discern those things which really matter and are of prime importance.
Keep the spirit of Christian joy burning in my heart. I desperately want to love, Lord. With the honesty of a person on his deathbed, I would like to say: "Lord, You know everything, You know that I love you!"
And I want to love my fellow-men with a sincere, unselfish and sacrificing love,
which breaks down all dividing walls and makes reconciliation a practical reality.
Lead me to a new understanding of faith, hope and love during the month of August!
Through the grace and love of Jesus Christ!
Amen.

August 1   Philippians 4:10-20

FAITH IS NOT A SPIRITUAL LUXURY
I have the strength to face all conditions by the power that Christ gives me (Phil 4:13)

It sometimes feels as if we are losing control of our lives and circumstances. Inevitably there are times when the demands of life overwhelm us. It then seems as though we do not have the faith to carry us through.

We may feel that our circumstances are deteriorating to the point of despair. Even our relationships become strained. We feel so helpless that we want to cry with Paul: "Who, then, is capable of such a task?" (2 Cor 2:16).

However, the problem is not that we cannot cope – no, everything only seems impossible because the balance is disturbed between our spiritual approach and the challenges of life. The demands of life have exceeded our faith.

If you have reached the end of your resources, you must return to the fundamental issues of life; those things which strengthen your faith and reassure you of the presence of the living Christ. Then you will regain your balance and see people and circumstances in the right perspective.

God does not want you to crack under stress. A living faith will be a stabilizing force in such times of pressure. Such a faith is not a spiritual luxury, but a compelling necessity. If you are driven to God by your distress and learn to trust Him unconditionally, He will support you from day to day. Then you will be capable of everything through Him who gives you strength.

Loving Father, I confess that I need You and that without You I am weak and powerless. Grant me the strength to accept the challenges of life, to wrestle with them and to be victorious through the power of your Holy Spirit.

August 2   Psalm 32:1-11

DESPERATELY NEEDED: ENTHUSIASTS!
I will teach you the way you should go; I will instruct you and advise you (Ps 32:8)

God wants to use all his children, but many of them pose a very real problem. They confess that they are willing to allow God to use them and work through them, but it seems as if they need royal commands every time, signed and sealed by God, before they even consider going into action.

The history of the Christian faith bears witness to astounding deeds performed by ordinary people, because they trusted God and demonstrated this faith with enthusiasm and lived out their commitment in joy. Occasionally these people were called fools, but because they were enthusiastic about their faith and obediently followed God's will for their lives, they were quite willing to be "fools for Christ"!

God can work miracles with a dedicated servant who not only talks and listens, but practises his faith with enthusiasm. When you listen to the voice of God in prayer and meditation and He shows you the way, you will accept the challenge in faith and proceed with courage in your heart. You will act in the knowledge that God leads and that He will inspire you to faith and action.

If God has mapped out part of the way for you, He expects you to proceed on that road. Don't demand to see the whole map of the completed journey. Trust Him and start out enthusiastically. You will be surprised by what God can do with an obedient servant. Place your hand in the hand of God and step out with enthusiasm – even into the dark. His eternal light will safely guide you.

Heavenly Leader, make me willing to follow enthusiastically wherever You may lead and to do whatever You expect from me.

August 3 Genesis 28:10-22

A TALKING STONE!
Jacob got up early next morning, took the stone that was under his head, and set it up as a memorial. Then he poured olive-oil on it to dedicate it to God (Gen 28:18)

Many things of great value and consequence happened in Jacob's life. But probably the most important event was connected with the stone at Bethel. Destitute and deeply distressed, he rested his head on this stone while fleeing from his angry brother.

And on this stone God granted Jacob his dream. There the God of Abraham and Isaac also became the God of Jacob. From that stone Jacob looked straight into heaven and saw God!

But it was also the place where the dream of the previous night faded the following day, because it could not endure the stark reality of day. It is difficult to cling to a dream in broad daylight.

Jacob, however, did not want to sacrifice his dream. He placed the stone in an upright position to prevent it from disappearing in the desert sand, so that he could repeatedly return to that sacred spot. He poured olive-oil over it, to sanctify it to the glory of God. Eventually this stone became a sign of Jacob's own consecration to his dream and to the God of Bethel; each day of his life! Bethel became a symbol of God's almighty presence and of his faithfulness – of the special mercy of God in Jacob's life.

From that moment his life changed radically and it could never be the same again. In this manner God lowers his ladder of mercy into the lives of his children, for Christ to descend to us personally.

Compassionate Lord, I want to consecrate my life to You and follow wherever You lead. Thank you for the message of hope and comfort which the stone of Bethel brings.

August 4 James 3:1-12

THE FIRE OF THE TONGUE

And the tongue is like a fire. It is a world of wrong, occupying its place in our bodies and spreading evil through our whole being (Jas 3:6)

If somebody were to compile a volume of all the misery of this world, he would have to devote many chapters to the suffering and sorrow, the many broken relationships, the destruction and pain caused by the human tongue.

With the tongue blatant untruths and half-truths are proclaimed; unfounded accusations are made; heartless judgements are made in the name of friendship, cold-blooded murder is committed; unthinking and cutting sarcasm and humiliating mockery are expressed – a never-ending list of all the painful accomplishments on which the uncontrolled tongue prides itself.

But the tongue is unbridled just until the owner commits his life to Christ. Then the tongue belongs to Him and there is a visible change which bears witness to spiritual discipline. As the disposition of Jesus Christ grows in the heart, the tongue is tamed. Eventually it becomes an instrument to sing the praises of God and to tell of his love.

If somebody else's tongue has hurt you, take your pain to the Lord in prayer. Don't repay evil with evil. Then it only becomes a vicious circle. Ask for grace to forgive and to forget.

But if you have harmed someone with your words, you must rectify the situation before it is too late. Confess it to Him who gives you strength to control your tongue. He will place a watch before your mouth and love in your heart.

Examine me, O God, and know my mind; test me, and discover my thoughts. Find out if there is any evil in me and guide me in the everlasting way (Ps 139:23-24).

August 5   1 John 3:11-18

TO LOVE IS AN ELEVATING TASK
This is how we know what love is: Christ gave his life for us (1 Jn 3:16)
Love is like a frail and tender plant. If we cherish it, care for it, and give it our sincere attention, it will prosper and flourish and eventually produce the most beautiful flowers. If we neglect our duty towards it, it will languish and eventually die – and with it all the promises of flowers.

The consequences are tragic when we treat love as a matter of course. Lovers enjoy demonstrating their love and will do anything to prove its quality. Many consider the marriage vows as the ultimate of sacrificial love. However, this attitude soon wilts in the face of selfish demands. So much unhappiness and many divorces could have been prevented if married couples had devoted as much loving care and compassion after the wedding as before.

However many ways there may be of revealing your love, unselfish self-sacrifice is always a prerequisite. That is how Jesus Christ disclosed his love to us. Kahlil Gibran says in *The Prophet*: "When I give of my possessions, I give but little. It is only when I give of myself that I truly give." Jesus gave Himself unconditionally for our benefit – the Paragon of true love!

To carry the positive power of love into the world, asks for consecration and hard work. This love must be revealed in practical terms, or else it changes to indifference, and eventually dies.

Loving Master, help me to labour faithfully at the loves in my life: my love to You and to my fellow-men. Grant me an abundance of the fragrant flowers from the plant of love which I cherish in my heart.

August 6　　　　　　　　　　　　　　　　　　　　Luke 12:13-21

THE TRUE WORTH OF MAN
Watch out and guard yourselves from every kind of greed; because a person's true life is not made up of the things he owns, no matter how rich he may be (Lk 12:15)

Impressions can be very deceptive. A person may seem outwardly joyful and happy, but inwardly his heart may be breaking. A businessman seeming extremely prosperous, may be on the brink of bankruptcy.

Don't allow yourself to be deceived by external appearances, because it often camouflages a moral weakness or a spiritual deficiency. The intrinsic and true value of a person is determined by his attachment to God and by his love to his fellow-men.

When you have risen above your desire to impress people, and strive to serve others in love, you have discovered your inherent value and true character. It no longer matters what people think of you – that's simply reputation. But what God knows you to be, that is whom you really are. This feeling of self-esteem is not born of a passing emotion, but is acquired by a conscientious adherence to noble principles, a firm spiritual foundation, and a single-minded faith in God.

When your life is controlled by the will of God and inspired by the Holy Spirit, you develop an inner disposition both compensating and enriching. This life originates from the true Vine and inevitably produces good fruit. Then you experience fulfilment and you become a source of joy and inspiration to those whom you live and work with.

Leader and Master, mercifully grant that by the work of your Holy Spirit, my life will reflect genuine spiritual values, singly to your greater honour and glory.

August 7　　　　　　　　　　　　　　　　　　　　Matthew 7:1-6

ABOUT LOGS AND SPECKS
Do not judge others, so that God will not judge you . . . Why, then, do you

look at the speck in your brother's eye, and pay no attention to the log in your own eye? (Mt 7:1, 3)
To Christians human relationships are of great importance. Intolerance, malignance and destructive criticism, spoil healthy relationships.

You are continuously in contact with other people. Sometimes their company is forced upon you: in your work, in your sport and in your daily life. In the social world there is a never-ending interaction of personalities.

Some people like you and you like them, but with others you find it difficult to get along. Then one must be extremely careful that you do not allow your inability to communicate to develop into aggression or intolerance.

Each person conveys his attitude to other people – consciously or unconsciously. If you don't like a person, he will invariably be aware of it. Even though your actions are correct, he will be conscious of your feelings of antagonism, and react to them.

The secret of successful human relationships is simply to love and respect people. Not in an exaggerated or sentimental manner, but absolutely sincere – in word and deed. You must love all people, in spite of their weaknesses and failures. To actively try to see only the best in others, and to expect only the noblest of motives from them, is a sure road to successful human relationships. This is only possible if you have the love of Jesus Christ in your heart.

Holy Father, according to the example of Jesus Christ, and through the guidance of the Holy Spirit, I want to try and come to a better understanding of my fellow-men.

August 8   Psalm 102:1-17

GOD WILL HOLD ME
When I am in trouble, don't turn away from me! Listen to me, and answer me quickly when I call! He will hear his forsaken people and listen to their prayer (Ps 102:2, 17)
Sometimes we find it difficult to pray. In such times we easily fall prey to despondency, because even that which keeps you going under all circumstances – a living and abiding awareness of the presence of God – no longer seems a reality to you.

It seems as if God no longer listens, as if your petitions and prayers fall on deaf ears. Suddenly God becomes an aloof and uncaring stranger – He who was always so near and available! When you feel this way, fear strikes at your heart and you feel that you are sinning against God Himself.

But what you should realize as a Christian, is that even these times – however strange it may sound – could mean a great deal to your spiritual life. Incorrectly you think that God has turned his face from you and does not care, because you now are lost.

In these times one must always remember that only by faith can you cling to the assurance of the presence of God in your life. You must learn to trust God under all circumstances; to hold his hand firmly in the sunshine, but also in the dark.

Faith does not depend on feelings and emotions. When you sincerely believe and trust in God, his presence becomes a joyful and reassuring reality. Then dark times can occur and you will know that God wil hold you in his hand – unto all eternity!

Holy and loving God, help me, when darkness settles over my life, to look away from myself and my problems; simply to seek You more vigorously and do your will more obediently, until You change the darkness into light.

August 9   Mark 4:35-41

THE STORMS OF LIFE
Teacher, don't You care that we are about to die? (Mk 4:38)
When you turn to Christ with a living faith in your heart, He helps to ease your distress and lighten your burden. He is capable of calming the storms of life. When Christ enters your life, you come to know the peaceful calm of a heart which has found its rest in God. Then problems can multiply and storms can arise – he who has his refuge in the living Christ, is safe and secure against the fury of the storm.

When the icy winds of sorrow and grief reach gale force in your life, you find peace and comfort in the knowledge that Christ is near you. With each storm raging in your heart, peace descends with the knowledge of his presence. This peace no storm can take from you.

A little boy sat playing peacefully on the floor of his father's cabin, while a devastating storm was raging and the ship was in danger of capsizing. Mountainous waves were threatening to drag them all to the depths of the ocean. When asked whether he was not afraid, he replied with childlike faith: "My father is the captain of this ship. Why should I be afraid?"

Christ is our peace in the storms of life. He changes the darkest night into glorious day. He brings contentment when problems whip up a storm of unbelief, doubt and uncertainty in our hearts. All He requires from you is to seek his will for your life and allow Him to lead you to peace and inner calm.

Dear Lord, I am so grateful to know that You control the storms in my life; that your hand holds me and leads me to green pastures and quiet waters.

August 10   Ecclesiastes 3:1-8

GOD'S CHRONOLOGY
Everything that happens in this world happens at the time God chooses (Ecc 3:1)

The peaceful, carefree days of the past are steadily disappearing and it seems as if each day is loaded with more and more activity – matters demanding our attention and consideration, calling for a decision. As a result we are placed increasingly at the mercy of pressure and strain.

If you try to keep up with the gruelling pace, you will find that you are tearing yourself apart in an effort to meet all the demands and to do the impossible. Eventually, all you attain is a feeling of unlimited frustration, because all your efforts have ended in failure.

The only way to bring your labours and efforts to fruition, is to become quiet before God in the first instance and before your hectic day begins. Give yourself to Him unconditionally. When you come to Him tired and overburdened, He willingly grants that reserve of strength and inward power you need.

If you start your day by placing your problems before Him, praying Him to grant you his guidance and to reveal to you his will for your life, you will be able to cope with your challenges with a novel calm and peace of mind. Then you see things in their true perspective, with Christ at the centre of your entire endeavour. Then the timeless Christ teaches you the secret of utilizing every moment of your precious time. So you come to live victoriously within God's chronology.

I dedicate and consecrate my daily labours to You, o Lord, and I pray that You will guide my thoughts and deeds in such a manner that I will constantly live according to your divine timetable.

August 11   1 Samuel 3:1-21

LISTEN TO THE LORD!
Then Eli realized that it was the Lord who was calling the boy, so he said to him, "Go back to bed; and if He calls you again, say, 'Speak, Lord, your servant is listening' (1 Sam 3:8)

It is of great importance for a child of God to spend a major part of his quiet time in communing with God: to praise and glorify his Name; to confess your sins and imperfections; to intercede for others; and to petition Him for your own needs and interests.

Nevertheless, do you ever give God an opportunity to speak to you? Or are you so tied up in your own needs and interests, that He never gets a chance to speak to you? God speaks in many and various ways with his children; if they would only listen for his voice. By Scripture, in nature, through your daily task, in your sorrow and grief, in joy and in confusion of spirit. God is not a God of silence or a God of speechless fate. "The sheep hear his voice as he calls his own sheep by name, and he leads them out" (Jn 10:3).

If you are sensitive to his voice, He will reveal his will to you. That is why it is imperative that every one of his children should spend enough time quietly listening to God. You must patiently wait upon the Lord as Samuel did, with a heart expressing the sole desire: "Speak, Lord, your servant is listening." You will hear his voice. You will never hear his words while you are assiduously stringing together line upon line of your own selfish words. Be still, and know that the Lord is God. You will unmistakably hear his voice and his Spirit will guide you to God's very presence.

I praise You, Lord, for the peace which I experience while I listen to You in quiet times, and for seeing and hearing your will for my life unfold.

August 12   1 John 4:7-21

FEAR AND LOVE CANNOT DWELL TOGETHER
There is no fear in love; perfect love drives out all fear (1 Jn 4:18)
We have so many fears and anxieties about insignificant and trifling matters – things of which we are only vaguely aware. While we live in the shadow of these countless fears and worries, we can never appreciate life with its sunshine and manifold of riches and joys. Not even to mention the great number of ominous things which we truly have reason to fear!

An attitude of love, however, can destroy fear and conquer anxiety, because if you can imagine but only something of God's love for you, and if you sincerely love God, there is no reason for fear. If you continue to fear, it simply means that you are not trusting God, because his love exorcises all fear. He carries you through and lovingly protects you, even in the depths of despair. Why then fear, if the almighty God is with you? Whether fear comes to you in any one of its thousand images, you will be safe in the hands of a loving God, and He is your guarantee against fear.

When you have been released from your paralysing fear, your life's work becomes a calling of love; sickness is a cord of love binding you to Him; even death becomes a friendly guide leading you through the dark valley up to the shining portals of heaven itself. When love has driven out all fear, all things work together for us, and as children of God we discover the wonder of true "life"!

Heavenly Comforter, You understand my fear. I kneel in gratitude for your great love, which drives out all fear and anxiety. Let the law of love rule my life, so that I can consecrate my life to You, the Source of all true love.

August 13   Psalm 50:1-15

PRAISE IS EXCELLENT THERAPY
Let the giving of thanks be your sacrifice to God, and give the Almighty all that you promised (Ps 50:14)
There are people with an inherent joy for living and they live totally – as if life is the greatest adventure of which each moment must be gladly

enjoyed. It seems as if they have no cares or worries and as if they never long for a different type of life.

One must never consider such happiness as a matter of course. Express your appreciation for what you have, because it is only when your heart breaks out in praise and thanks to God, that his blessings and benedictions become a joyful reality in your life.

If your cup runs over with joy and you feel it virtually impossible to experience greater happiness, you must look around you and share your joy with somebody less fortunate than yourself. It is excellent medicine, not only for the other person, but perhaps more so for yourself. Your own joy multiplies so greatly when you share it with another person. If you are selfish and petty in the midst of your happiness, you will not find joy in your prosperity for very long. Happiness was born a twin and must be shared to gain the greatest profit from it.

Each perfect gift comes from God. When you receive your blessings from his bounty with humility and share it with others to the glory of his Name, you bring God a sacrifice of praise and joy to your fellow-men.

Lord, You bless me beyond my wildest expectations. Help me to humbly and willingly share my happiness with others.

August 14 Isaiah 45:1-8

GOD OF THE DARK SECRET PLACES
I will give you treasures from dark, secret places; then you will know that I am the Lord . . . (Is 45:3)
Your memories after the death of a loved one, may bring a limited degree of comfort. But it may also increase the depth of your sorrow and aggravate your sense of loss. Holiday times, Christmas and birthdays bring an unbearable nostalgia which keeps you wandering in the dark and barren country of sorrow.

Everyday there are so many memories which are revived: a tune over the radio, a photo, a dried flower between the pages of a book . . . all these reminders carry you back to the past with unbearable pain.

But also this is beneficial: you must express your sorrow. A flood of tears often calms the storm.

The company of friends can be wonderfully enriching and comforting, and you will have to make time for this. But there is another Friend who wants to listen and to whom you may go with your sorrows. Then you are never alone in the abyss of sorrow and grief. When you regularly speak to God, He will alleviate your pain: ". . . He will wipe away all tears from their eyes" (Rev 21:4).

Through his Spirit, God gently guides us back to life and teaches us to say with Paul: "The one thing I do, however, is to forget what is behind me and do my best to reach what is ahead" (Phil 3:13).

Even though I pass through the dark, secret places of sorrow, good Shepherd, I shall not fear, because You are with me. Keep me close to You, comforting Redeemer, so that I will always be sure of your presence through Jesus Christ.

August 15   John 8:12-20

AFRAID OF THE DARK?

"I am the light of the world," He said. *"Whoever follows Me will have the light of life and will never walk in darkness"* (Jn 8:12)

Only when you find yourself in pitch-black darkness, do you learn to appreciate the light. On a grey, rainy day with the sky overcast with threatening clouds, or in the darkest night, you long for the sun. When there is a power failure and there is no light to dispel the darkness, you look with new eyes at the humble lamp which supplies light. Whatever source of power may be lacking – the darkness leaves you with a feeling of helplessness, despondency and even despair. It has a negative influence on your life, your thoughts and your attitudes.

Our spiritual life can be influenced by light and darkness, and changes according to our emotions. One moment you may be filled with overwhelming joy and all things seem bright. In the wink of an eye, however, happiness can be changed to depression, when your plans go awry and everything becomes a failure.

If only we would set aside our trust in human ingenuity and rather follow the road Christ shows to us! This road is illumined with the light of his love and mercy. Of Him John proclaims: "God is light, and there is no darkness at all in Him" (1 Jn 1:5).

God of eternal light and love, help me in my darkest moments to remember that You are the light of my life and that You will never let me go or keep me in darkness longer than your love allows or I can bear.

August 16   Colossians 4:1-6

CHRISTIAN UNDERSTANDING
Your speech should always be pleasant and interesting, and you should know how to give the right answer to everyone (Col 4:6)

If we would only spend more time making an effort to understand people, our lives would be much more interesting and meaningful. But we are too possessed with our own problems and afflictions. We refuse to consider their heartache, despondency, joy, ideals or changing moods.

The well-known writer, Berta Smit, once said: "I wanted to press past my neighbour. I was afraid that he would make demands which I did not want to meet in my selfishness. But when I fleetingly looked up into his face, I saw the eyes of Jesus looking at me through his eyes."

Do you ever purposefully plan a discussion with a fellow-man? Do you know or care about what his interests are? Have you ever tried to understand the difficult time he is passing through? To understand a person you must make a definite effort to gauge his needs and to be sensitive to his physical and spiritual distress.

The deepest yearning of a human heart is often never expressed. Very seldom can one in a conversation penetrate the deepest recesses of another's yearnings. Try to understand what a person does not say. If you don't understand his silences, you will never understand his words. To listen – also to the unspoken needs of another – is part of the art of Christian living.

Merciful God, give me the grace to make a sincere effort to understand my fellow-men, so that I can love and serve him according to the example of your son, Jesus Christ.

August 17   Matthew 14:22-32

ISOLATION CAN BE A BLESSING
After sending the people away, He went up a hill by Himself to pray. When evening came, Jesus was there alone . . . (Mt 14:23)

Man flourishes in company and in a crowd he will do things he would otherwise never have dreamt of. He fears isolation and must continually be surrounded by others. He can't endure his own company and is afraid of his own thoughts.

It is natural for man to have a need for company and it is also true that good company can be very stimulating. But one's true character is revealed when you are alone. In seclusion the riches or the poverty of your spirit is divulged. If you are restless or unhappy when you are alone, you are not yet spiritually mature. If you are able to fix your thoughts upon eternal matters when you are alone, you possess one of the richest treasures on earth.

You must develop the capability to be satisfied with your own company at times when you are isolated from the company of others. You must keep your mind constructively busy in unbroken communion with God. If you use your isolation to communicate with God, you are strengthened and renewed in body and spirit. Then you regain balance in life, your judgement is sound and you will be able to make wise decisions.

When you return to society this strength and wisdom will benefit others. In this manner your time alone with God becomes a blessing to others.

Loving Lord and Master, I thank You for inspiring moments alone with You. Let me never complain about my isolation; rather let me use it as an opportunity to serve others.

August 18 Matthew 6:24-34

BURDENED WITH TOMORROW'S WORRIES TODAY?
So do not worry about tomorrow; it will have enough worries of its own. There is no need to add to the troubles each day brings (Mt 6:34)

Are you perhaps one of those unhappy people constantly fretting and worrying about what may happen tomorrow? It seems as if life is making impossible demands on you. Responsibilities multiply and threaten to overwhelm you. In this breeding-ground worry flourishes like weeds among the wheat.

To free yourself from the grip of worry, you must be able to identify its cause. Too many people are ignorant of what causes their worry, but yet they let if fester and undermine their peace of mind with calamitous results. It is a profitable exercise to make a list of those things which you consider the causes of your worry and distress. Lay them before the Lord in prayer and see them in the right perspective so that you can decide how important or insignificant they are.

If you believe that you can triumph over your problems through the power of Jesus Christ, and if you live with this conviction in your heart, it will greatly help you to approach your problems with a calm mind. If you face your problems bravely, you will prevent today's problems spilling over into tomorrow – neither will you be burdened today by the imaginary problems of tomorrow.

When you live positively and in the knowledge that Jesus Christ is a living reality in your life, you discover that Christ also holds your problems of today in his hands and that He is already part of all your tomorrows. He is sufficient for today and He also becomes a calming and assuring presence for all your tomorrows.

Lord and Saviour, I worship You as a living reality in my life. I thank You for the emancipating knowledge that I can conquer my worries through your mercy.

August 19 Psalm 23:1-6

COMFORT IN LONELINESS
Even if I go through the deepest darkness, I will not be afraid, Lord, for You are with me (Ps 23:4)

All of us experience times of loneliness, but in actual fact nobody is ever entirely alone. Indeed, Jesus Himself said: "And I will be with you always, to the end of the age" (Mt 28:20).

However, we so easily forget this promise of our Lord, because loneliness is such a painful reality. There is the loneliness of the sick-bed, where our illness isolates us totally from the great stream of life; the loneliness within a family when members of a family long for each other with aching hearts because of forced parting; the loneliness of old age when your strength fails and your world grows smaller and smaller. But you can also feel desperately lonely in the teeming crowds of a city.

Then there is also the loneliness caused by sin; the comfortless prison of drug addiction, alcoholism, crime, and the loneliness of death from which there is no escape.

Christ knows what loneliness means. In Gethsemane He had a lonely struggle. On the cross He was forsaken by God. For this reason we may trust his promises, even when going through the dark valleys of life and death. In spite of all our fears and loneliness let us remember his comforting words: "I will be with you always."

I praise You, Lord Jesus, and worship You as the one who redeems me from my loneliness and isolation. Thank you for your constant presence. Help me to remain with You always.

August 20   Job 30:16-31

A SILENT GOD?
I call to You, O God, but You never answer; and when I pray, You pay no attention (Job 30:20)
Job knew great suffering. He lost all his children and earthly possessions. He was infected with ghastly sores and sat on a rubbish-dump scratching himself with a potsherd. He had to listen to the specious arguments of hopeless comforters.

Job's deepest suffering, however, was due to the painful experience that, in his deepest need, he called to God – and apparently received no answers. Countless numbers of Christ's followers have had this experience: a God who refuses to listen! A heaven of copper above him, which a poor mortal cannot penetrate.

In his humiliation and suffering Job felt rejected and deserted by God. The tormenting idea that God does not care, is a traumatic experience. Thus it was with Job, but God was purifying and refining him, to make his faith invincible.

God loves you dearly! He will never allow you to drift beyond his love and care. In his own good time, as with Job, He will crown you with his blessing and mercy – more than you could ever dream of.

Once, long ago, when his Son was dying on a cross, He was silent. His Son lamented: "My God, My God, why have You forsaken Me?" But never was God nearer to his Son than at that appalling moment. If you persevere in faith and keep on trusting Him, this will also be your experience.

Redeemer and Lord, I praise your holy Name, because I know that I will never be forsaken by God because You have redeemed me from that utter loneliness. I rejoice in the knowledge: I know my Redeemer lives!

August 21   2 Corinthians 5:1-10

THE GHOST OF OLD AGE UNMASKED
For we know that when this tent we live in – our body here on earth – is torn

down, God will have a house in heaven for us to live in, a home He Himself has made, which will last for ever (2 Cor 5:1)

The total dependence of a new-born baby; the high expectations of youth; the surging force of adulthood; the wisdom, equilibrium and peace of old age – these are all parts of that rousing symphony of God which we call "life".

One can easily fall into the trap of self-pity under the burden of memories of the past; especially when you consider your faults and sins: worldliness – when the bright lights of wordly pleasure meant everything to you; sensuality – when passion burnt high; infidelity – when you said with Peter: "I don't know the Man!"

Yet, God has forgiven you! He does not reproach you. He heals you of worldliness by loosening the fetters which bind you to the world, with a tender hand. The world decreases in importance and God becomes more important to you. You become more loyal and obedient, and with Peter you come to confess: "Lord, You know everything; You know that I love You!" Your passions are at rest and you have but one great passion: your love for God! Now you look forward to the eternal home which Christ has prepared for you. Your last great desire is not for earthly possessions, but for the eternal and the divine. The prodigal son has returned home and the feast is set in the house of the Father.

I thank You, redeeming Lord, that You do not forsake me in my old age. I accept old age as a loving gift out of your hand and praise You for each new day.

August 22 Galatians 1:1-24

ALONE WITH GOD
And when He decided to reveal his Son to me . . . I went at once to Arabia . . . (Gal 1:15-17)

The moment Jesus Christ became a living reality in your life, you were amazed by what had happened to you. Your values changed dramatically and your whole attitude towards life became different.

After Paul had met Christ on his way to Damascus, he was so overwhelmed that he immediately sought the seclusion of Arabia, instead of the company of the other apostles.

No doubt, your first reaction after an experience with Christ, is to talk about it with anybody who is willing to listen. However, this experience is so sanctified and deeply personal that it takes time to grow to that deeper knowledge of Christ's love, power and constant presence in your life.

It is only when you are alone with God that you can in honesty handle your transgressions and imperfections. Then you see yourself as you truly are. You can only confess to Christ and receive his purifying and redeeming mercy.

It is imperative to be alone with God. In the silence you become aware of his holy presence. You receive his all-wise guidance. The noise of the world is silenced and your mind becomes receptive for the influence of the Holy Spirit.

In these sanctified, never to be forgotten moments, God reveals his way to you and grants you the strength to do his will.

Merciful Father, impress upon my mind the necessity of spending time alone with You.

August 23 — Hebrews 5:1-10

THE MYSTERY OF SUFFERING
But even though He was God's Son, He learnt through his sufferings to be obedient (Heb 5:8)
One of the greatest mysteries of human existence, is that of suffering. Through all the ages man has been seeking an answer to this problem. Some have tried to ignore the existence of suffering, but that does not diminish the pain and confusion.

The Son of God experienced every imaginable type of suffering during his life: at the hands of friends and foe, in the garden of Gethsemane and on the cross of Calvary – intellectual, physical and spiritual. But He submitted to it in obedience to his Father's will. Nobody can maintain that He brought his suffering upon Himself by his own negative thoughts or deeds. He suffered because He was truly and completely human and identified totally with a suffering humanity.

Nobody suffers of his own free will. Neither is it the will of God that we should suffer. But suffering is an inescapable part of our human existence. It is but a faint reflection of what Christ had to suffer. Through his suffering He redeemed the world. This He could only achieve by being obedient to God through suffering and death.

Jesus Christ, through his indescribable suffering, taught us to accept it as part of God's perfect plan for our lives, and to follow the road God has mapped out, in total obedience. When in future you feel inclined to ask: "Why do bad things happen to good people?" – think of Jesus on the cross, suffering in obedience to God's will and thereby redeeming humanity!

Praise and glory to Jesus my Redeemer, for enduring my suffering and dying for my sins. Through the blows He received I was made whole! I thank You, God, for your promise that my cross will never be heavier than my strength!

August 24   **Luke 6:46-49**

LIVING ACCORDING TO GOD'S WILL
Why do you call Me, "Lord, Lord," and yet don't do what I tell you? (Lk 6:46)
The only option for the Christian believer is the way of total commitment to the will of God. It is disastrous to try and force God to fit into our preconceived agenda for life.

One is often unaware of the fact that you are trying to force God to comply with your plans – it is done so subtly. Often you mislead yourself in thinking that God is leading you, while in actual fact you want your own way, without seriously seeking the will of God. To you, your plans seem quite innocent and you simply can't see anything wrong with them. God, however, sees the total picture. What you are doing, possibly causes no permanent damage, but it also does no good, except for satisfying yourself.

True consecration means absolute obedience to God and living according to his will every moment of your life. It can either be a joyful privilege or an unbearable burden of strict religious laws. It all depends on your attitude. If your love for Christ is genuine, your obedience to Him will not be a burden, or something you have to endure while life passes by. It will reflect your love and appreciation for Him.

True consecration and commitment is reached only through joyous obedience. Then you learn the fulness and wealth of God's gifts.

Heavenly Father, I glorify your Name for the privilege of being able to prove my love through my obedience. Support me through your good Spirit.

August 25 Luke 15:11-24

DISCOVER YOUR TRUE SELF
At last he came to his senses and said, "All my father's hired workers have more than they can eat, and here I am about to starve!" (Lk 15:17)

Very few people have the courage to see themselves as they truly are. For a while you can mislead your friends as to who you really are. But in moments of absolute truth and meditation, you have to confess that the person you reflect to the world around you, is not your true "self".

When you sincerely go to God in prayer, He reveals your true self to you. This is not always a flattering experience. Hidden and forgotten sins are laid bare. A feeling of regret grips your heart and you are called to confession in order to experience God's complete forgiveness. To see yourself as God knows you really are, can simultaneously be a humbling and enriching experience.

When you start accepting yourself as you are, you also become aware of the redeeming and recreating love of God. You realize what you can be by the grace of Jesus Christ. If you allow Him to cleanse you of hypocrisy, pettiness, bitterness, hate and other negative powers in your life, you experience a mighty inflow of the Holy Spirit into your life. Stripped of all deceit and duplicity – and absolutely forgiven by God – you start a new life. This indescribable experience is a gift from God. To accept it with gratitude is the start of discovering your true self.

Lord my God, I sincerely want to be what You intended me to be. Let your Holy Spirit be my guide in this exciting adventure.

August 26 Isaiah 30:8-18

INSPIRATION AND GUIDANCE
Come back and quietly trust in Me. Then you will be strong and secure (Is 30:15)

We live in an era in which action plays a vital role. Everthing is judged by results and there is very little time for meditation and planning. If a person isolates himself in prayer, he is written off as an unpractical dreamer. Without planning, however, there can be no worthwhile, constructive action. To be a dreamer, simply for the sake of inactive dreaming, is a recipe for an unproductive life. A well-balanced person is one who can combine effective planning with constructive action.

When, as a Christian, you make your mind available to the Lord, open your life to his inspiring influence, and become sensitive to the whispering of his Spirit; then you experience an exciting and creative power which rises above all human knowledge. The living Christ is the great inspiration, inspiring you with dynamic action. No other source can supply you with so much power.

Christ does not only inspire your spiritual life, He is Lord of each area of your life. Each action bearing his approval will be carried out by his inspiration. Before you start an important project, or enter a new period of your life, you must first spend time alone with God, to receive his inspiration and guidance.

Teach me, dear Lord, to wait in silent prayer for your inspiration and guidance in my daily life.

August 27   Proverbs 11:1-16

APPRECIATION CONQUERS JEALOUSY
A city is happy when honest people have good fortune . . . (Prov 11:10)
We must guard against jealousy entering our hearts, like sentries guarding a border-post. It is not always easy to recognise, because it comes disguised in so many different shapes. The seed of it is so small and insignificant that we often ignore it, but it grows into a monster which spoils our communion with God, and makes it difficult for others to get along with us.

One of the most common forms of jealousy is the inability to be happy when somebody whom you know well, is successful in his achievements. You loathe the fact that somebody else has succeeded. With cutting remarks or a sharp retort as to how advantageous it is "to know the right people", you try to deny another's success. Strangely enough, everybody but you are aware of the fact that it is plain jealousy which makes you act in such a manner.

To conquer this sin, you must reconsider your relationship with Christ. Allow Him to control your life through the Holy Spirit. He will renew and cleanse your thoughts. Then you will be able to rejoice in the success of others. If you find this difficult, confess it to the Lord and plead for his mercy to forget yourself. He will give you love in your heart and strength to do the right thing. Then you learn to show appreciation for the success of others and you are freed from the slavery of jealousy.

Thank you, Lord Jesus, for releasing me from the fetters of jealousy and for the ability to have appreciation for the achievements of others.

August 28 2 Timothy 1:3-18

VARIETY IN GOD'S CREATION
He saved us and called us to be his own people, not because of what we have done, but because of his own purpose and grace. He gave us this grace by means of Christ Jesus before the beginning of time . . . (2 Tim 1:9)

Each person experiences Christianity in a different manner. Some reveal it in exuberant joy, others in quiet service. You must always allow for the fact that the experience of other people can differ from yours. You must restrain yourself from being critical or derogatory, or of thinking that your religious experience is superior to those of others. Then you are denying the glorious variety of God's creation and, in spiritual pride, set yourself up as an example to others.

The Christian with a quiet disposition is often misunderstood and blamed for being "lukewarm". As a result, these people feel inferior in the company of other Christians. However, some of God's greatest servants were quiet, withdrawn people.

True Christian experience is achieved by the Holy Spirit in a person's heart. How it is revealed in his life, will depend on his disposition, temperament and background. The Lord needs different types of people in his Kingdom. Consider for a moment how his disciples differed from one another.

When one lives entirely for the honour and glory of Jesus Christ, you do not compare your life and actions with those of other Christians. You may admire the enthusiasm and fervour of others, but it is only by your commitment to Him – in your own way – that you serve Him best.

Lord, take my personality and my temperament into your keeping and help me to live to your glory and the establishment of your Kingdom.

August 29   John 14:15-31

PEACE!
Peace is what I leave with you; it is my own peace that I give you. I do not give it as the world does. Do not be worried and upset; do not be afraid (Jn 14:27)

Without God, peace is impossible. However hard man tries to attain peace, it will be all in vain if it does not lead to peace in God. God gives the peace for which men strive, without them having to lift a finger.

Man seeks peace in the wrong places. He allows trivialities to interfere with his inner being, with the result that the peace he is seeking, evades him. Peace is not dependent upon your outward circumstances, but upon your inward attitude towards your Creator, your fellow-men and life in general.

The road to peace is not necessarily the changing of your circumstances, but the renewal of your thoughts. When you commit your life to God and allow Him to make you a witness of his love through the work of the Holy Spirit, then you miraculously find peace with God, with yourself, with your neighbour and with your daily task.

It was never God's intention that we should all be rich, or powerful, or important – but that we should all be heirs to his peace. To obtain this peace, we need not do great and mighty deeds for the applause of the world. We need only carry out the humble and quiet act of the commitment to the love of God. When we do that, we receive his peace in our sleep. "It is my own peace that I give you!" Honest and loving service to others is peace in concrete form.

Lord of love and peace, lead me on the way to perfect peace.

August 30   Romans 8:18-39

THE VICTORY OVER DEPRESSION
No, in all these things we are more than conquerors through Him who loved us! (Rom 8:37)

You can conquer depression by faith if you are willing to do something constructive. You must believe that God is greater than your circumstances or your problems which cause your despondency. Speak about it honestly and openly to God and listen to what He wants to say to you through his Spirit. It is just possible that God has a divine purpose with this dark period in your life. Acceptance of your circumstances is virtually acceptance of God's will for your life. Frustration and worry solve no problems; on the contrary, they aggravate them.

Look for something in your life for which you can praise and thank God; think positively of all the benefits you still receive from God. Make a definite decision to do everything necessary to conquer your frustration. Get up and go out. Accept the realities of your situation, but look past them and see God at work behind them. It is a fallacy to think that God does not love you because you are despondent.

You are a royal child and you must live and act as one. Place God in the central spot of your life. Forget yourself and stop expecting everything and everybody to revolve around your personal problems. See God at work in your life. Become involved with the problems of others. Look away from yourself and see the world around you. Then you will see the loving purpose of God in all things – even when you feel deeply depressed.

As a deer longs for a stream of cool water, so I long for You, o God. Thank you for not deserting me in my depression, and grant me victory through Jesus Christ, my Lord.

August 31 Mark 1:29-39

JESUS OUR EXAMPLE IN PRAYER
Very early the next morning, long before daylight, Jesus got up and left the house. He went out of the town to a lonely place, where He prayed (Mk 1:35)

Prayer played a very important role in the earthly life of Jesus Christ. Right at the beginning of his ministry, when He was baptized, He prayed and the Holy Spirit descended upon Him. When Jesus had to make a choice of disciples, He spent the whole night praying to God. While He was ministering to people, prayer played a prominent part. In this way He was equipped for his task. When the cross became inevitable, Jesus prayed in Gethsemane. Even on the cross He prayed for those who crucified Him.

When we have to make choices or important decisions in our lives, prayer is indispensable. We must have knowledge of the strengthening power of prayer in our moments of deep disappointment and confusion;

in the execution of our task or calling; in moments of crises, and distorted human relationships. And when we suffer injustice, we must also know: through prayer we are capable of forgiving.

Through prayer Jesus was in a continuous conversation with God. He prayed for his disciples and He still intercedes for us.

With Jesus Christ as our perfect example, we must also strive after an unbroken communication with our heavenly Father. "Prayer is the unconditional prerequisite for everything God wants to do on earth" (Andrew Murray).

Help me, Lord Jesus, to follow your example and to grow in my sincere communication with my heavenly Father.

SEPTEMBER

PRAYER

Loving Father, we worship You as the sustainer of your
creation.
Thank you for spring; for new life
breaking out all around us.
Thank you for the trees in blossom, spreading
their beauty like giant bouquets.
Tender, young, green life in thousands of
shades, everywhere around, as though You
have just spoken the word of creation.
The earth awakens and rejoices in new life –
the winter is over, the time of singing has
arrived.
Grant that everybody – farmer, artist, poet, economist,
teacher – will see your hand behind
it all and will know: You have visited the land!
Redeemer, also touch my heart and life:
bring new life to my barren heart; grant that
the grain of wheat which was put in the ground,
will bear fruit which is acceptable to You.
Let me join joyfully in the triumphant, stirring
song of spring coming from the depth of my being:
Praise the Lord, my soul.
Amen.

September 1 2 Peter 3:1-18

GROWTH IS IMPERATIVE
But continue to grow in the grace and knowledge of our Lord and Saviour Jesus Christ. To Him be the glory, now and for ever! (2 Pet 3:18)

Every Christian who experienced a spiritual rebirth, has reason to rejoice. Some people give expression to their experience with great enthusiasm and regard everybody who does not share in their spiritual elation, with suspicion.

However, every one of us experiences his spiritual rebirth in a very personal manner. There is the sudden and dramatic conversion, when a profane sinner becomes a consecrated follower of Christ. There are also those whose spiritual growth and renewal is a gradual process. Like Lydia who went to the place of prayer regularly and simply opened her heart to God. We read of the jailer of Philippi whose dramatic conversion was sensational; yet there is Timothy, who simply learnt to believe from his mother and grandmother.

There are many Christians who can name the day and date, even the very hour of their conversion. Yet, there are many who cannot do so, but the quality of their commitment, love and service leave no question as to the reality of their spiritual experience with Christ.

True discipleship is a process of growth to maturity in Jesus Christ. It is not always possible to tell exactly when the seed germinated, but eventually the fruit is visible proof. On the other hand, if you do not grow, there is stagnation and eventually death. The choice is yours.

Master and Saviour, help me to remain in You like the branch on the tree, so that I will grow and bear fruit.

September 2 Psalm 62:1-12

FOR PEOPLE UNDER PRESSURE
He alone protects and saves me; He is my defender, and I shall never be defeated (Ps 62:2)

Man is obsessed by the idea of progress. Progress is the slogan of our time. However good that may be, it inevitably causes unbearable pressure. Increasingly higher standards are set and greater demands are made upon the individual.

There are many kinds of tranquillisers, all claiming to release people from the stress under which they work and live. Nevertheless, there is only one guarantee of peace and calm for body and soul. That is to know God and to become quiet in his presence. This is the only way to be released from the stress and strain of life. Then we join the Prince of peace in his triumphal journey to eternal peace.

There is no purpose in having a fleeting or temporary relationship with God. It must be enduring and stem from prayer, meditation and obedience. We must develop a sensitive awareness of the work of the Holy Spirit within us. This was the way in which Jesus Christ was able to stand the worst test for his earthly existence. He invites those who are burdened and tired to come to Him for rest. Follow Him obediently and you will experience the permanent rest which is so evasive in the pressurised life we lead. No longer will you be buffeted by the storms of life, but you will find strength, shelter and support in the power of the living Christ.

O God my Father, I have found peace and rest in You. You are the Comforter of my soul. I praise your holy Name for being able to live a life of peace and calm amidst the storms of life.

September 3 Psalm 37:23-40

A CURE FOR CARE
I am an old man now; I have lived a long time, but I have never seen a good man abandoned by the Lord or his children begging for food (Ps 37:25)
Many of the things we fear, never become a reality. But it is an integral part of our sinful nature to torture ourselves with thoughts of things we think are going to happen. We often live in such fear of some would-be disaster that we are incapable of enjoying the happy moments God grants us today. We are like the man who complained because his neighbour's cock crowed every night. "But he only crows at daybreak!" the surprised neighbour exclaimed. "Yes, but do you know what agony I endure, waiting all night for that cock to crow?"

Sometimes we become totally paralysed in the grip of a number of petty worries. In the well-known story of the shipwrecked Gulliver, he lies on the beach, totally exhausted, and then the little people of Lilliput tie him with thousands of gossamery threads. These ropes were as thin as cotton, and separately, he would have been able to break them with his little finger, but combined they rendered him powerless.

When we go to the Lord with all our cares – however insignificant – He will grant us calm and peace of mind. Test this cure, and you will not only be surprised but also cured and able to start a life of joy and praise.

Lord Jesus, teach me to trust You so completely that I will walk each step of the way without undue care and worry.

September 4   Ephesians 3:14-21

OBSTACLES BECOME OPPORTUNITIES
To Him who by means of his power working in us is able to do so much more than we can ever ask for, or even think of: to God be the glory . . . (Eph 3:20-21)
It often happens that we are more aware of our limitations than of our potential. The long list of what is lacking in our lives – according to our judgement – seems endless. We are dominated in such a manner by our own imperfections, that we see no further than our failures.

To constantly be aware of your failures, is to be blind to all the wondrous things God has placed within your grasp. When you have come to look beyond the limitations you have placed upon yourself, you can truly start living. God grants you this freedom when you seek his will and carry it out in prayer.

You never know to which heights you can rise, or to what extent God can use you to do glorious things in his Name. It is only when you open your mind and spirit to the influence of his Holy Spirit, that He reveals this to you.

When you discover to your surprise that God is willing to work through you, that you can commit yourself entirely to Him, your own sense of inferiority can no longer have a limiting influence on you. You also discover that all the riches of God are at your disposal. Then even the obstacles in your life are transformed into precious opportunities by the almighty hand of God. When God considers you good enough for his service, you dare not underestimate yourself.

Jesus my Lord, teach me to trust You so completely, that I will allow your Spirit to teach me to develop my potential to the full.

September 5   Matthew 22:34-40

RELIGION IS A WAY OF LIFE
The whole Law of Moses and the teachings of the prophets depend on these two commandments (Mt 22:40)

Religion means different things to different people. Some people find great pleasure in theological debate and are at their happiest when they can argue for hours about some concealed dogmatic question. Others again are so enthusiastic to practise their faith, that they disregard all theology and meditation.

Between these two extremes there are many ways to experience your religion and it is easy to become confused.

This state of affairs is not new. When Christ was ministering in Palestine, He often met people who were groping in spiritual darkness and were intent upon making religion incomprehensible and unattractive to others. These people tried to set a trap for Jesus by asking Him which was the greatest of God's laws. However, He summarised the entire law in the following words: Love the Lord your God with all your heart, with all your soul, and with all your mind. Love your neighbour as you love yourself. So simple, that even a child can understand it.

We must, however, remember that faith is not limited to what Jesus teaches us. It is imperative that we should practise our religion – in obedience and love to God and our fellow-men.

God of love, by the work of your Son, Jesus Christ, make your love a practical reality to me so that my religion will no longer be a theory but a way of life.

September 6   Isaiah 40:1-11

SORROW IS A PAINFUL REALITY
He will take care of his flock like a shepherd; He will gather the lambs together and carry them in his arms . . . (Is 40:11)

Even in the most beautiful garden, tended by the most expert gardener, there are rosebuds which never bloom. For some unknown reason the rosebud develops according to botanical laws, just like every other rose, but it never flowers and the breathtaking beauty which was expected, remains a futile promise in the bud.

Many parents have experienced the pain of losing a little child in death – a child whom they cherished and loved, but only for a short period of time. Such parents identify with the words of many poets who tried to describe this pain burning in their hearts like a poisoned arrow. Especially the Afrikaans poet, Totius, knew this experience as he had lost two children at a very young age.

The lives of these children, however, are not a total loss. They go back to God's heavenly garden, where the little loved one's are safe in the arms of Jesus; the great Friend of little children. Never will they be tormented by the cruelties of life. And there is the wonderful prospect of being reunited with them, when God Himself will allay the pain in our hearts.

But while you are still here on earth, you have the responsibility and calling, by virtue of your own sorrow, to notice the sorrow of others around you and to comfort them in their hour of pain and confusion. You cannot bring comfort to others, without receiving comfort in your own distress.

Gentle Jesus, You called little children to You, laid your hands upon them and blessed them. Help us to trust You with our little ones, even in death. And grant us, by our own painful experience, to bring comfort to other sorrowing parents.

September 7 2 Corinthians 5:11-21

RECONCILED WITH GOD
Our message is that God was making all mankind his friends through Christ. God did not keep an account of their sins, and He has given us the message which tells how He makes them his friends (2 Cor 5:19)

Sin is a terrifying reality. We may call it by diffcrent mitigating names, but any act which separates man from God, can be called sin. This estrangement is always man's doing. God desires that the crown of his creation will live in perfect harmony with Him. To this purpose He sent his Son into this world – so that He could reconcile God with fallen mankind.

Sin is obviously such an overwhelming reality, that we easily forget that man is created after the image of God. Even though the image is disfigured beyond recognition, it is still there. Jesus Christ appeals to the divinity in the soul of man, and when man reacts to this appeal of love, a unique and powerful experience with the living Christ is set in motion. He becomes united with God, as indeed Jesus said: "Whoever loves Me will obey my teaching. My Father will love him, and my Father will come to him and live with him" (Jn 14:23).

If you love Jesus, your thoughts are renewed and your life changes radically. When God comes to live in your heart, you will try to live from day to day in the knowledge of his presence. You will put your life entirely in his care. Then you will know real peace because you are reconciled with God.

In the knowledge, o Lord, that You live in me, I continuously strive to do your will.

September 8 1 Samuel 16:14-23

MOODINESS
From then on, whenever the evil spirit sent by God came on Saul, David would get his harp and play on it. The evil spirit would leave, and Saul would feel better and be all right again (1 Sam 16:23)
Moodiness, sad to say, is a general occurence, even amongst the children of the Lord. Unfortunately many people think that it has to be accepted as a normal part of life and that other people have to bear with it. At its root, however, moodiness is simply a sign of a lack of self-control.

There are many ways to combat moodiness. Saul tried to control his moodiness by listening to the soothing music of David's harp. Also that which you read can be uplifting and can serve as an inspiration for your spirit. A long walk can purify your spirit and remove all pettiness and despondency. It can broaden your outlook and help you to rise above your dismal mood. If you really want to conquer this weakness, there are many ways in which it can be done.

When you make time for a meaningful meeting with the Lord, it will be very difficult for this darkness of the spirit to dominate your life. If the living Christ is a reality to you, the shadows will disappear. The more He takes control of your life, the easier it will become to control your moods.

When you allow the Spirit of God to take control of your life, moodiness and depression will be things of the past. Christ makes all things new.

Fill my life, heavenly Father, so totally with your Holy Spirit, that He will also control my moods.

September 9 Revelation 2:1-7

ENTHUSIASM IS NOT ENOUGH
But this is what I have against you: You do not love Me now as you did at first. Think how far you have fallen! (Rev 2:4-5)

Very few people ever forget that first glow of Christian experience when Christ became a glorious reality to them; when they could rejoice in the blessed assurance that all their sins were forgiven; when their joy knew no bounds and they could hardly suppress the desire to share this experience with the whole world.

To testify to others about your salvation, strengthens your spirit, but a strong testimony demands more than just enthusiasm. You must constantly be aware of the presence of the living Christ. This you can only achieve through Bible study, prayer and communion with fellow-Christians.

There is indeed a dangerous possibility to talk about Jesus and yet loose touch with Him. Enthusiasm must grow into a positive, strong and practical faith which can testify to that in which you believe.

When you confess with your lips that you believe in Jesus Christ, you must be willing to commit your life to Him and follow Him obediently. Your entire life, body, spirit and mind are involved. In all these aspects you must grow in your love for and consecration to Christ. If this growth is absent, your first love has cooled down. This is a tragic situation which only the Holy Spirit can rectify.

Gracious Lord, grant that the enthusiasm I display in spiritual matters will also extend to my body and my mind. Make me a practical witness of your love and mercy.

September 10 Psalm 46:1-11

THE SEARCH FOR PEACE
God is our shelter and strength . . . so we will not be afraid . . . (Ps 46:1-2)

Stress, anxiety, fear and worry have become such an ordinary part of our daily existence, that we come to think of them as normal. Fact is that God did not intend it that way. If we allow these negative attitudes to dominate our lives, we limit God in his work of mercy. Hence the admonition in Psalm 46:10: "Stop fighting and know that I am God."

To genuinely find peace, to really know complete peace of mind, it is imperative that we set aside time on a daily basis for prayer and meditation, and give God the opportunity to calm the inner turmoil of our spirit by his holy Word. This is God's highway to peace.

If we are under pressure and unhappy, it is because we can think of nothing else but our burdens and that which we still have to do. It is time to clearly say to ourselves: "Stop fighting! Relax! Be calm! Let go and let God!" By allowing stress and anxiety to dominate our lives or to crack under the strain, is to deny the power of God and to refuse to take Him at his word.

The search for peace is not a passive or negative perception; the search for peace is a mighty, active deed by which we glorify God and enrich the quality of our lives.

I thank You, faithful heavenly Father, that in spending time with You, and through the consolation of your Word, I am freed of all pressure and strain. Thank you, Lord Jesus, for making it possible for me to spend time with my heavenly Father through your redeeming work.

September 11   Colossians 1:24-29

UNLIMITED POSSIBILITIES IN CHRIST
And the secret is that Christ is in you, which means that you will share in the glory of God. So we preach Christ to everyone (Col 1:27-28)

Few people really believe in themselves. This is not because of humility, but because they refuse to believe in their Godgiven potential. You meet people who seem to act with great self-confidence and apparently think highly of themselves, but often this is pure bravado and exhibition.

Our feelings of inferiority do not have their origin in God, but are products of man himself. God created us to his own image and He considers each individual of great value. God has a divine purpose with your life, and you are committing a sin if you refuse Him to realise it. We are inclined to remember only our defeats, our concealed sins and our failures. God, however, sees what you can be: the conquests you can make; the successes you can achieve, the confession of sins which can cleanse and strengthen you.

It is encouraging to know that Christ is fully aware of our potential, even when we are ignorant of it. Why then subject yourself to the humdrum routine of a monotonous existence, when Christ can lead you to the mountain tops of achievement? He knows what you can accomplish if his Spirit works in you and fills you with hope, faith and self-confidence. All He asks of you, is obedient submission to his will.

Lord Jesus, take my life and develop my possibilities to their utmost potential, solely to the glory and honour of your holy Name.

September 12   Hebrews 11:1-7

FAITH IS ESSENTIAL
No one can please God without faith . . . (Heb 11:6)
Often people claim to be working for the Lord, but they remain ineffective in his service. This may be because they are trying to serve God according to their own will and desires, and not as He wants them to. They drive themselves forward on paths which they have planned in their blindness.

They want to please God – but they also want to please themselves! In many cases this is impossible. If you want to serve Him, you will have to act according to his divine will and make sure that you are not simply using God as a front to execute your own plans and live according to your own will.

To discover God's will for your life, demands total commitment of your life to Him. When you declare yourself willing to follow Him, He will lead you without a doubt. You must only seek his guidance in prayer and with a faithful heart.

There is no fixed pattern according to which the Lord leads his servants. He can use circumstances to map out the way. Or He can lead you step by step. But He can only lead you if you have the courage to take the first few halting steps in simple faith.

No-one knows beforehand exactly how God is going to lead him. But you can simplify the task of finding out, by putting Him first in your life and spending a lot of time in his holy presence. Then the Holy Spirit will guide you and grant you peace of mind, and the work you do for Him will be of great value and abundantly blessed.

Heavenly Father, through Jesus Christ my Lord, please strengthen my faith. Fill my life with your Holy Spirit and lead me step by step.

September 13 Romans 8:31-39

WHERE DO I GO WITH MY DEPRESSION?
No, in all these things we have complete victory through Him who loved us! (Rom 8:37)
Medication and professional help are of great importance, but not enough to conquer depression. You must be willing to do something constructive about it yourself. If you believe that God is greater than your circumstances or the problems which are causing your depression, you can conquer them in his Name.

Take your problems and pressures to your heavenly Father in prayer. Don't just mumble a few words by force of habit – talk to God! Make a list of the problems in your life and pray for a solution for each specific problem. Believe with unwavering faith that He has a purpose with this dark period in your life. Do not try to oppose God if He is trying to reach a divine purpose in your life, even though it means suffering.

You must realise that you cannot always have your way. Acceptance of your circumstances is in actual fact acceptance of God's will for you. Frustration and worry solve no problems. On the contrary – they only aggravate them. Find something positive for which you can praise God and live in praise and gratitude from hour to hour. Confess and lay down sinful acts and thoughts. Think as a child of God ought to think and act as if you believe in the privilege of being a child!

Look away from yourself. Look up at Christ in his great love and mercy. Look at the world around you and endeavour to see God's purpose in everything. This will give you enough reason for joy and hope.

Good Master, help me to believe sincerely that You are with me even in my darkest hour and that You can change the darkness into a new dawn.

September 14   Philippians 1:1-11

PAUL'S PRAYER FOR YOU

I pray that your love will keep on growing more and more, together with true knowledge and perfect judgement, so that you will be able to choose what is best. Then you will be free from all impurity and blame on the Day of Christ. Your lives will be filled with the truly good qualities which only Jesus Christ can produce, for the glory and praise of God (Phil 1:9-11)

This inspiring prayer of Paul was for the congregation of Philippi, but it is also the treasured possession of Christians through the ages. He prays "that your love will keep on growing". They must not only hoard it in their hearts, but allow it to flow freely to others. This love must not only grow in volume, but also in quality.

When Paul proceeds and prays: ". . . so that you will be able to choose what is best", his prayer provides not only for the emotions, but also for the mind. He pleads for the power of discrimination – to be able to put first things first.

When a Christian is granted these spiritual virtues by grace, it will inevitably lead him to being "free from all impurity and blame". Here Paul prays not only for the heart and the mind, but also for the character of the Christian. It means an unblemished and pure life, not only in the eyes of people, but also of God. Our example and actions must always be to the greater glory and honour of God. Then the coming of the Lord will not be a day of judgement but a day of joyful reunion with our Saviour.

This does not come about through our own strength, it is something "which only Jesus can achieve, for the glory and praise of God!"

God of infinite love, let my love flow freely to others; grant me the power of discrimination and make my whole life acceptable to You. Do this through Jesus Christ and the Holy Spirit.

September 15   Matthew 5:1-11

FROM TEARS TO COMFORT

Happy are those who mourn; God will comfort them! (Mt 5:4)

Sorrow and grief are an integral part of human life. Therefore it is a wonderful comfort to hear from Jesus Himself that those who mourn will be comforted. He was a Man of Sorrow, and He knew grief and suffering in his own life.

Is there need or want in your home? He also knew that – He had no place of his own. Therefore He understands and cares.

Are you struggling with a deep grief? He struggled in Gethsemane until his sweat became like drops of blood.

Do you feel lonely and forsaken, even by God? He questioned God for forsaking Him on the cross.

There is so much adversity in life – sickness, want and poverty; so much care and worry. But Christ comes to us with his abundant comfort and brings peace to our hearts and our minds.

Not far from the bitter fountain of Mara, one finds Elim, with its twelve fountains and many palm trees. There you will once more be able to pitch your tent in peace and realize that the bitter Mara was a porch giving entrance to the comfort and abundance of Elim.

May you experience the comfort of God in your hour of deepest need. Allow Him to minister to your broken spirit. He is not only the great Comforter but also the great Healer who makes all things new!

Thank you, Lord Jesus, for sending the Comforter to be with us for ever. Thank you that my suffering and grief have taught me that it is not what I have lost which counts, but that which I have received through grace – your divine comfort!

September 16 Proverbs 12:1-11

CONSTRUCTIVE CRITICISM
Anyone who loves knowledge wants to be told when he is wrong. It is stupid to hate being corrected (Prov 12:1)

No human being is infallible. You must never act as if you are the exception. If you make a mistake, don't waste time with empty explanations to try and justify your actions. Listen to constructive criticism and endeavour to learn from your mistakes. Don't take it amiss when people criticise you, otherwise you will reveal a pettiness which can have disastrous results. Rather be grateful that there are people who love you so much that they will take the trouble to help you.

If you believe that you are above criticism or reproval, you are deceiving yourself. It is far wiser to admit that you are still developing and growing and that you need all the advice you can get. Nobody knows all the answers, and to acknowledge your mistakes is a sure sign of maturity.

However, there are people who express only derogatory criticism. With their negative and unkind attitude, they reveal their own inferiority and immaturity. One must be able to know when criticism is well-meant and when it is negative and derogatory.

As you grow in understanding and insight, you will be able to cope with criticism. In this Jesus was our perfect example. He could pray for his worst critics.

Don't reject constructive criticism – it can only contribute to your spiritual growth and development of character.

Father of mercy, I stumble so often that I constantly need reprimanding. Grant that I will allow it to enrich my life and, through your Holy Spirit, give me the power of discrimination.

September 17 Psalm 84:1-12

LEARN TO RECEIVE GRACIOUSLY
The Lord is our protector and glorious king, blessing us with kindness and honour. He does not refuse any good thing to those who do what is right (Ps 84:11)

To some people it is embarrassing – even humiliating – to receive. They are often generous givers, but when a gift of love is given to them, they immediately start planning to return the gift with interest, or to go one better with a present that far exceeds that gift in value. Such an attitude brings joy to nobody.

It is also true that you are constantly at the receiving end of life – whether you want to accept it or not. Look around you for a moment and see all the things you receive for free and even before you ask. Life itself is a gift; to be able to make choices in life is a wonderful gift; the love and loyalty of dear ones in spite of your shortcomings and failures; your faith and redemption are free gifts through the grace of God. It all comes to you from the bounty of God.

Don't accept your blessings as a right, or a matter of course, or a prize for your good behaviour. Count them and appreciate them. As you become more aware of God's bountiful supply, you will become less afraid of distress and need. Thanksgiving and praise will fill your life and you will come to realise that the purpose of life is to give and not to receive. You also have to learn to receive gracefully. Life will then grant you its richest fulfilment and you will become a worthy receiver of the untold blessings of your heavenly Father.

Grant, o heavenly Benefactor, that I will be willing to give myself before I can receive from your bounty.

September 18 Romans 2:1-16

GOD IS FORBEARING
Or perhaps you despise his great kindness, tolerance, and patience. Surely you know that God is kind, because He is trying to lead you to repent (Rom 2:4)

We should judge God's acts according to Holy Scripture and not according to our own wishes and desires. Don't make the mistake of thinking that God never judges or damns, and that He will eventually forgive everything because his being is love.

It is true that God loves the sinner, but He also hates sin. Often people are confused and unable to distinguish between the two. They believe that God will condone sin because He loves the sinner.

The goodness, forbearance and love which God reveals to unworthy people, must not be seen as glossing over of our sins. It is simply a part of the divine nature of our heavenly Father. He not only bestows his love upon us, but He also gives Himself to us through Jesus Christ.

We hurt and torment the loving heart of God, and yet He shows only understanding and sympathy for our weaknesses, temptations and peculiarities. He treats us with so much patience, mercy and love, because He wants to draw us into a new relationship with Himself. He wants to renew our lives and make us sensitive to the pain caused by sin. Don't ever think of God's tolerance as weakness or take it for granted. It is a precious and liberating gift of mercy, whereby God wants to bring us back to Him and make us his children again.

Lord and Master, keep me from considering your forbearance as a sign of weakness. Let your Holy Spirit make my soul always sensitive to your love and tender care.

September 19   Philippians 4:1-9

YOU ARE AS HAPPY AS YOU THINK YOU ARE
May you always be joyful in your union with the Lord. I say it again: rejoice! (Phil 4:4)

Some people flourish on bad luck. It is part of their philosophy of life to feel unhappy. They are prophets of doom and disaster. Every silver lining is only the outline of a dark and threatening cloud of ill omen bringing storm and destruction.

It is simply because they allow their thoughts constantly to dwell on negative things. God did not create them that way and neither did He intend them to become what they are, but over the years this attitude has become an inseparable part of their lives.

It lies within one's power to decide whether one is going to be happy or unhappy. If you despair when circumstances are against you and believe that it is impossible for you to be happy, then you ignore and deny the fact that the Spirit of God can rule your life, if you would only allow Him to do so. The choice is entirely yours.

One can only be happy if you live in total spiritual commitment and firmly believe that Christ is in control of every part of your life. Only then do you discover the true meaning of peace of mind and inner calm. Then you see the silver lining for what it truly is: a promise of the sunshine of God's mercy which breaks through every cloud and you will sing a song of praise.

Thank you, Lord Jesus Christ, that my inner happiness does not depend on external things, but is brought about by your Spirit. I am your child. You are the source of my joy.

September 20   2 Corinthians 3:1-18

OH, TO BE LIKE JESUS!
You yourselves are the letter we have, written on our hearts for everyone to know and read. It is written, not with ink but with the Spirit of the living God, and not on stone tablets but on human hearts (2 Cor 3:2-3)

Many dedicated Christians waste their strength and energy on futile projects. They become involved in some dynamic political or social organisation and convince themselves that this is the will of God. But, alas, in their enthusiasm for "the cause" they become increasingly less aware of the presence of the living Christ in their lives.

It is a sobering thought to consider that it is possible to become a Christian without Christ, active in worthwhile causes and yet without the experience of the redeeming love of Jesus Christ in your life.

As a Christian your main loyalty is not to a "cause" but to Christ! If He is at the centre of your life, and you allow Him to send you into this world as his "letter", your faith comes alive and everybody will recognise the power and love of Jesus in your life. You will become his ambassador in the world. In this manner you will not only glorify God, but also experience joy, happiness and peace which up till now were lacking in your life.

The world is sick and tired of religious slogans founded on the so-called teachings of Jesus Christ. What the world desperately needs is to see Christ in his disciples. Only then you become a blessing to those with whom you live and work, and make a positive contribution to the age in which you live.

Merciful God and Father, help me to consecrate myself to You to such an extent that the world will only see Jesus in me.

September 21 Romans 8:18-30

VICTORY OVER GRIEF
I consider that what we suffer at this present time cannot be compared at all with the glory that is going to be revealed to us (Rom 8:18)

If you are absolutely sure that you are a child of God, you have a guarantee that you will be able to endure sorrow and pain. You will accept, like Jesus did, that it is God's will that your path must take you past Gethsemane and Golgotha. It is not a sin to grieve. However, ask God to grant you the wisdom to see life and death in their true perspective.

Being a Christian is no guarantee that you will be spared sorrow, but God has promised to be with you and give you his support. He leads you to make adjustments and to find the meaning of sorrowful experiences. It brings you closer to God – alone with Him you can vent your sorrow, be comforted as nowhere else, and receive help for the future.

But your responsibility is to reaffirm your faith in life and to bear your grief with dignity. You must also notice the sorrow of others around you. You must stop asking: "Why did it happen to me?" Rather ask: "What am I to do, now that it has happened?"

The most important experiences of life are not found in superficial pleasures, but in the hour of your deepest sorrow. You are closer to God when your heart is broken than in the halcyon days of joy and laughter. Then your grief serves a divine purpose and eventually leads to victory over grief.

Dear God of comfort, You have taught us to find strength in quietness and trust. Grant us your strength in our hours of sorrow and bring joy and comfort into our hearts.

September 22 Ephesians 4:1-16

THE TRUTH EXPRESSED IN LOVE BRINGS GROWTH
Instead, by speaking the truth in a spirit of love, we must grow up in every way to Christ, who is the head (Eph 4:15)

You find people who pride themselves on their honesty. This obviously gives them the right to ride roughshod over the feelings of other people – at least, so they think. They can make life very complicated and confusing when their honesty lacks love.

There are times when it is better to remain silent; but to suppress the truth, just to prevent a difficult situation from arising, often creates more problems than it solves. That is why we should remember that the balm of truth is love.

If you speak the truth without mercy, you may cause a wound which can never be healed. When the truth is spoken in love, it loses none of its power or influence and it is to the advantage of both the speaker and the listener.

To express the truth in love is a sign of healthy spiritual growth and maturity. You need not necessarily be a Christian to speak the truth – it is considered a universal virtue. But to serve the truth because the living Spirit of Christ is working in your heart, gives it an added dimension which cannot be obtained from any other source. Truth spoken in love brings forgiveness and healing to the trespasser. Link truth to love inseparably, and allow it to be revealed in your life.

O Lord my God, grant that both your love and truth find expression in my life – to your glory and honour!

September 23 Psalm 27:1-14

A CHALLENGE FOR TIMES OF AFFLICTION
Even if a whole army surrounds me, I will not be afraid; even if enemies attack me, I will still trust God (Ps 27:3)

We are experiencing confusing and disturbing times. Trusted and tried values are disregarded or neglected. Truth is rejected and the lie is hailed as the highest good. Atheism and materialism are on the increase. It often seems as if we have come to the end of an era, and one wonders whether our generation is witnessing the death throes of an obsolete age or the birth pangs of a new one. Few people like what they see in the world around them.

Because of the serious times in which we live, it is imperative to have anchors to trust in the storm; to develop a strong faith. It will enable us to remain standing and retain a balanced judgement. It will also strengthen mankind and serve society. More than ever before, the world needs faith and peace which represent the true hallmark of Christianity.

Only when man's spirit is destroyed, is he really conquered. This can only happen when faith dies and hope for the future dwindles. Therefore, more than ever before, Christians must place their trust and faith in the living Christ. This is still his world, and He has promised to be with us, even to the end of time.

Lord Jesus, I meet the disturbing challenges of our time in the strength and wisdom of the Holy Spirit. It encourages me to know that You are always with me.

September 24 Philippians 4:1-9

POSITIVE THINKING
In conclusion, my brothers, fill your minds with those things that are good and that deserve praise: things that are true, noble, right, pure, lovely and honourable (Phil 4:8)

No intelligent person can doubt the value of positive thinking. If it is practised with dedication, it often surpasses the expectations of the person who practises it.

A positive thinker welcomes the challenges of life without fear of failure. He thinks constructively and creatively in the most trying circumstances and never allows thoughts of defeat to enter his mind. Such a person develops the capability to rise above his circumstances and he lives and works with enthusiasm and self-confidence.

We must, however, remember that positive thinking is not necessarily a guarantee for faith. You need not even be a Christian to believe in the power of positive thinking. But this approach must never take the place of Jesus Christ in your life.

Guard against trusting exclusively in your own strength and capability. True positive thinking has a spiritual undertone. If you are aware that Christ is living within you, this knowledge renews your thinking. Then you understand the meaning of Paul's plea in Philippians 2:5: "The attitude you should have is the one that Jesus Christ had." This is true creative and positive thinking.

Holy Spirit of God, help me to think positively so that I can have the peace and joy which Jesus Christ has achieved for me.

September 25 Mark 4:35-41

FAITH VERSUS FEAR
Why are you frightened? Have you still no faith? (Mk 4:40)
You can't enjoy life as God intended you to, if you are constantly living in fear. And fear reveals itself in so many different shapes: fear of illness; fear for your children's safety; fear of losing your material possessions; fear of not being able to meet your responsibilities; fear of life ... and fear of death.

Your world is possibly so permeated with fear, that you can hardly visualise a life without fear. And it leaves you in a constant state of self-pity.

Some fears are necessary and constructive. The fear which retains a child from placing his hand on a hot stove, or keeps people away from danger, is constructive. It protects you against recklessness and self-destruction.

However, to have a living and powerful faith, you must learn to cope with life without living under a burden of fear that destroys all peace and harmony.

Faith in the goodness and mercy of a loving heavenly Father, cannot grow in a heart constantly harbouring fear. It is detrimental to your faith to live in fear of what may happen.

Trust firmly in the goodness of your Father and when destructive and fearsome thoughts enter your mind, you must focus your mind on God and cling to Him in faith.

Master and Lord, only by your grace and mercy can I conquer my fears and grow in faith.

September 26   1 Corinthians 1:1-17

UNITED IN CHRIST
God is to be trusted, the God who called you to have fellowship with his Son Jesus Christ, our Lord (1 Cor 1:9)
One of the greatest privileges of a Christian, is being part of a living community. If you attend church only when you feel like it, or if you go without identifying with the rest of the congregation, you must not be surprised if you feel isolated and lonely.

The true church or body of believers, are people who are involved with each other, who care and love. Their faith is not limited to one or two opportunities for worship every week. They are constantly seeking opportunities to serve each other in love. If somebody is lonely, the others comfort him by their presence and prayers. If somebody is sad, the others surround him with their love and sympathy.

The community of the faithful is not a passive deed of worship, but is a dynamic and active "caring" for others as well as respect and understanding of their individuality.

But this association works in two directions. When you are in need, you must learn to accept the help of others in the spirit in which it is offered. And when you give, your sacrifice of love must contribute to the well-being of others through love and understanding. Then you are no longer a Sunday Christian, but your life will also be a demonstration of your faith during the rest of the week.

My Redeemer and Saviour, grant that I will always give of my noblest and best, and help me to receive gracefully when I am in need.

September 27 Matthew 12:15-21

CHRIST HEALS
... and large crowds followed Him. He healed all those who were ill ... (Mt 12:15)

In the epistles we read of many people who were healed by Jesus in various ways. Those who came to Him with a spiritual ailment, were often unaware of their condition. They simply knew there was something wanting in their lives which caused them to be deeply unhappy. The Lord gave them a glimpse into their own hearts, like the woman from Samaria of whom we read in John 4. When they realised their need, He healed them and gave them spiritual peace.

Many people who came to Jesus, were desperate for peace of mind and healing of the spirit. He saw how unwillingness to forgive poisoned their souls. He saw how jealousy, anger and hatred led to self-destruction. Therefore He taught that perfect healing of mind and heart could only be reached by reconciliation and forgiveness brought about by love.

He knew of the intimate interplay between spirit, body and mind; that painful and negative thoughts and emotions can make the body sick. We need inner healing and forgiveness before our bodies can be healed. When Christ heals, He heals the whole being: body, mind and spirit. A new, positive outlook on life is the inevitable result of a whole spirit, and this leads to a healthy body in the service of the great Healer.

By your wonder-working and healing power, o Saviour, the old things in my life have passed away and I am a new, whole being. I praise your holy Name!

September 28 Ecclesiastes 7:15-21

SELF-DESTRUCTION
So don't be too good or too wise – why kill yourself? (Ecc 7:16)

Never pass hasty or unkind judgement on somebody who has committed suicide. Only God can judge, and only He knows the circumstances and the frame of mind of somebody who took his own life.

There is also a kind of moral and spiritual suicide against which we must guard, because it destroys the personality and deprives life of its beauty and equilibrium. There are people who seem just about perfect, but deep in their hearts destructive forces are at work: hatred, bitterness, lust, greed, jealousy and anger. These things undermine everything which is noble, loving, honest and true.

The astounding fact is that some people harbour these detrimental attitudes unknowingly and in this way commit spiritual suicide. No human being can allow destructive thoughts to fester, without paying an extremely high price.

Self-destroying forces of evil can only be conquered by a greater power. The power of Jesus purifies, heals, restores and opens up new possibilities. To have this power become a reality in our lives, we must accept Him and allow Him to reveal Himself in our thoughts and actions.

Make the living Christ the Lord of your life, so that you can truly "live"!

God, my Father through Jesus Christ, may my love for You always be so great and real, that destructive forces will never enter into my mind or spirit.

September 29 — Isaiah 55:1-13

GOD CONTROLS MY THOUGHTS AND DEEDS
"My thoughts," says the Lord, "are not like yours, and my ways are different from yours" (Is 55:8)

No human being can be truly objective in his thinking. Tradition, background and culture all play an important role when you have to make a decision. The thoughts of the masses are conditioned by the media, to propagate certain political, social and racial issues. Unfortunately very few people take the trouble to think over their problems carefully and come to a satisfactory solution. They allow others to do their thinking for them.

If you have accepted that Christ rules your life, you no longer belong to yourself – you belong to Christ. This means that your mind and your thoughts are at his disposal, to use how and when He sees fit.

When you open your mind to the guidance of the Holy Spirit you no longer have preconceived ideas. Your own feelings are of secondary importance to the glorious knowledge that you are now a child of God.

You live in expectation of the next inspiring thought which will lead to a deeper practical relationship with Jesus, your Saviour and Redeemer.

Before Christ has perfect control of your life, you must learn to subject your mind and thoughts to his love and wisdom. It is a worthwhile and compensating excercise.

Holy Spirit of God, fill my mind with thoughts and desires befitting a child of Jesus Christ.

September 30 Romans 8:31-39

DEFEAT OR VICTORY?
No, in all these things we have complete victory through Him who loved us! (Rom 8:37)

Defeat and victory are two of the most fundamental things in one's life. It also reveals character. Nobody enjoys failure – but when it does occur, one must handle it positively and creatively.

You often have to battle against overwhelming and fearsome forces, and as a child of the living God you cannot allow yourself to be trampled underfoot. Many people live in a constant fear of failure. They refuse to start a new project. This destroys their initiative and obstructs their approach to the challenges of life.

History teaches us that many people who had to cope with initial failure, tried again and eventually succeeded. Paul was one of them.

One is never a failure until he has decided that he is. God never denounces the work of his hands. Jesus Christ is the power in our lives, recreating and renewing us. He understands your heart and if you trust Him utterly, He will grant you victory. Approach life with its variety of demands, trust Him unconditionally and He will grant you victory.

Lord, my Saviour, I often lack strength for life's battles, but I thank You, that by your grace, You grant me victory – especially over sin and failure.

OCTOBER

PRAYER

Eternal God, we know that the aged amongst us are
many – people whose earthly tent-dwellings
seem to become more dilapidated with each passing day –
though, inwardly they are growing and becoming
stronger.
We worship You as the Unchangeable, and when we
notice the change and decay around us and
within ourselves, we rejoice in You, our God!
We worship You as the one who controls all of our lives:
youth with its strength and invincibility,
its life expectancy and its dauntlessness;
but also as the God who blesses us as we grow older,
granting us wisdom born of experience,
calmness in spirit and mind,
and cautiousness.
We praise and thank You, Creator God, for making
our whole world beautiful:
the early morning with its colourful sunrise;
the plenitude of the midday;
the glory of sunset;
the evening with its twilight;
and the quiet of night-time.
Thank you, good Lord, for being our faithful
companion,
even right up to the final stage of our pilgrimage.
We rely on your loving promise that You will always
be with us, that You will never abandon us;
that You are still with us, just as You were in the
days of our youth.
Make us increasingly aware of your
everlasting arms reaching towards us,
open and lovingly.
In the Name of Jesus our Redeemer.
Amen.

October 1 James 2:14-26

FAITH AND PRACTICE
My brothers, what good is it for someone to say that he has faith if his actions do not prove it? Can that faith save him? (Jas 2:14)
Being aware of the presence of God in times of prayer, Bible reading and meditation, can touch a deep emotional chord in one's heart. Thereafter it might seem as if nothing is impossible any more; as if, by your faith, you will be able to move mountains.

But when you are confronted with the harsh realities of the world again, this mountain-top experience which you had with God, will have to compete with the stark realities of life. Strong emotions will not be enough to keep you going. Your experiences with Christ should be of such a strength that He will be revealed in every sphere of your life. When you are filled with his Spirit and his closeness fills you with joy, your highest aim in life will be to do his will, whatever your circumstances.

A practical faith which has its origin in the living Christ, is vastly more precious than mere enthusiasm. Such a faith allows the Spirit of God to take effect in the everyday occurrences of our existence, inspiring us to a full life committed to God.

We will even find it possible to move amongst people who have no interest in the faith which means so much to us. However, as we reveal the disposition of our Lord and Master, we will discover that our faith grows stronger, and that we are able to draw people to Christ because we practise our faith in everyday situations.

Holy Spirit of God, teach me daily how to apply my faith in everyday matters, according to the example of Jesus, my Saviour.

October 2 2 Corinthians 4:16-5:10

IN THE DEPTH OF DESPAIR?
... He gave us his Spirit as the guarantee of all that He has in store for us. So we are always full of courage (2 Cor 5:5-6)
When we obey God unconditionally, it is easy to keep a strong heart. If we do not live according to his will, we won't have the self-confidence to live purposefully and with gladness. Obedience does not imply your

reluctant subjection to that which you cannot avoid, but rather a joyous acceptance of his will as the highest good for your life.

At times we all experience moments of depression which border on despair. However, it is during these times that the Holy Spirit rekindles the hope in your heart. Once you have learnt to obey the Spirit, your greatest wish will be to do God's will – even though it is in a Gethsemane of sweat and blood.

Initially it may be difficult, but the Holy Spirit equips us to lead a life which pleases God. It demands a special brand of faith not to act according to your own desires, but to fulfil the will of God. Surely one will then grow in self-assurance and develop a faith which works miracles.

The Holy Spirit will guide you towards spiritual daring. This new approach to life is based on love, which is a gift from the Holy Spirit. Love drives out all fear. It is impossible to walk in the love of God, obey Him in all things, and yet lose courage. This is the lesson the Spirit of God wants to teach us from day to day.

Forgive me, Lord, for my moments of fear and disobedience. Accompany me over the dark and desolate plains of despair and lift me up to the heights of your love, through the blessed work of the Holy Spirit.

October 3 Isaiah 46:1-13

IN THE LECTURE-ROOM OF OLD AGE
I am your God and will take care of you until you are old and your hair is grey. I made you and will care for you; I will give you help and rescue you (Is 46:4)

Some people age more quickly than others. There are those who are physically healthy, and yet they are old at forty. Others again have reached the Biblical three-score and ten, but their spirits are still young. Thus it all depends on how one approaches old age.

It is a wonderful experience to meet an aged person who has a living faith and trusts in God and who bravely struggles to understand the problems of modern times. Growing old does not mean that you have to lose your grip on life or your interest in the world and your fellow-men.

As the years go by, one gains knowledge through experience in every area of life. Some of these experiences are enriching and others are of little value, but all of them should give you a better understanding and a greater appreciation of the problems which the younger generation have to contend with.

One can gain the optimum for this period of life, by being more tolerant, considerate, noble and sympathetic and by showing greater understanding for others. In fact, this stage is the finishing school before one passes on to eternity. It is wonderful to grow old gracefully, to be able to have a spirit which remains youthful because you have placed your trust in the eternal God.

Heavenly Father, grant that with the increase in years, I will be able to retain my tolerance and sympathy, and still be a source of inspiration and encouragement to others.

October 4 Job 38:1-15

MEET GOD IN THE STORM
Then out of the storm the Lord spoke to Job (Job 38:1)
God reveals Himself to different people in different ways. Elijah, sitting under a bush in the wilderness, was on the verge of despair. God saw his suffering and came to him to strengthen and encourage him. At first there was a strong wind which rented the mountains; then came the earthquake; after the earthquake a scorching fire – and the Lord was in none of them. God came to Elijah in the whispering of the evening breeze. Meeting God in the silence often makes one deeply aware of his guidance, healing power and love, and He becomes a living reality at these times.

But God does not only meet with us in the quiet. His voice is audible in the storm, the hurricane and the tornado. He is not only the God who speaks in the silence, He is also to be met in the pulsing, restless and agitated world in which we live.

This is why God can also grant you his guidance during the storms of life, if only you are willing to listen to his voice and obey his revealed will for your life. Whatever your circumstances may be, you can be sure of his loving presence. Frenzied activity may never prevent your meeting with Him.

If you have an intense desire to meet Him, you will find Him waiting for you – whether it is in the midst of the storm or during meditation.

I praise your Name, loving Master, that You make me aware of your presence, even amidst the bustle of our lives. Grant me, especially in difficult times, your peace that passes all understanding.

October 5   Matthew 14:22-33

ALONE WITH GOD
After sending the people away, He went up a hill by Himself to pray. When evening came, Jesus was there alone (Mt 14:23)

Jesus Christ valued his private meetings with his Father highly. Had it not been for these invigorating moments the burden of his ministry would have become unbearable. Crowds followed Him everywhere He went: religious leaders demanded answers to their questions; sick people pleaded to be healed; people experiencing sincere spiritual hunger or intense confusion sought his guidance; poor and hungry people desired to be fed. Jesus could always help, because He was constantly being strengthened by his Father. However busy Jesus might have been, He always made time to spend a period of quiet in the company of his Father.

If you consider yourself too busy to pray, it is simply proof of how low prayer appears on your priority list. One is always able to find time for those things you really want to do. Your prayer times should highlight your day and there should be a burning desire in your heart to use these times for maximum replenishment.

Perhaps you are unsure of what to say to God in your quiet time. If this is the case then read aloud one of the beautiful prayers in the Bible and make it your own. Prayer requires concentration, but if you really want to communicate with God, you will not find it difficult. If you sincerely and regularly honour your quiet time with God, He will answer your petitions, and talking to Him will become a pure joy. You will start looking forward to be alone in prayer with God.

Jesus, my Lord and Saviour, through your Holy Spirit, I am able to enter your presence with a feeling of joy and expectation.

October 6   Job 17:1-10

COPING WITH YOUR SORROW
My grief has almost made me blind; my arms and legs are as thin as shadows (Job 17:7)

Grief enters our hearts in many different ways and causes disruption: the death of a loved one; a tragic occurrence; an unexpected failure or disappointment. However, the way in which you cope with your sorrow, will determine how much control it is likely to gain over your life. If you fold up under your grief, you are allowing it complete control and authority over your life. It is important to make an effort to be positive, or else you will court failure and eventually fall into despair.

If you really want to conquer grief, a genuine faith in the living God is essential. If your faith can gain victory over your sorrow, you will be able to live a full life in the Lord.

If you have to greet a loved one for the last time, your faith in eternal life will give you the courage to endure. If your hopes, dreams and ideals are shattered and failure seems inevitable, faith will enable you to rise from the ashes like a phoenix, so that you can start anew. Whatever the cause of your sorrows, you can triumph over it if you have a sincere and living faith.

By believing in the eternal goodness and love of God and Jesus Christ, who has saved you – also from grief – you will be strengthened to accept your sorrow as part of his divine purpose. Approach your grief with faith in your heart and consider your sorrow a challenge to your faith in Christ. In Him we find victory and peace of mind.

I worship You, Lord Jesus, as the Man of sorrow who knows my grief and cares about me. Help me to continue growing in faith and love so that I may gain victory over my sorrow.

October 7 Isaiah 50:1-11

THE CALL TO TESTIFY
Why did my people fail to respond when I went to them to save them? Why did they not answer when I called? (Is 50:2)

Christ's earthly ministry was characterised by a spirit of love and charity. He used to seek the will of his Father in prayer and obediently did what his Father expected of Him. He healed the sick; He gave hearing to the deaf; He gave sight to the blind; the crippled could miraculously use their limbs and even the dead were raised! Jesus warned, taught, encouraged and reprimanded in the holy Name of his Father.

After his death on Calvary and his triumphant resurrection just before He was taken up to heaven, Jesus instructed his disciples to continue this ministry. For ages this same ministry was passed on from one generation of followers to the next, and today the assignment is just as valid as it was then. It is the calling of all who accept Him as their Saviour and Redeemer and who are willing to consecrate their lives and labour to his service. God offers you the privilege of serving Him as his witness.

In a world which is darkened by hate, jealousy, tragedy, uncertainty and strife; a world on its way to self-destruction, Jesus calls simple people to serve Him. Through their example and testimony they are able to lead lost souls to Him. Your relationship with the Master must therefore be of such a nature, that your ear and heart will be sensitive to his call. And your answer? "Send me! I will go!"

Lord, I am extremely honoured that You want to use me in your divine service. Make me a faithful and obedient witness.

October 8 1 Corinthians 10:1-17

WHO IS ON THE THRONE?
Whoever thinks he is standing firm had better be careful that he does not fall. But God keeps his promise, and He will not allow you to be tested beyond your power to remain firm . . . (1 Cor 10:12-13)

Religious assurance is a wonderful gift from the Holy Spirit. It enriches the life of the Christian beyond all description. This assurance instills calm and courage in those who are afraid, strength in those who are weak, and comforts those who are despondent. Its blessing spreads like a fragrance and encourages other Christians whose faith is weaker than yours.

The borderland between spiritual assurance and spiritual pride is very indistinct. To act as if you have monopoly on Christ, is to invite spiritual disaster and failure. If you glory in your experiences with Christ, and with a proud heart compare yourself to others, to their disadvantage and humiliation, your actions will speak of foolishness and childishness. Such an attitude can cause incalculable harm to your relationship with God, because He detests pride.

The moment you allow God on to the throne of your life instead of your proud self, you will be able to start giving spiritually. Each religious failure can be traced back to that moment when God was dethroned in favour of our personal pride and self-reliance.

If you remain deeply aware of your dependence on God and focus your thoughts and emotions entirely on Him, you will be able to place your trust in Him at all times, and never have to fear the sin of self-glorification.

Most gracious God and Father, protect me from allowing my self a place on the throne of my life – by the work of Jesus my Lord and the Holy Spirit.

October 9 Psalm 32:1-11

GOD'S EDUCATION IS EFFECTIVE
The Lord says, "I will teach you the way you should go; I will instruct you and advise you" (Ps 32:8)

God guides those who trust in Him completely. This is a promise to remember, especially at the beginning of every new year, at the dawn of every demanding day and every unknown night.

The sincere belief that your life is in God's hands, is not based on theological speculation or wishful thinking. It is the essential and meaningful experience of thousands who trust in Him and lead an active and obedient life to his glory.

However, you can only really experience the guidance of God in your life, if you are absolutely and entirely dedicated to Him; if you live in accordance with his holy will, unquestioningly. This, again, can only be achieved if you maintain unbroken contact with the living Christ – through regular Bible study and a dynamic and meaningful prayer life.

As a Christian in the school of life, you should live positively from day to day, bearing the knowledge that He is watching over you. You should also be willing to conscientiously do your share and contribute to the expansion of his kingdom. Jesus Christ will unlock the doors, but you will have to show your complete willingness and obedience by turning the knob and entering. It demands supreme courage to follow Him without hesitation and to be convinced that you are doing his will and following his example. However, if you accept the challenge, a surprising experience awaits you: with Christianlike insight you will be able to see his divine will for your life and how his road is mapped out for you.

Lord, You are my shelter and my strength. Keep me an obedient and diligent student in the school of your love so as to fulfil your will in my life.

October 10   Matthew 4:1-11

DON'T UNDERESTIMATE TEMPTATIONS
Then the Spirit led Jesus into the desert to be tempted by the Devil (Mt 4:1)
How different life would have been if man could be safeguarded against all forms of temptation! But now nobody escapes it – not even the Lord Jesus could!

It is important to be able to recognize temptation because it always seems very attractive. In order to resist it, we need mercy to look beyond the tempting exterior and see the venomous damage it can cause.

Many Christians underestimate the power of temptation and overestimate their own power for survival. Satan fabricates all kinds of images in our mind. He whispers of glorious things to come, and we play a naive game with danger.

Those who have fallen prey to these dark powers, live in a world of fantasy, thinking that they are in absolute command of their actions and emotions. Only a moment of weakness and temptation had become a disastrous reality which harmed their spiritual integrity beyond recognition.

To be able to truly conquer temptation, it must be rejected before it develops into a compelling passion. The aim of the tempter is to humiliate us and make us prisoners, confined by our despicable deeds. Therefore we should plead for wisdom to recognize temptation for what it really is. The Holy Spirit will grant us the power to conquer it before it becomes our master. ". . . at the time you are put to the test, He will give you the strength to endure it . . ." (1 Cor 10:13).

Thank you, Lord Jesus, for your shining example when You were being tempted. Do not bring me to hard testing but keep me safe from the Evil One. Give me strength to withstand temptation, and humility in victory.

October 11   Psalm 56:1-13

A LIFE THAT SPEAKS OF QUALITY
And so I walk in the presence of God, in the light that shines on the living (Ps 56:13)
There are many people whose hope and ideals are being smothered by the monotony of their existence. They are willing to do just about any-

thing to escape from this unhappy situation. They may start off by gathering possessions and undertaking exciting risks – anything which makes the adrenaline flow. They believe that being alive actually means being on the move at all times, doing new things and tasting new experiences.

There may be a trace of truth in this philosophy, but then the intention is to satisfy only your mental and emotional needs, while your spiritual life is being neglected. Soon you will experience a feeling of emptiness, unfulfilment, basically because you have forgotten that you are mainly a spiritual being.

It is only when God takes his legitimate place in your life and you follow the road of the living Christ, that you will be able to experience that life which God has intended for his children. Thus, a meaningful life means a life committed to God through and through. To give Christ partial dominion over your life is to choose a second-class existence. It is only when He is in full control that life gains in quality and perfection. Remember: "In Him we live and move and exist" (Acts 17:28). He is the Way to go; the Truth to know; and the Life to live!

Redeeming Christ, I kneel in worship and appreciation that by your love and power I may know a full and satisfying life. Lead me through your Holy Spirit to a deeper knowledge and total commitment.

October 12   John 11:17-27

FEAR OF DEATH
I am the resurrection and the life. Whoever believes in Me will live, even though he dies; and whoever lives and believes in Me will never die. Do you believe this? (Jn 11:25-26)

It often happens that people confess their fear for death with a sense of shame in their hearts. Death poses a problem to many people – even for dedicated Christians – and one must be careful not to ingore it by uttering pious clichés or reprimands about the lack of faith.

Very few people travel this lonely road without hesitation in their hearts. Fear for death remains a constant companion.

The Word of God is a fountain of comfort for the dying, especially for the aged, for those who are weary of life and the terminally ill. Through God's glorious promises man is assured that he is never alone, not even on that solitary road. God is with us in the valley of the shadow of death. Therefore we need not approach death encumbered with fear. Jesus Christ gained victory over death. In Christ, death is stripped of its menace. By our union with the resurrected Lord our fear is conquered.

When one is present at the deathbed of a believer, one cannot help but recognize the final great peace with which he meets death. By the grace of God also this difficult road is being levelled for us. In the moment of our deepest loneliness and crisis, God grants us his peace. That is why we are able to rejoice: "Even if I go through the deepest darkness, I will not be afraid, Lord, for You are with me" (Ps 23:4).

Lord, my Saviour and Redeemer, grant that my love for You will drive all fear from my heart – also when I enter the valley of the shadow of death.

October 13 1 John 2:1-6

THE TRUE TEST
If we obey God's commands, then we are sure that we know Him (1 Jn 2:3)
It is sad but true: many people become Christians on their own terms. They simply adjust the Word of God to suit their own needs and desires. They will accept the word of consolation pronounced by Christ, but sidestep the challenges which true discipleship demands.

To become a true Christian, you have to consecrate your whole life to God's dominion. If not, you will experience a type of inferior Christianity which is unacceptable to the Lord, while it curtails your spiritual growth even further.

There is no use in confessing your faith verbally, if it is not being confirmed in practice. Faith and good deeds are inseparable when it comes to a real and dynamic relationship with Christ. If this cannot be said of you, then you have never yet really committed your life to God. True Christianity demands a willing obedience regarding God's desires as revealed in his Word. It is just as important to keep his commandments as it is to read your Bible, to pray and to meditate.

Through these matters your love for Him becomes visible. If your heart is filled with love for Christ, you will be eager to serve Him, be obedient to his will and live according to his perfect example. Only then can you hope to pass the test of true discipleship.

Loving Master, grant that my greatest desire will be to know your will and to execute it obediently.

October 14   2 Corinthians 7:2-16

FAITH COMFORTS THOSE IN GRIEF
For the sadness that is used by God brings a change of heart that leads to salvation – and there is no regret in that! (2 Cor 7:10)

Sorrow is part of our human existence. No one can escape its onslaughts. Neither can one prepare oneself for it, because you never know when it is going to strike. And had you known, you would have been powerless to prevent it.

What is dangerous about sorrow is that it can confuse and paralyse you in such a way that clear and logical thinking becomes impossible. It is only some time later that you will be able to estimate in what degree it has touched your life.

One must also guard against self-pity, because this may hinder you in mastering your sorrow. Another negative effect of intense grief is that it can cloud your outlook on life itself, and cause you to become bitter and cynical. It then becomes very difficult for others to support you or even live with you.

The only way to emerge from this quagmire is to take your sorrow to your heavenly Father in prayer. He grants wisdom and strength so that you can fight your grief courageously and be released from its negative results in your heart. Thus, even your sorrow is turned to your advantage by God and He leads you to discover new meaning in life. However, the richest blessing which sorrow can bring, is a deeper knowledge of a caring and loving Father.

God of sympathy and comfort, I worship your holy Name for granting me a song of praise, even in the hour of my deepest sorrow, because through Jesus my Lord, I am bound to your love and mercy.

October 15   1 Peter 5:1-11

AN ANXIOUS COUNTENANCE DOES GOD NO HONOUR
Leave all your worries with Him, because He cares for you (1 Pet 5:7)

It is encouraging to know that God is not only the creator, but also the provider for his creation.

Why then do we worry and torment ourselves if we know that we have an almighty Father who cares for us and supports us in the hour of our need? His love is the only constant factor in our lives. Therefore, it is not to God's honour that we worry, it rather reveals a lack of faith and trust in his care: "In view of all this, what can we say? If God is for us, who can be against us? Certainly not God, who did not even keep back his own Son, but offered Him for us all!" (Rom 8:31-32).

Problems are not being solved simply because you worry. On the contrary, more troubles seem to appear from nowhere. When you subject yourself to this weakness of the spirit, it becomes very easy to forget about the love of God and that He is always ready to reach out a helping hand, whatever cares you may have. Racked by worries you can't feel anything else but despondency, because without God all your efforts are fruitless.

God offers you his loving care, however dismal your situation may be. He will put his arms around you and tenderly and safely lead you to the solution of your problems.

God knows everything. He cares for you from day to day. He gave us his beloved Son – the most precious and only one He had! Therefore you should never live under the misconception that you have to carry life's burden all by yourself. A life without God is a hopeless end, but a life with God creates an endless hope.

Eternal God of love and mercy, I worship You in this day because You so tenderly care for your children. I place myself and my troubles at the feet of your Son, Jesus Christ, in the knowledge that He will solve my problems.

October 16　　　　　　　　　　　　　　　　Matthew 9:27-31

FAITH RESTORES THE SIGHT OF THE BLIND
Then Jesus touched their eyes and said, "Let it happen, then, just as you believe!" – and their sight was restored (Mt 9:29)
Many people, when they passionately desire something, believe deep down in their heart that it is unattainable in any case. To them life seems drab and colourless, without any excitement, because they do not have

the courage to pursue their dreams. Usually they also remain without spiritual conviction, strength or vision.

When you sincerely believe, all things become possible. Experience will teach you that your every noble desire which is in accordance with the will of God, can be claimed by faith.

That does not mean that you are striving for the unattainable in your own strength, but rather that you are faithfully and trustingly awaiting a revelation of the omnipotence of God in your everyday life.

A faith which is to bear fruit, must have its inspiration and origin in God. If we ask great things from God, we will receive great things from Him, enabling us to perform miraculous deeds in his Name. This was the experience of the blind men of whom we read in the Holy Scriptures.

If your faith is rooted in God and implemented entirely to his glory, you can become a channel through which He executes his mighty deeds. A whole new world of spiritual power will be revealed to you, and in his Name you will be able to recognize all the colourful possibilities for your life.

These wonderful things can happen if the power of God is not limited by disbelief or stunted faith. Through your consecration to God, your faith will become a living reality and you will come to see the invisible.

Omnipotent God and Father, I praise your Name for enriching my life with the seed of your faith in my heart, and for letting it grow to bear fruit which is acceptable to You. Strengthen my faith from day to day through the indwelling power of the Holy Spirit.

October 17 Psalm 103:1-22

PAINFUL MEMORIES
He does not keep on rebuking; He is not angry for ever (Ps 103:9)
Every one of us carries memories which we would rather forget. We have done so many things which we would so much like to erase from our minds and hearts. There was the cutting word spoken in haste. It inflicted such pain that even time cannot heal it. There is the rumour which was spread maliciously and can never be recalled; the foolish decisions which must be executed; love that was denied and can never again be restored. No wonder we are being borne down by the weight of our negative memories.

It is possible that you have tried everything in your power to compensate for your actions – that is what God expects of you. Or perhaps you have accepted Jesus Christ as your Saviour and Redeemer and come to know the extreme joy of being forgiven – yet you refuse to forgive yourself. Face this fact: Christ forgave you – you will have to learn to forgive yourself.

If, after mastering self-forgiveness, you still have moments of painful remorse, you will have to learn to cope with it. Never allow these memories to take control of your mind and thereby force you to despair. The truth is that you have gained wisdom through your experiences, you have learnt some valuable lessons. You have gained a deeper insight into and a better understanding of human behaviour, and therefore you will be able to warn and council others who find themselves in the same predicament. Thus, by the grace of God we even benefit from our painful memories.

It is comforting to know, dear Lord, that even my most painful memories can be used to honour your Name. Thank you for cleansing my conscience through your love and forgiveness.

October 18 John 8:31-47

TRUE FREEDOM IS TO FULFIL GOD'S WILL
If the Son sets you free, then you will be really free (Jn 8:36)
Freedom is a word which is used very frequently, but most of the times in the wrong context. The oppressed are usually keen to answer to the call of freedom, only to find themselves under a new, and perhaps harsher regime. True freedom encompasses much more than lofty political or social ideals.

Most people think that freedom gives you the right to say and do as you like – anything that restricts this right is considered as oppression and is therefore vigorously opposed. However, freedom must never be confused with lawlessness. Freedom does not imply the right to do as you like, but that which God expects of you. You can only be truly free if you accept the responsibilities God entrusts you with. The highest form of freedom is obtained when we subject ourselves to the sovereignty of God. On the other hand, the freedom that is offered by Satan, always ends in slavery.

It is only after the living Christ has become the Lord of your life, that you will come to know the real meaning of freedom: that is to be cut loose from the tyranny of sin. Faith then takes the place of fear; hate makes way for love, and negative attitudes are transformed into a new obedience. Only as a new person in Christ will you truly be free!

Having committed yourself to the living Christ and having given Him full control of your entire life, you will now be free to serve Him faithfully and joyfully. Your freedom will no longer be an illusion, but a glorious reality.

Jesus, my Redeemer, You have set me free from the slavery of sin. Help me to utilize my freedom to your honour and glory.

October 19 — Jeremiah 8:1-17

FROM DEFEAT TO VICTORY
When someone falls down, doesn't he get back up? If someone misses the road, doesn't he turn back? (Jer 8:4)

It is not uncommon to experience failure occasionally. At such times it is one's positive approach to life that enables you to keep your footing. However, if you have been knocked down by circumstances, you should get up and tackle life with renewed zeal.

It is unfortunate that many people who suffer, believe that they will never again be able to face the challenges of life. Overwhelmed with self-pity, they seem to take pleasure in the supposed ruins of their life while they proclaim to all the world what an injustice they have suffered. Their role as martyrs surely suits them. These people travel along a lonely road, because as time goes by, their friends get bored listening to their lamentations

However hard life has beaten you, you have to remember that it is not God's will that you should constantly suffer defeat. On the contrary, He wants you to live victoriously and constructively. Even amidst disappointment and failure He will support you and lead you to a new dawn of victory in his Name.

Don't waste time with useless self-reproach and self-pity. Place yourself in the hands of Him who makes all things new. Strive for the good which is ahead and forget the past. The Spirit of God will lead you to recovery and eventually to victory. Faith is the tender thread that keeps our lives from falling apart.

Almighty God, You are my shelter and strength. Grant me the courage to rise above my failures and the wisdom to live faithfully and victoriously.

October 20   Psalm 42:1-11

CONQUER DEPRESSION BY ACTING POSITIVELY

Why am I so sad? Why am I so troubled? I will put my hope in God, and once again I will praise Him, my Saviour and my God (Ps 42:11)

One should never allow despondency to rob you of your spiritual poise. Many of God's most dedicated followers do feel depressed at times. However, the knowledge that your experience is not unique, that it stems from our innermost self, that it has never been part of God's plan for our lives, should comfort us greatly.

When you are being plagued by doubt, it might be because you are not utilising your spiritual potential to the full. You know what you are – and you know what you should be. And these two realities don't always correspond.

If your spiritual life is but lukewarm, and if you don't live in absolute commitment to God, you are actually giving way to feelings of sadness and hopelessness. Obedience to his will demands an effective and dynamic faith.

It is especially when you rebel against the will of God that you become depressed very easily. Anger takes the place of enthusiasm and the spiritual road does not seem so exciting any more. Do you still wonder why your faith has lost its sparkle?

Start on something positive! You should never be satisfied with inactivity or simply be caught in a trap of self-pity. Build a new life! Begin by being what God intended you to be and do his will enthusiastically. Turn your thoughts to the Lord and forget about yourself. Trust Him with your despair and depression as you trust Him with your life. By the love and mercy of God the shadows will flee.

Lord, guide me to do your will obediently. Lift my spirits through the work and love of the living Christ.

October 21 — John 20:19-29

FAITH AT YOUR FINGERTIPS

Unless I see the scars of the nails in his hands and put my finger on those scars and my hand in his side, I will not believe (Jn 20:25)

When Jesus lived on earth, many people proclaimed that they would believe in Him if only He would, by means of a sign, prove that He was the Messiah. The fact that He restored the sight of the blind, opened the ears of the deaf, healed the crippled and even raised the dead, passed them by unnoticed. The divine wisdom of his words did not impress the unbelieving crowds. They only saw what they wanted to see. Nothing could make the light shine on the darkness of their spiritual lives.

That's the way it was with Thomas. Though, not only Thomas – we too have to contend with the same type of Christian followers in our day. Unless something sensational happens to convince them of the existence of God or the divinity of Jesus Christ, they refuse to believe. They simply turn a blind eye to the mighty works of God as revealed in creation. They fail to recognize the divine power of Christ even as He recreates the lives of those who have entrusted themselves to Him. God's patience with these faithless people passes all understanding.

When Jesus came and stood among the disciples where they were gathered behind locked doors, He invited Thomas to use his fingertips in order to find out whether He was indeed alive. And then the miracle! Thomas no longer wanted to see or to feel – he simply confessed: "My Lord and my God!"

Lord and Saviour, grant me a childlike faith so that I may accept your dominion over my life unconditionally. Keep me from seeking your presence in sensational miracles. Restore my sight so that I may see the invisible through faith.

October 22 — Romans 12:9-21

LIVING WITH DIFFICULT PEOPLE

Do not let evil defeat you; instead, conquer evil with good (Rom 12:21)

People's personalities differ, and therefore all people don't get along equally well. Perhaps you have to live or work with somebody who is impossible. If this person is an authoritive figure, he can make life very miserable for you. If you find yourself in a position where you have to keep on suppressing the anger and aggression which his actions cause you, your health will eventually suffer.

The solutions which the world offers for these situations, seldom work. If someone purposefully tries to make life unbearable for you and you retaliate, you are actually degrading yourself. At such a level where you are less deserving of respect, you will hardly be able to help conquer hate and discord in this strife-torn world.

Whatever the situation, a Christian's performance should always reveal a constructive and positive attitude. When you harbour the spirit of Jesus Christ in your heart, you won't see "difficult" people as enemies who have to be opposed, but as people who need to be supported by love. Some people may consider such an attitude as foolishness or weakness, but by praying for unjust people, you are discarding all hatred and antagonism. They will not be able to withstand the impact of your unceasing love and understanding, and eventually they will react in a positive manner. When you have gained this victory in Christ's Name, you will be able to make friends of your enemies.

O Holy Spirit of God, teach me your love and understanding so that I may get along with other people. Guard me against their bitterness and hostility.

October 23   Ephesians 4:1-16

WILL A SECOND BIRTH BE ENOUGH?
Instead, by speaking the truth in a spirit of love, we must grow up in every way to Christ, who is the head (Eph 4:15)

In order to become members of God's eternal family we have to be born again. Christ Himself commented on this issue when He was on earth: "No one can see the Kingdom of God unless he is born again" (Jn 3:3). There are many Christians who are able to name the precise day and date, even the hour of their rebirth, and yet hardly any progress is noticed in their spiritual lives.

Before we can lead a fruit-bearing religious life, we have to be born again. Thus, our second birth should always be seen as the point of departure on our spiritual pilgrimage and not as a goal in itself. The moment you accept Jesus Christ as your Saviour and Redeemer, you will receive clear guidance as to God's reasons and purposes for your life. Living by a new set of standards which is in accordance with God's will, now becomes second nature.

There are many followers of Christ who never realize how important it is to keep on growing in your knowledge of Jesus Christ. They call Him Lord, yet they refuse to accept the challenge to enter the deeper waters of the spirit. However, an effective and richer life in Christ demands daily renewal and growth in spiritual stature. Quite possibly you will find that you tend to backslide at times and revert to your old ways and sinful habits. If you grow toward Christ with singleness of purpose, you will be able to break the old bonds and establish a meaningful relationship with Him. Only then will you be able to bear the fruit which is expected of a truly reborn child of God.

Holy Master, help me to persevere on the road of spiritual growth.

October 24 John 1:35-42

BEHIND THE SCENES FOR CHRIST
One of them was Andrew, Simon Peter's brother. At once he found his brother Simon and told him, "We have found the Messiah." Then he took Simon to Jesus (Jn 1:40-42)

Andrew did not mind playing second fiddle. He is known to us as "Simon Peter's brother". He was able to live in the shadow of his famous brother without harbouring feelings of bitterness or jealousy. He willingly allowed others the limelight. Social status, honour and esteem were of no major importance to him. It was enough for him just to be near Jesus and to enjoy his company and friendship. Though, he couldn't keep the wonder of this friendship to himself. He was always ready to introduce people to Christ.

John 1.41-42 tells us that Andrew found his brother and brought him to Jesus. To be a witness for Christ in one's own family is probably the most difficult challenge which a disciple has to face.

In John 6:8 we are introduced to the boy who brought five barley loaves and two fish. With so little at his disposal, Jesus was able to perform a miracle – He fed the multitude. Our testimony for Christ may trigger off many a great miracle in the lives of people.

John 12:20-22 tells us that Andrew introduced a number of Greeks to Jesus. He wanted that all should hear the gospel. Having met Jesus,

Andrew wanted to share the joy of this experience with others so that they could also believe.

We are partners working together for God, therefore we should be willing to step out of the limelight at times and also perform our duties behind the scenes. Whether in or out of the public eye, our work for Christ is important.

Loving Lord and Master, thank you that I have a wonderful message to convey to this sinful world. Make me a faithful disciple.

October 25 Isaiah 26:1-11

TRUSTING THE LORD!
You, Lord, give perfect peace to those who keep their purpose firm and put their trust in You (Is 26:3)

The peace of God is far beyond human understanding or thought. Peace can never be created artificially – it is of a quality the world can never hope to equal.

Paul declared repeatedly that Christ is the only source of peace. He creates peace and He proclaims peace. No human being is capable of erasing any estrangement between the Creator God and his creation, mankind. Only God can put us right with Him. He does it by the free gift of this grace through Jesus Christ.

The riches of the peace of God are incalculable and exceeds our wildest dreams or expectations. However, there are definite conditions we have to adhere to before we can make it our own.

We have to place our trust in God unconditionally. We have to renounce our self-sufficiency and trust in Him for our strength. We have to focus our thoughts on God and place them under his control. At times we also have to come to a standstill in order to get in touch with the magnificence of the wonder-working power of God.

Because we have placed our trust in the Lord, we are able to experience the calm of spirit and the peace of mind which God grants his children. No disappointment, persecution, affliction, poverty or hardship can ever separate us from Him. If you search for peace beyond yourself, in Jesus Christ, God's heavenly peace will fill your life.

I know that my greatest strength is to be found in prayer and trust, o

Father. Support me through your Holy Spirit and grant me the peace of God which passes all understanding.

October 26 Mark 2:1-12

VICARIOUS FAITH
Seeing how much faith they had, Jesus said to the paralysed man, "My son, your sins are forgiven" (Mk 2:5)
Through the faith of his friends the paralysed man was healed in body and soul. By their act of faith we are taught that there is a trust which quietly surmounts all obstacles on behalf of another.

Fear for ridicule make it impossible for some Christians to bear witness to the living Christ or to confess their faith in public. They are the so-called "secret disciples". However, Christ cannot be served in secret. This secretiveness will either destroy the new life in Christ, or God's triumph in our lives will conquer it. Our love for Christ transforms us into alive, radiant and dynamic people, so that the world will know beyond doubt that we belong to Him.

If you are his follower, the world should see Christ's image reflected in your life. You have to share your faith by confidently proclaiming it in word and deed. Your life should at all times reveal a great deal about your relationship with Christ. When you are truly reborn, you will never tire of sharing the wonder of God's grace and mercy in your life.

Antagonism can easily flare up if we force others to listen to our witness. Beautiful and pious words can never take the place of beautiful and pious deeds. Our loving actions should stem from a life consecrated to God. To this purpose we should place ourselves in God's hands unconditionally.

Lord, I sincerely want to become less so that You can become more in my life. Help me not to confess my faith only verbally, but also to do the will of my heavenly Father.

October 27 Luke 2:8-20

PEACE – GOD'S GIFT OF LOVE
Glory to God in the highest heaven, and peace on earth to those with whom He is pleased! (Lk 2:14)

There are mainly two types of people in this world – those who give and those who take! The one group approaches life with this philosophy: "What do I get out of it?" Even as they carry the gifts, they silently hope to receive something more valuable. However, the child of Gods asks: "What can I give?" He expects nothing and no price-tag is attached to his love.

If you are following Christ only for what may come your way and not for what you may be able to give, you simply don't understand the first thing about God's peace. "Giving" is a divine principle – that is why God gave his Son!

By accepting God's gift of love, your life becomes a song of joy to his glory. Under the guidance of the Holy Spirit, your glorification of God becomes a liberating force which empowers you to love God and become a peacemaker.

When the living Christ and his disciples were at supper on the day before the Passover Festival, He promised that He would send his helper. The Holy Spirit came upon them and filled them with power; He equipped them for service; taught, guided and comforted them. He warmed their hearts and souls, and gave them understanding: these and other gifts were not only for themselves, but also for others – so that God's peace may reign. In this manner God's gift of love can become a reality in our lives – if only we accept another gift from God – the Holy Spirit, and the peace that He brings!

Dear Lord, I desperately want to be your missionary of peace in this world. I want to share the glory of your love and peace with others. Make me willing and obedient in this ministry and strengthen me through your Spirit.

October 28 Job 23:1-17

SEEKING GOD IN PRAYER
How I wish I knew where to find Him, and knew how to go where He is. I would state my case before Him and present all the arguments in my favour. I want to know what He would say and how He would answer me (Job 23:3-5)

This deeply moving sigh of Job reflects the silent wish in millions of seeking human hearts! Won't we all like to know where to find God? Some people try to suppress this yearning by proclaiming that they have no interest in religion whatsoever. Yet, deep down in their hearts they have a longing for the Truth which will bring meaning and purpose to their lives.

When a person realizes and acknowledges his dependence on God, he immediately wants to know: "Where can I find God?" He then either rejoices when he finds Him, or he experiences the paralysing frustration as he continues to search.

We may search far and wide for God: in churches, among other Christians, or in quiet meditation. In our struggle to find God, we can passionately dedicate ourselves to be of service to the poor and the destitute. Yet, all will be in vain, and you may feel like giving up hope.

It is only when you realize that the One you are looking for, is actually with you, that you meet Him. God can be reached immediately – by prayer. Stop looking for Him, and accept his comforting presence in faith. When Christ becomes the beginning and the end of your faith, your thoughts and acts will be controlled by Him. You will experience his loving work in your life, every moment of every day. Rejoice – you have found Him!

Lord and Master, I accept and welcome You into my life with joy and appreciation. Thank you that I may experience your indwelling presence at all times.

October 29   John 16:25-33

BE BRAVE!
The world will make you suffer. But be brave! I have defeated the world (Jn 16:33)

People are inclined to confuse courage with fearlessness or even recklessness. Robert Louis Stevenson said something very true: "Courage is not the absence of fear; courage is the conquest of fear!" Courage is to do what you have to do in the conviction that, if you do your duty, you can trust upon God for the outcome.

When a coast-guard station on the west coast of America received a SOS one stormy night, the officers risked their lives on a raging sea to perform their rescue work. A young man who had to go out for the first time, said anxiously to his commander: "Sir, we won't come back again!" The experienced old seaman answered: "Son, our order and duty is to go out. Nobody can guarantee our safe return."

Courage is to speak the truth at all times; to be honest and fair under all circumstances; to be able to say "No!" firmly when it is required.

Courage is to work at your problems until you are victorious – and not to succumb to them in self-pity; to be honest with yourself and exercise to have self-control over body, mind and soul – and never to hide behind your failings or imperfections.

Courage is to commit yourself to witnessing for Christ, even if it is to your disadvantage here on earth. Those who consecrate their lives to God, will be strengthened by the Holy Spirit so that they are able to face the trials and tribulations.

Holy God, fear sometimes threatens to overwhelm me. Lead me to true Christian courage and victory through my Lord, Jesus Christ. Strengthen me to conquer the problems of every day and guide me through your Holy Spirit.

October 30   Colossians 4:2-6

WAIT FOR GOD TO ANSWER

Be persistent in prayer, and keep alert as you pray, giving thanks to God (Col 4:2)

"If I have asked something of God in prayer, should I leave it to Him to answer in his own time, or do I have to remind Him repeatedly of my needs and desires?" Since the very early days this has been a matter of debate amongst the followers of Jesus Christ.

Truth is, both arguments can be correct. Sincere prayers cannot be governed by rigid laws. The Holy Spirit is at work in the hearts and minds of God's children and He considers every individual's being, background and personality. With this information at his disposal He leads every one of us to the presence of God by any one of the many different roads.

Under the guidance of the Holy Spirit, our prayers do not always travel a well-known route, but often goes along that way which God chose to suit our personal needs. This is part of God's merciful plan. The style of your prayer does not matter, as long as you pray faithfully and purposefully, always aware of his loving and divine presence. Soon you'll know when God answers your prayers and you will rejoice as God's Holy Spirit transforms your life. As a new being in Christ it does not matter whether you remind God humbly every day, or whether you wait for his answer in faith and trust.

I shall wait upon Thee patiently, o Lord. Holy Spirit of God, guard me against impatience and help me to watch and pray persistently, so that I may see You at work in my life.

October 31   Ephesians 4:17-32

TO RECEIVE AND TO GRANT FORGIVENESS
Instead, be kind and tender-hearted to one another, and forgive one another, as God has forgiven you through Christ (Eph 4:32)
If you consider yourself a Christian, you have to be able to forgive. Christ Himself thought it such an important matter that He specifically mentioned it in his prayer: "Forgive us the wrongs we have done, as we forgive the wrongs that others have done to us" (Mt 6:12).

We are by nature inclined to harbour grudges and we find it extremely difficult to forgive others. It is especially at such times that we have to allow the mercy and love of God to work in our lives. If we are unable to help ourselves, the Spirit of the living Christ will do it through us and for us. If you find it difficult to forgive, you will have to allow the purifying love of Christ to remove all the bitterness and hatred. Don't allow your unforgiving disposition to poison and undermine your physical, mental and spiritual health.

Many people proclaim that they are willing to forgive, but that they will not forget. There is no suggestion of forgiveness in such a remark and attitude! A Christian can never forgive someone only half-heartedly. To harbour and nurse a grievance, is to cause yourself irreparable spiritual harm.

Christ could forgive unconditionally, even while hanging on the cross on Calvary; therefore we, his followers, will have to learn to forgive. When we allow the Spirit of God to teach us forgiveness, the joy of our salvation will become a reality in our lives.

Saviour and Friend, save me by the purifying power of the Holy Spirit from the sin of an unforgiving heart. Because You have pardoned me so greatly, Father, I will gladly grant my pardon to others.

NOVEMBER

PRAYER

Eternal God, heavenly Teacher, I worship You as
the Source of all knowledge during this month.
It is exam-time for thousands of scholars and students –
but also for thousands of others who will be wrestling
with the exams of life.
During this trying time:
Grant me the peace of God which passes all
understanding.
Keep me healthy in body and mind and grant me peace
and calm under pressure.
Be in my heart and give me assurance and composure
when I have to give account of my responsibilities.
Be in my eyes, that I will be able to study and
understand with discrimination.
Be in my mind, that I will be able to arrange my
thoughts logically and think clearly.
Be in my hands and make them firm and strong
to reproduce what I have so painstakingly learnt.
Thank you for loved ones who remember me with love
and care during this exacting time – and pray for me!
Be to me – today and every day –
the Way to go;
the Truth to know;
the Life to live.
In the strong and redeeming Name of
Jesus Christ my Lord.
Amen.

November 1 Hebrews 12:1-11

NEVER GIVE UP!
So do not let yourselves become discouraged and give up (Heb 12:3)
Even the most dynamic and energetic Christians may become exhausted and weary when their burden of responsibilities become too great. If you are striving after an ideal and suddenly realize that the years are swiftly passing, without the aim being reached, it becomes a very discouraging experience – even to a devoted Christian.

Often the problems of the present moment absorb so much of your everyday time, that you lose sight of your ideals. The excitement vanishes from your existence and you become spiritually tired and weary.

When your life and work threatens to become meaningless, it is imperative that you remain positive and always aware of the presence of the living Christ in your life. Christ enables you to regain a true perspective of the present situation and casts the light of hope and joy upon your depressed spirit.

Life becomes meaningless if you neglect its spiritual demands. Prayer and meditation is not the privilege of only the great men of God, but a divine gift to each of his children with meaningful spiritual ideals and who lives according to the will of God.

If you converse with God in prayer regularly and meditate upon his Word faithfully; if you keep your eyes fixed on Jesus, the Beginner and Finisher of our faith; if you never give in, you will be able to complete the race by perseverance and courage. Otherwise your spiritual gains may become a tragic loss. Christ does not so much need "starters", as He needs "stickers" in his kingdom.

Thank you, Lord and Master, for the Holy Spirit, who gives me the capability to triumph over disappointment. I kneel in amazement before your love which comforts and encourages me.

November 2 Psalm 42:1-12

ETERNITY IN OUR HEARTS
As a deer longs for a stream of cool water, so I long for You, O God (Psalm 42:1)
Modern man calls it depression, this painful yearning and melancholy

which settles over the spirit like a dark shadow. We all have experience of it: the student in a hostel on a Sunday-evening; the national serviceman at the border-base; the lonely young person in the teeming city; parents and grandparents longing for their children and grandchildren; loved ones separated from each other. As you grow older you pine for things which are long past, and for people you have known but who have been taken away by death.

David felt this yearning so strongly that he experienced the strange desire to drink water from the well at the gates of Bethlehem just once more (2 Sam 23:15). He was yearning for the environment where he had spent many happy and carefree days in his enchanted youth. When his brave soldiers, in contempt of the danger of death, brought him of the water, he didn't drink it, but poured it on the ground as a libation to God.

All our human yearnings are but a shadow of our eternal longing for God. He placed eternity in our hearts. God grants comfort for all our yearning and melancholy. He sent the Comforter to be with us for ever. The Spirit gives us the blessed assurance that we are God's children and that we shall find no peace until we have found our peace in God. The Spirit reminds us of the banquet in the Father's house and of the undying love of the Father's heart. Then yearning and depression disappear and our hearts rejoice with a hymn of home-coming.

Jesus, Lord, I worship You as the one who opened the way to the Father's house and the Father's heart where we receive healing for all our human ailments and all our yearnings are realized.

November 3   Psalm 38:1-22

THE POWER OF REPENTANCE
I am about to fall and am in constant pain. I confess my sins; they fill me with anxiety (Ps 38:17-18)
One of the most difficult things in life to do, is to confess that you were wrong. It is painful to acknowledge: "I am also guilty!" The burden of his feelings of guilt forced Dawid to the confession: "My sins fill me with anxiety!"

A confession can bridge the chasm of estrangement between friends; it can rectify a relationship of love which has gone awry; it can expel bitterness and jealousy. But every time we want to confess a wrong we have done, we find enough reason to keep us from doing so: I have done nothing wrong; people will think I am weak; I will lose my dignity; he will be filled with delight to hear me confess. And this is exactly why we never taste the joy of emancipation through confession. Our life becomes impoverished and a breeding-ground for bitterness, hatred and the inability to forgive and to forget.

But if we do not repent and confess, relationships can never be corrected. Neither with God nor with our fellow-men. We can't afford to be too proud to accept fault. Ask God to grant you courage through the Holy Spirit to confess your guilt and to be cleansed and healed. This will make you heir to the joy and freedom which is the portion of those who experience the power of repentance in their daily lives.

Loving Lord Jesus, grant me the grace to forgive as You have forgiven me. Help me to rectify all the broken relationships which sin has caused in my life by the way of confession and repentance. You can make all things new and I am waiting upon your redeeming power.

November 4   James 5:7-20

PRAYER IN TIMES OF AFFLICTION
Is anyone among you in trouble? He should pray (Jas 5:13)
He who prays builds a rampart against the ills of life; a bulwark which is stronger than granite. It is the powerline by which the grace of God is conveyed to each domain of our lives, especially in times of problems and affliction.

To be able to cope with pain, you must have peace with God. That you can obtain only through a disciplined prayer life. There is but one highway to God out of our needs, failure, disappointment, sorrow and affliction: the highway of prayer.

God is always available and through prayer we have free entry to the throne of Grace. Jesus Christ gave his life to make it possible for us to go directly to the throne of God.

It is just possible that at this moment you are bearing a load of care. Take it to the Lord in prayer. He will listen and He can help! If you pray with sincerity, faith and dependence, the Lord will grant what He knows to be best for you in his wisdom.

Sometimes God's anwer is entirely different to your desires and at other times it seems as if He is unwilling to answer. However, He is always testing and strengthening your faith. You must persevere in prayer and obediently follow wherever He leads. Then your afflictions become blessed experiences which bring you closer to God. To neglect prayer in times of affliction, is to miss the riches God offers to those who trust Him under every circumstance of life.

I praise You, Lord my God, that You are willing to listen to me. I need You so much, especially in times of affliction and despair. I confess my love to You, in the Name of Jesus Christ, my Intercessor and Saviour.

November 5   Ecclesiastes 11:9-12:8

CREATE INSPIRING MEMORIES
So remember your Creator while you are still young, before those dismal days and years come when you will say, "I don't enjoy life" (Ecc 12:1)
Your memories of tomorrow are created by what you do today. If you persevere with one or other action, convinced that you will be able to escape its bitter results, life takes its revenge. Even though nobody knows what you have done, you will have to live with your conscience. Even though you don't consider it important, the tragic results will not be absent from your future life.

If you choose an inferior road to the road of communion with the Holy Spirit, you are filling the store-rooms of your conscience with unworthy memories. Then you allow ghosts from the past to destroy your peace of mind.

However exciting you may find the ways of the world, there is a better self in you which yearns for God. Your answer to this longing for God can influence your life for better or for worse. What you choose, is not only important for today, but is responsible for tomorrow's joy or sadness, success or failure.

Many aged people have an intense desire to wipe deeds of foolishness of the past from their memories, but the pain is there indelibly.

When you trust in God's forgiveness and you live according to his divine will, in obedience to his instructions, you will have beautiful memories at the eventide of your life, to warm your heart.

Merciful God and Father, teach me to plan wisely and carefully for all the tomorrows of my life.

November 6   1 John 5:1-5

CONQUER YOUR FEAR BY FAITH

And we win the victory over the world by means of our faith. Who can defeat the world? Only the person who believes that Jesus is the Son of God (1 Jn 5:4-5)

Nobody can tell with absolute assurance what the future holds in store. There are times when threatening clouds seem intent on destroying your peace of mind and robbing you of the joy of life.

There is absolutely nothing you can do to free yourself from the fear of the unknown, but to go to God in prayer. A living faith in the goodness and love of God as your heavenly Father is a wonderful antidote for fear and anxiety. And there is no fear which God Almighty cannot handle.

When you believe unflinchingly in the love and power of God, you can confront your fear with confidence and resist it so that it cannot control your life. Then you learn to shake off all self-pity; to avoid all negative thoughts which cause despondency and cause your mind and spirit to fear.

It is when your faith strengthens you inwardly, that you develop the ability to cope with your fear and to revert it to something positive. When the Holy Spirit takes over the government of your life, you no longer fear the unknown future. Then you know with certainty that God is in control of your life.

Where previously there was fear, God now rules with love and power. Fear is conquered and life gains a new dimension of joy and freedom.

Lord, my God, by your mercy I have a faith which can conquer my fear. I want to live close to You – the Source of my power and confidence.

November 7   1 Corinthians 13:1-13

SERVING WITH LOVE

. . . and the greatest of these is love (1 Cor 13:13)

The danger of a destructive world war seems more possible today than a few years ago. The world is constantly implementing emergency measures to fend off crises. And these very measures are often the cause of division and strife.

God has the ideal solution to the problems of the world, but modern man rejects it, and classifies it as impractical, idealistic and too simplistic. The Word of God has a singular demand: that we love Him and our fellow-men. If this strife-torn world would only learn to love, the ailments and problems of the world would be remedied.

Most people accept this truth, but they lack the courage and faith to practise it. If the Christians of our time would proclaim the gospel of love, and commit themselves to serving in love, they would make the greatest contribution possible to world peace.

Love is not a purely sentimental or emotional approach to problems. To truly serve in love, is to bring God into each situation of life where injustice, hatred, bitterness and other negative evil forces are at work without resistance.

Allow the love of God to inspire and guide you, and you will discover that God can use you powerfully. By proclaiming and practising love, you make a contribution to the healing of society and the spiritual reconstruction of our generation.

Loving God and Father, fill me so entirely with your divine love, that I will be able to share it with others willingly and productively.

November 8   Romans 3:1-8

GOD ALWAYS REMAINS FAITHFUL

But what if some of them were not faithful? Does this mean that God will not be faithful? Certainly not! God must be true, even though every man is a liar (Rom 3:3-4)

When a person you trust disappoints you, you feel hurt and disillusioned and you will find it difficult to trust him again. It is a problem to know whom you can trust, but sometimes you must risk a chance, because all relationships – family ties, friendships, business transactions and social support – have trust as a prerequisite. Without it society would crumble.

But because human nature is so unreliable, it is probable that he will cause all these relationships to be marred by distrust. People don't always intend to be unreliable; it is inevitably part of their imperfect nature.

With God it is entirely different. In this changing and imperfect world, God alone is eternal, perfect and unchanging. The promises of his Word can be trusted and relied upon. He has kept his promises through all the ages. Even though his will often differs from our desires. He proves his faithfulness repeatedly and He is busy completing his plan with our lives.

What God expects of you is an unshakeable faith and trust. When the clouds of doubt and disappointment cast a shadow over your life and it feels as if everybody has forsaken you, you must desperately cling to the knowledge that God always remains faithful. Your heavenly Father will never fail or disappoint you.

Unchanging God of love, I do not always understand, but I trust in your faithfulness unconditionally.

November 9   Acts 8:4-13

THE SECRET OF TRIUMPH
The believers who were scattered went everywhere, preaching the message (Acts 8:4)
Bloody persecution broke loose against the early church. The apostles courageously stood firm in the heart of the storm and persevered, but the new Christians were scattered over the whole known world of those days.

It would have been easy for them to fall into self-pity and in rebellion they could demand to know how God could allow such a situation to develop. But they didn't – they changed their obstacles into opportunities. Within the limitations placed upon them, they sought for positive action. They used the opportunity to witness that the Messiah had come, that He had died for mankind and that He was raised from death. The message they had to bring, was so much greater than their temporary tribulation. They subjected themselves willingly to the desires of Christ – even though it meant bitter persecution and a martyr's death.

The ability to transform defeat into victory, can only be attained if our faith is greater than the disaster which we experience. If you are convinced of this great and glorious fact, nothing can conquer you. Life will still have its steep inclines and dark valleys, but you are assured of your eventual triumph through Jesus Christ.

When Christ has complete control of your life, you see further than your disappointments and failures of the present moment. You have a balanced outlook on life. Then you know without a doubt that Jesus Christ will lead you to victory, even through failure.

I thank You, merciful and almighty God, that I experience the daily miracle of defeat being transformed into victory. Keep me courageous in my struggle by the power of Jesus, my Redeemer.

November 10   Isaiah 35:1-10

DRAW INSPIRATION FROM YOUR SPIRITUAL RESERVES
Tell everyone who is discouraged, "Be strong and don't be afraid! God is coming to your rescue . . ." (Is 35:4)

We are easily discouraged. It can happen in the wink of an eye, and we are left in dismay and despair. In such moments we question the wisdom of persevering and wonder whether all our efforts are worthwhile.

When your ideals are shattered and all your efforts seem in vain, you dare not allow self-pity or bitterness to drive you to despair.

God has given you spiritual reserves from which to draw. From them you can gain new hope and purpose in life. Perhaps, in the past, you have had sources of inspiration and encouragement, which suddenly are not available any more. Without a permanent source of encouragement, it feels as if life has lost its purpose.

But God is always present. He is an inexhaustable source of inspiration and courage. Draw freely and abundantly from this rich reservoir of power and grace. Then your idealism will be rekindled and you will be able to face the challenges of life. You will find a new joy and happiness in living.

God wants to help you to do great and glorious deeds to his honour. He wants to conquer the influences which depress you and paralyse you. He wants to make the wonder of his mercy a reality in your everyday life.

You are not fighting a lonely battle. God is on your side. One faithful person with God, is a majority. He will keep his everlasting arms under you and sustain you.

Thank you, merciful Lord, for the endless reservoir of spiritual reserves You make available and from which I can draw in my battle against discouragement and despair.

November 11   Philippians 3:1-16

FREE OF SPECTRES FROM THE PAST
... the one thing I do, however, is to forget what is behind me and do my best to reach what is ahead (Phil 3:13)

Memories can be a cause for inspiration or for despair; can allow you to submit or drive you to rebellion; can make you joyous or sad. It also influences the present and the future.

Unpleasant memories have a way of clinging to one's mind obstinately as the years pass by, and even becoming more painful.

What you often do not realize is that, by continuously reliving each painful particular of these memories, or relating them in detail with each available opportunity, you nurse your bitterness and allow it full dominion over your life. This vicious circle can only be broken by the work of grace by the Holy Spirit. He makes you willing to forgive seventy times seven.

To hate those who have wronged you, is just human and part of your sinful nature. It is, however, not the will of God for your life and forms a dangerous obstacle in your spiritual progress. If you refuse to forgive, it is impossible to experience true spiritual release from the bondage of hatred. As a result your physical and spiritual health suffers a setback.

When you experience God's forgiveness, only then can you freely forgive. Then you have a divine duty to forgive – and you are freed of haunting memories. On this road the Holy Spirit is your guide.

Holy God, and in Jesus Christ, my heavenly Father, I thank You that I can cope with the past, because your Holy Spirit has done his redeeming and healing work in my life.

November 12   John 11:1-27

WITH GOD IT IS NEVER TOO LATE
If You had been here, Lord, my brother would not have died! (Jn 11:21)

When Jesus heard that Lazarus was ill, He waited two days before going there – even though He loved Lazarus, Mary and Martha dearly.

Perhaps you have also sincerely wanted God to do a certain thing for you immediately – before it was too late. And then nothing happened! Like Mary and Martha, with the death of their brother Lazarus, you also had to learn this lesson: God has his own timetable and you can't force Him to act at times prescribed by human desires.

When Jesus was informed of the very serious illness of Lazarus, He made no effort to go to the help of his friends immediately. But when He eventually arrived, He could revert the tragedy of the death of Lazarus into an opportunity to glorify God, his Father.

Perhaps there were times in your life when you also felt that God had left matters too late. But God is never late! His timing is always perfect. We have a temporary and earthly perspective, but He sees things from an eternal perspective. We know only the present moment, but God sees what the future holds and He knows what is best for you.

If you love and trust Him, He will cause all things to work together for your highest good, according to his perfect timing. Don't put demands to God. Allow Him to unfold his will in his own good time. Then you live according to God's timetable and you experience peace of mind.

God who hears our prayers, forgive me my sins of impatience. I place my life in your hands and submit to your divine time. Help me in this through the power of your Son, Jesus Christ.

November 13   Job 21:1-16

QUESTIONING THE POWER OF PRAYER
They think that there is no need to serve God nor any advantage in praying to Him (Job 21:15)
There are many people who wonder whether it is worthwhile or serves any useful purpose to pray. They know that painful feeling of disillusionment after sincerely praying for something and not receiving it.

However, this disenchantment of many people can be traced back to their own ignorance regarding prayer. Prayer is not a vending machine from which you extract what you desire simply by the insertion of a coin.

True prayer is primarily seeking the kingdom of God and his glory. You can only discover this kingdom after you have met the King and have consecrated yourself to Him. Christ must be the focal point of your entire prayer life, because it is only through Him that you can enter into the presence of God.

If you feel that your prayer life is inadequate and causes you to harbour a sense of disappointment, you are required to do a bit of honest introspection. Do you sincerely desire the will of God in your prayers and in your life? Do you elevate Him above all other things you treasure in your life? Are you aware of God's holy presence when you pray? Or do you use God as a pawn in your own game of chess?

Being honest and sincere with yourself in answering these questions, may be the point of departure to a new, dynamic and meaningful prayer life. Then your prayers are no longer question marks, but exclamation marks!

I glorify your Name, Almighty God, who through the power of your Holy Spirit has taught me to know that effective prayer depends on my relationship with You, my living Saviour.

November 14   Luke 8:40-48

A LORD WHO CARES

Jesus asked, "Who touched Me?" Jesus said to her, "My daughter, your faith has made you well. Go in peace" (Lk 8:45, 48)

When Jesus was here on earth, people came from near and far to listen to his message. Sick people were conveyed over many kilometres, so that He could heal them. But, in spite of the overwhelming demands of his ministry, he was never so busy that He couldn't find time for the personal needs of people.

On his way to the home of Jairus, where his little daughter lay dying, the crowd thronged around Him. In that crowd was a woman with a desperate need. When she touched the hem of his garment, in the faith that she would thereby be healed, Jesus first ministered to her need, before He proceeded on his way.

Jesus always cares about people in distress. That is why we can confidently approach Him. His love, understanding and healing power is available to everybody: to Jairus and his little daughter; to the counsillor of the synagogue, and to a nameless woman in her desperate need.

In a simple act of faith this woman stretched out her hands to Jesus and He cared enough to heal her body and spirit so that she could start a new life in his peace.

Christ is aware of our need, but He wants us to confess them to Him in faith and trust. He will ease our burdens and we need never feel helpless or destitute – Jesus cares!

Saviour Christ, thank you that I have heard You say to me: "Your faith has made you well. Go in peace!" Glory and honour to your holy Name!

November 15 Philippians 1:3-11

BE CAREFUL OF IMBALANCE
I pray that your love will keep on growing more and more, together with true knowledge and perfect judgement, so that you will be able to choose what is best (Phil 1:9-10)

There are people who are extremely health-conscious and they will go to great pains to develop their bodies to their full potential. Others again will do anything possible to develop their mental powers. Eventually they form the intellectual nucleus of society and make a great contribution.

Man was created body, mind and soul by God. If one of these areas is developed to the exclusion of the other two, there is an imbalance. Each aspect must receive its share of serious attention.

In modern society more than enough is done to develop the body and the mind, while the spirit is often neglected. Perhaps this is why the world has become the dismal place it is. When man denies his origin, he becomes a tragic phenomenon.

To live a fulfilled and compensating life, you must care for your body, develop your mind and acknowledge God as the Source of spiritual growth through the Holy Spirit. If your spirit is in harmony and balance with your Creator, through the ministry of Jesus Christ, you will live a balanced and satisfying life. By the work of the Spirit we develop to our full potential in all the departments of our life – body, mind and soul.

Jesus my Lord, I worship You as the Master who made it possible for the

Holy Spirit to live and work in me and lead me to a balanced and satisfying life.

November 16   Romans 12:1-21

MY LIFE AS A SACRIFICE
Offer yourselves as a living sacrifice to God, dedicated to his service and pleasing to Him. This is the true worship that you should offer (Rom 12:1) Your body is a breathtaking and awe-inspiring mechanism created by the artistic hand of God, to house your spirit so that it can function in a visible and practical fashion. Therefore it deserves all the respect and attention you can devote to it.

Scripture teaches us that our bodies are temples of God and that the Spirit of God dwells within us (1 Cor 6:19). Therefore you must take great care of your body by healthy exercise and enough rest. Your periods of exercise can become a spiritual blessing, and your times of rest can be opportunities for recuperation of powers to be able to serve God better.

If your body is consecrated to God and used to his honour, you won't want to harm it by over-indulgence in any form. An unhealthy diet and incorrect eating habits can weaken your body and make you mentally sluggish and spiritually inactive. Nicotine is poison to the body and alcohol destroys personalities, homes and human happiness. When you sacrifice yourself to Christ, you should avoid all harmful habits which may be to the detriment of your consecration to Him.

You cannot pass your responsibility towards your body to someone else. It is not a matter of self-exaltation of self-glorification, but it is a sacrifice to the service of God.

Dear God, I renew my consecration to You and place my body on your altar. Use it in your service and to the glory of your Name.

November 17   Exodus 3:1-12

TRYING TO SIDE-STEP YOUR RESPONSIBILITIES
But Moses said to God, "I am nobody. How can I go to the king and bring the Israelites out of Egypt?" (Ex 3:11)

Most people try to avoid their responsibilities. When we meet a challenge, we are immediately convinced of our inability to succeed – even before we have seriously contemplated the matter.

It is also true, however, that one cannot always do everything. Some commands demand specialised training and are beyond the capabilities of the average person. Yet, many of the things we convince ourselves we cannot do, are not beyond our powers. We underestimate ourselves because we feel inferior and become afraid to get involved or to accept our responsibilities.

If you allow a challenge to pass without even trying, you deprive yourself of an opportunity to widen your abilities – physically, mentally and spiritually – or to develop your potential. You never know what you are capable of doing until you have honestly made an effort to do something which you thought was beyond your power.

You must stop thinking only of your limitations. Cast yourself upon the strength of God. Like Paul, you may discover: "I have the strength to face all conditions by the power that Christ gives me" (Phil 4:13). Stop disparaging yourself. Convince yourself that you can accept all the challenges and responsibilities by the help of the almighty God. He is your constant campanion.

God of Power, grant me your grace which makes all things possible. Keep me from trying to shirk my challenges and responsibilities and help me to trust in your wisdom and power in faithfully doing my duty.

November 18 2 Corinthians 4:16-5:10

COMPENSATION
Even though our physical being is gradually decaying, yet our spiritual being is renewed day after day (2 Cor 4:16)

It is sad to think that your youth has passed forever. With this realization there often comes an unlimited loneliness: people you have known along the road have fallen away; the environment in which you find yourself is not the one in which you grew up or completed your life's task; your strength has decreased; and perhaps the most difficult of all – you are so dependent on others. The powers you once had in faculty and mind are reduced: your eyes don't search the horizons; your hands holding the cup are shaking; your ears refuse to catch up all the sounds;

the road seems steep and difficult; the heart does its work with great effort.

Yet, God compensates us for all this. When the Lord takes away physical power, He grants increased spiritual power. External strength is replaced by a new, exciting form of internal strength. Then we start to understand the word of God to Zechariah: "You will succeed, not by military might or by your own strength, but by my Spirit" (Zech 4:6).

We must not obstinately contemplate only the losses of old age. We must learn to see and appreciate the good things God grants us in these years of our lives. Let us praise God who compensates his children for every earthly loss.

Heavenly Father, I kneel in worship and gratitude for all You give to me as the years increase. Teach me to trust, Lord, so that in my old age this will not be a new lesson.

November 19 Colossians 2:1-5

JOY IN ACHIEVEMENT
For even though I am absent in body, yet I am with you in spirit, and I am glad as I see the resolute firmness with which you stand together in your faith in Christ (Col 2:5)

When you have painstakingly completed a worthwhile task, it gives you great satisfaction. Especially if you have laboured over a long period of time and have often been discouraged by failure. But if you persevere and eventually reach success and realise your ideals, your mind and spirit will be elevated by a sense of accomplishment and joy.

The only thing that can motivate you to persevere until the end, is whether your ideals or goals are worthwhile. If they are of no importance or intrinsic value, it really doesn't matter whether you succeed or not. That is why we must learn to make great demands upon ourselves, so that we really have a challenge and the reaching of our goals will bring satisfaction. Don't underestimate yourself. Higher demands often offer the opportunity of discovering new possibilities within yourself and developing them to the greatest extent.

The highest ideal of each Christian should be to grow in faith until the stature of Christ is reached. This calls for devotion, love and faithfulness to Jesus Christ. Such a purpose may seem impossible and impractical. But the Lord Himself gives you strength and grace.

The presence of the Holy Spirit in your life makes the impossible possible! Through his mercy we attain to the joy of achievement in all our striving and labour.

Not in my own strength, o Lord, but only through your love and power, I gain the knowledge of growth in Jesus Christ and the indwelling inspiration of the Holy Spirit.

November 20 Psalm 33:1-22

DAWN AFTER DARKNESS
The Lord loves what is righteous and just; his constant love fills the earth (Ps 33:5)
There are times when we can't see the silver lining around the dark, threatening clouds. But if you start counting your blessings, you discover that God gives you many more days of sunshine and joy, than days of darkness and shadow.

To be able to appreciate the good moments of life, it is necessary to always see the love and justice of God in all things. You can't expect the good gifts of life if you are ignorant of God Himself.

To know the bounteous kind-heartedness of God, does not mean that you will be spared problems and sorrows. These things are also part of your life. But you won't allow the darkness to obscure the love and light which the living Christ brings to your life.

The darker and more ominous the moment, the greater your need to be united with Him who is the Light of the world. If you spend time in his presence, you are injected with new strength and courage to conquer the darkness.

You can turn to Him confidently in your distress and despair. Open your life to Him and you will discover that He has always been there – your constant companion even in the shadow of darkness. In times of trials and tribulations, you discover that, when all other hope has fled, He is with you always. In this way even the darkness becomes a blessing through his love and mercy.

Holy Lord and Father, I sincerely thank You that You bear with me so patiently and lovingly while I am a scholar in your school of faith. I praise your holy Name for the assurance of your love in my darkness.

November 21 Isaiah 49:14-26

DON'T LIMIT YOURSELF
Then you will know that I am the Lord; no one who waits for my help will be disappointed (Is 49:23)
There are many people who know deep in their hearts that they have many talents which have not yet been fully developed. Their excuse is that circumstances were against them: lack of opportunities; a reserved spirit; humility bordering on an inferiority complex; fear of failure. They are unwilling to tax themselves and can enumerate many reasons why their ideals have not been realised.

A weak self-image is extremely limiting. To attain to anything worthwhile, you must have faith in God and in yourself – in that order. If you feel at this moment that you are not utilizing your talents to their full capacity, you must not doubt your own ability. Formulate your plans and identify definite aims for yourself. Don't be led by emotion only, but be practical and constructive.

If you know what you want to reach, you must plan your route to reach your destination. He who fails to plan, plans to fail. Be enthusiastic and excited. To give yourself to a project which is worthwhile, is the secret of joy and fulfillment in life.

You will often have to remotivate yourself. Make sure you are within the will of God, because to obey his will is to taste the joy of fulfillment in life. Then you will be able to unshackle yourself from the limitations that are binding you. Remember, the Lord promises: "No one who waits for my help will be disappointed."

Master and Saviour, by your Holy Spirit I have complete freedom to reach my full potential. I thank You for your ever-present help. Grant me noble ideals and the courage to fulfil them.

November 22 Psalm 24:1-10

THIS IS STILL GOD'S WORLD!
The world and all that is in it belong to the Lord; the earth and all who live on it are His (Ps 24:1)
A living faith is absolutely essential in the world in which we live. In these unsure times, when we all wonder what the future holds, it is

important to have a faith which will hold unshakeably when everything around you falls to ruin.

Even though evil flourishes, and even though the forces of destruction cause justice and right to seem ridiculous and without influence, God is still in control. Don't let appearances deceive you. This world still belongs to God without a doubt.

Man wants to be sure that God cares and that He is still in control. This yearning and desire has caused many people to be side-tracked. Without faith in the wise and loving God, who has the times and destinies of nations and individuals in his hand, we are lost.

Jesus Christ didn't come to this world to proclaim a new philosophy, but to bring abundant life to humanity. To all who accept Him, He gives the power to believe, so that they can live victoriously and purposefully – even in the most confusing situations of life.

With faith in your heart you can approach the future with courage and know that He will be your guide and anchor in these uncertain times. Then the future of this world holds no terror for his children.

Almighty God and heavenly Father, thank you that I can know by faith that, even amidst the confusion of this world, You are in control, and that I can have your peace in my heart and mind. In the Name of Jesus my Lord I pray.

November 23 Matthew 7:1-6

BE CAREFUL TO CRITICISE
Do not judge others, so that God will not judge you, for God will judge you in the same way as you judge others . . . (Mt 7:1-2)

Embittered people are inclined to pass harsh judgement on others. They don't see any good in their fellow-men and they have absolutely no appreciation for the accomplishments of others. However noble the deed may be, they will denigrate it with bitter criticism. If somebody reaches success in the business world, they allude to fraud. There is no room for appreciation for the success of others. These are very lonely people.

Destructive criticism in a non-Christian is bad enough – it can possibly be understood. But a Christian who acts in this way is an obstacle to the kingdom of God. He partakes in character murder. He doesn't use the God-given opportunities granted him unstintingly to encourage and inspire others. He is rather serving the Devil than the Lord.

As a disciple of Jesus Christ, you are called to a positive and constructive way of life. If you are in a company where derogatory remarks are made about someone not present, it is your duty to defend him.

There are, however, times when constructive criticism is necessary. But then you must talk to the person involved privately and with love and understanding. If you desire criticism to serve a purpose, you must pray about it and make sure that it is to the benefit of the person involved.

To this end we need the guidance and the help of the Holy Spirit.

Father, protect me from pride. Help me to act in love and understanding and if I must criticise, to do it constructively.

November 24 Hebrews 2:5-18

ARE YOUR AFRAID OF DEATH?
He did this so that through his death He might destroy the Devil, who has the power over death, and in this way set free those who were slaves all their lives because of their fear of death (Heb 2:14-15)

Death is inevitable to every human being. Even the children of God go through life burdened with this dismal fear of death.

As Christians we must unmask this enemy and wrestle with it until we are victorious and can honestly confess that we have eternal life in Jesus – even though we die. We need not live in fear of death. According to medical witness, the dying moments are painless. To the incurably sick, death is a kind release from suffering.

Possibly it is the fear of the unknown that overwhelms most people. Yet, with our birth we came into a world of which we knew nothing; after death we are going to a place of which we know a great deal, because Christ Himself has told us about it. So much in joy and happiness and glory as the eye has not seen and the ear has not heard, God has prepared for those who love Him.

Charles Kingsley said: "It is not darkness to which I am going, for God is Light; it is not loneliness, because Christ is with me; it is not an unknown country, because my resurrected Lord is there!"

All we really have to fear is spiritual death, when we are separated from God. Our Saviour, Jesus Christ, saves us also from the fear of death. The Holy Spirit comforts us and cultivates that love in our hearts which drives out all fear.

Ever-present Lord, I thank You for your eternal love, which enfolds me also in my moments of fear. Grant me the love that drives out all fear from my life.

November 25 Matthew 28:16-20

A COMPANION FOR EACH DAY
And I will be with you always, to the end of the age (Mt 28:20)

We are not made to live alone. And to bear responsibility on your own, is an experience nobody enjoys. The managing director of a company, who has to make important decisions on his own; the single parent who has to struggle with overwhelming odds to raise a family; the captain of a ship, who knows the loneliness of command – all these people experience a painful desire for somebody with whom they can share the burden of responsibility.

When you feel lonely, you must be very sure that you are not the cause of your loneliness. Perhaps somebody has offered help and you have refused it in pride or self-sufficiency. Pride may also have prevented you from accepting good advice. Somebody may have offered you friendship, but you turned it down because you questioned his motives.

Perhaps you are a loner by nature, and yet you feel deeply hurt because you have no friends. If you are unhappy because of your loneliness and you can't carry on that way, you must do something constructive about it. Be friendly and see how people react. Give yourself in love and service to others, and you will be too busy to be lonely.

When one is empty of your self-sufficiency and filled with the love of Christ, life takes on a new meaning. God, in Jesus Christ, is your constant companion. Experience his comfort and guidance as you live within his will and share in his love.

Immanuel, God with us, your daily presence is the joy of my life and my comfort in days of loneliness and desolation.

November 26 Ephesians 5:1-20

THE VIRTUE OF GRATITUDE
In the Name of our Lord Jesus Christ, always give thanks for everything to God the Father (Eph 5:20)

Paul calls upon us all to live as people of the Light. His inspired speech reaches a joyous climax in which he urges us to give thanks to the Lord "for everything". To a Christian it is important to learn how to express gratitude, because it gives a special quality to life.

Each child of God has enough reason for gratitude. The secret of being thankful is to live a life of gratitude. It is to practise the philosophy of Albert Schweitzer of Lambarene: "In gratitude for the blessings you receive, you must make some sacrifice in your life for others."

Because you have received the gift of life, you must use it positively and victoriously, through the power of the living Christ.

Because you are happy, you must endeavour to make others happy.

Because you see so much beauty in God's creation, you must strive to enrich and beautify the world around you.

Because you are strong and healthy, you must care for your body as a temple of God and use it in service of others.

Always add a life of thanksgiving to your prayers, in gratitude for God's love.

The miracle of God's mercy is that then your cup will run over!

Dear Father, make my whole life a hymn of gratitude for all your abundant love and mercy. Help me, through your Spirit, to live a life of gratitude.

November 27   1 Corinthians 15:50-58

VICTORIOUS LIVING
But thanks be to God who gives us the victory through our Lord Jesus Christ! (1 Cor 15:57)
God's children are destined for a life of victory, and not of defeat and failure. Life is not for bitterness or frustration, but for truimphant fulfilment. A person who is always complaining bitterly, has lost his vision and has lost view of God's plan with his life. When this happens he will not be able to experience a life of victory.

You can't reach your aim in life without meticulous planning. Without something to strive after, you will attain nothing. The brook would lose its song if it weren't for the stones over which the water has to flow.

Plant the seed of victory in your heart. However small or delicate it may be, it will germinate and grow through the work of the Holy Spirit, prayer and Scripture-reading. If the weeds of doubt threaten to smother it, you must remember that God is the gardener who sincerely wants to see the seed grow to fruition. Think, pray and act victoriously. The man who moves mountains, starts by carrying stones.

When defeat or failure threatens to overwhelm you, you must cling to Him who offers you a life of victory. When the tide of opposition has receded, you stand strong and conquering in the strength of Jesus Christ.

Redeemer and Saviour, there are some defeats which inevitably lead to victory, because they bring me closer to You, the Source of victorious living.

November 28 John 15:1-17

THE INDWELLING CHRIST
Remain united to Me, and I will remain united to you. A branch cannot bear fruit by itself; it can do so only if it remains in the vine. In the same way you cannot bear fruit unless you remain in Me (Jn 15:4)

We dare never consider our Christianity as a matter of course. Many people believe that they are born Christians and that it is part of their heritage, without them ever having a definite and meaningful experience with the living Christ.

An active faith is much more than a noble tradition. It is an awareness of the amazing fact that Jesus Christ occupies the lives of those who accept Him as Saviour and Redeemer and acknowledge his dominion over their lives. They allow the Holy Spirit to work in and through them.

To be aware of the presence of the Holy Spirit, demands an act of faith. You take your Saviour at his word and believe that He dwells within you.

When you are tempted or afflicted, ask yourself: "How would Jesus Christ handle it?" Change this question into a prayer and ask for his guidance. God will answer according to your needs.

Christ can talk to you by inspiring you spiritually, or by changing your circumstances. However He answers, you will know that He is with you and in you. By his power you grow to the stature of Jesus Christ and you have the assurance of his indwelling presence.

Lord Jesus, You are the true vine and I desire to be united with You like a branch. Help me never to drift away from your love and care.

November 29 Matthew 26:36-46

ARE YOU SOMETIMES TOO TIRED TO PRAY?
How is it that you three were not able to keep watch with Me even for one hour? Keep watch and pray that you will not fall into temptation. The spirit is willing, but the flesh is weak (Mt 26:40-41)

Often one starts your quiet time with God with the best intentions, but you are physically exhausted and you find it difficult to concentrate. Then your prayer life is a failure and ineffective.

Hard work and long hours are not the only reasons for this fatigue and exhaustion. Heartache, depression, frustration, relationships which have gone wrong, grief, and many other things can disrupt your prayer life.

Jesus also became tired and weary. Yet He persevered in prayer and He was refreshed and strengthened by it. He was overwhelmed by grief and anguish, but He only prayed with greater concentration. If we are tired or upset, we become sleepy and lose concentration. Christ teaches us that prayer is as important as the air we breathe.

Many people see prayer as something supplementary, while it is an indispensable component of pulsating and creative life. To quickly mutter a prayer without your heart and mind in it, is a joyless duty. But if your life is committed to Christ and his Spirit dwells in you, your prayer time becomes a joyful time of renewal.

If you are tired and weary, talk to God aloud. Read the Bible. Find time early during the day, while you are still fresh and before the demands of life have tired you, to spend in prayer with God. Let prayer be the key to each day and the bolt to each night.

Dear Lord and Master, thank you for your example in prayer. I often lay awake about the cares of this world, yet I am sleepy when I must pray. Help me conquer this weakness through the guidance of your Spirit.

November 30 Psalm 90:1-17

PERSPECTIVE ON OLD AGE
Teach us how short our life is, so that we may become wise (Ps 90:12)

Old age is relative: Some people are old long before their time, while others stay young, even in old age. It all depends upon "how" you live, and not upon "how long" you live!

We must guard against growing too old to welcome new experiences. Live every day to its full capacity. Don't let age prevent you from adapting to a new, meaningful style of life. Change and renewal are the essence of life. Every time spring comes around we are reminded of this.

We fear the unknown and as a result we often miss some of life's most exciting experiences. We desperately cling to our possessions – and yet we can't take anything with us on our pilgrimage to eternity.

We refuse to go to a home for senior citizens where we can be professionally cared for and where we can make new friends of our own age. We forget that God is with us at all times and all places.

Don't let age obscure the beauty of God's creation around you. God intended our whole life – also our twilight years – to be beautiful: spring with its sparkling life; summer with its strength, growth and ripening; autumn with its myriad of colours and the glory of the harvest; and also winter with its own enchantment.

It is wonderful to grow old if you remain young while ageing. Each new day is a new beginning and we must ask God for wisdom to use each day to his honour.

Teach me, heavenly Father, to appreciate life as a divine gift, and to measure my life in deeds, attitudes and love – and not in years.

DECEMBER

PRAYER

Jesus of Bethlehem, Lord and Master:
during this month we worship You as the promised One,
who came from the glory of heaven to this sinful world, as a baby in the crook of a mother's arm, inviting us back to God from a bed of straw in a humble manger!
We yearn for a true celebration of Christmas, which will meet with your divine approval.
Renew our hearts and our attitudes as we celebrate your birthday, Lord.
Purify us from all bitterness and hatred and cleanse us from sin.
Let each gift be given in sincere love and let each Christmas card be a confession of our faith in You, our Saviour and Redeemer.
Give new meaning to all the well-known and well-loved carols as we sing them again and again.
Give that Christmas-tide will bring reconciliation between man and God, so that all men shall name You "Father!"
Give reconciliation between man and man, so that the "Peace" of which the angels sang, will not be an idle dream or an impossible ideal,
but a glorious reality of our faith in You – the Prince of Peace!
Grant that the spirit of Christmas will fill our hearts: not only for a few short weeks, but that it will stay with us when we take up our duties and responsibilities for the new year; and let it abide with us – even in the cold of June!
We ask this in the powerful Name of Him who came to free us from our sin and who is to us:
Immanuel – God with us!
Amen.

December 1   1 John 4:7-21

THE GOSPEL IN A NUTSHELL

God is love, and whoever lives in love lives in union with God and God lives in union with him (1 Jn 4:16)

Jesus Christ had the superb ability to proclaim the gospel so simply that even the humblest could understand it, without the message losing its deepest meaning. The theme of each message was the eternal and unchanging truth: God is love!

To share in this love, we must open our hearts to Him: "Whoever loves Me will obey my teaching. My Father will love him, and my Father and I will come to him and live with him (Jn 14:23).

Love for God assumes obedience to his will and the opening of your heart and mind to the influence of his Holy Spirit. He must reign as sovereign over every area of your life and control your thinking and your deeds.

To piously declare "God is love" is more than a sentimental or emotional confession of faith. It demands a way of life which will confirm your unspoken faith in the unfathomable love of God and it is your duty to reflect that love in the world around you.

This is what Paul said in his letter to the Ephesians when he prayed that Christ would live in their hearts by faith and that "you may have your roots and foundation in love, so that you, together with all God's people, may have the power to understand how broad and long, how high and deep, is Christ's love" (Eph 3:17-18). He prays that we shall know this love and be filled with the abundance of God's love so that we shall understand and appreciate the gospel of his love.

God of love, my heart breaks out in praise when I consider all the dimensions of your love. I thank You for your love. Help me to reflect it to hearts who hunger for it.

December 2   Genesis 1:26-2:4

BREAK THE MURDEROUS RHYTHM

By the seventh day God finished what He had been doing and stopped working. He blessed the seventh day and set it apart as a special day . . . (Gen 2:2-3)

Until quite recently Sunday was a day of absolute rest and all activity was reduced to a minimum. Unfortunately, there is today very little difference between the day of the Lord and any ordinary day of the week.

After completing his creation, God rested on the seventh day. Many people are under the impression that this act of God had only a religious meaning and that it is enough simply to go to church on Sunday. As a result the day of rest is seen as a compulsory enforcement of religious principles of which the world desires to be freed. Therefore they propagate more activity and entertainment on Sunday.

At this time in which we live, more than ever before, the demands of life become increasingly great. More and more is expected of us and the pressures brought to bear upon us, reach gigantic proportions. Therefore it becomes imperative that we will come to a standstill and break the murderous routine in which we are trapped.

Our intellectual, physical and spiritual powers must be replenished. God is our Source of power and only by meaningful communion with Him, can we meet the challenges of life.

Observing a day of rest, is not a limitation or violation of your freedom. On the contrary: it is a God-given opportunity to obtain strength from Almighty God for the task ahead. Let us be grateful to God for this.

Lord and Master, teach me to reap the full benefit from the day of the Lord and send me back to life and its challenges with strength and renewed inspiration.

December 3 Romans 8:18-30

PURPOSEFUL INTERCESSION
In the same way the Spirit also comes to help us, weak as we are. For we do not know how we ought to pray; the Spirit Himself pleads with God for us in groans that words cannot express (Rom 8:26)
When your relationship with God is imperfect and insincere, your prayer life cannot function purposefully. It is of the greatest importance that you will be unimpeachably honest and that you allow yourself to be guided by the Holy Spirit.

It is no problem praying for people who are close to you. You pray for their temptations and tribulations, their hopes and expectations – yes, you speak to God regarding each facet of their lives. Here the guidance of the Holy Spirit is necessary, because even though you love them passionately, you don't know what is best for them. When the Holy Spirit teaches you to pray that God's will shall be done, those for whom you pray can receive the richest blessings God has in store for his children.

Always pray in a spirit of expectation. If you petition without expecting great things from God, you receive according to your requests. Pray and believe that God will answer your prayers in his good time. Charles Trumbell said: "Prayer is the releasing of the energy of God, because prayer means asking God to do that which is impossible for us." Then God's will is dramatically revealed in your own life and in the lives of those for whom you pray. It is exciting and strengthens your faith to live in this expectation.

Identify with those for whom you are praying. Keep the lines open between yourself and God and make sure you are aware of the needs for those whom you will be interceding for. Be convinced that God's divine will shall prevail, because God is almighty and He listens to purposive intercession.

Dear Lord who listens, You have called me to the ministry of intercession. Make me faithful, sincere and obedient in this glorious privilege.

December 4 Romans 8:1-17

CHILDREN OF THE KING

... instead, the Spirit makes you God's children, and by the Spirit's power we cry to God, "Father! my Father!" (Rom 8:15)

There is a world of difference between professing that you are a child of God and actually experiencing this miraculous relationship. Many people profess faith, and then live in constant fear. They suffer a destructive inferiority complex and they are not capable of coping with the problems of life. The contrast between what they know they should be and what they really are, is so great that they are inclined to despair and lay down their principles.

When God called you to be his child and you reacted joyfully, you started an entirely new life. Your sins are forgiven and you live in a new relationship to the King. Because his Spirit lives and works in your life, a total change is made in your behaviour towards people.

As a child of the King you must live in confidence and approach life without fear. Your Father is the mightiest King. The knowledge that He loves you and cares for you, should give you peace of mind. The assurance that He will safely lead you if you are obedient to Him and return his love, should be a great comfort to you. He lovingly invites you to call Him "Father"!

God's divine love flows through your life like the blood of royalty flows in the veins of the children of earthly kings. This relationship grows in depth and becomes a greater reality as you grow spiritually and God becomes an indispensable part of your everyday existence.

Thank you for the inexpressable grace that I may call You Father, through the merit of Jesus Christ, my Saviour. Make me a worthy child of the King, through the work of the Holy Spirit.

December 5 — Matthew 6:19-34

GOD OR GOLD

No one can be a slave of two masters; he will hate one and love the other; he will be loyal to one and despise the other. You cannot serve both God and money (Mt 6:24)

Gold is part of the magnificent creation of God. It fascinated men over all the ages. Poets and writers have raised songs of praise about it since time immemorial. It is also one of the most important foundations upon which trade is built.

When Solomon built a temple for the Lord, he used a great amount of gold to symbolise the glory of God. The Wise Men from the East brought gold as one of their gifts to the Child of Bethlehem.

But gold also carries with it its own dangers and perversions. Materialism is often an obstacle on our way to faith in God. It causes us to lose our perspective when we are faced with choices of great importance. This happened to the Israelites when they demanded of Aaron to make a god which could lead them. Hence the worship of the golden calf – gold elevated to an idol!

For Israel the result was disastrous. This is a danger which faces each individual person: your gold is either a sacrifice in the service of the Child of Bethlehem, or an idol which takes the place of God in your life.

When God takes the primary place, gold and all other earthly possessions will take their rightful, but secondary place. Paul prays for the Philippians "true knowledge and perfect judgement, so that you will be able to choose what is best" (Phil 1:9). And Christ said in his sermon on the mountain: "Instead, be concerned above everything else with the Kingdom of God and with what He requires of you, and He will provide you with all these other things" (Mt 6:33).

Heavenly Father, keep me from subjection or enslavement to material possessions. Let all my possessions be a sacrifice to your service, through Jesus Christ my Lord.

December 6 Matthew 5:13-20

WAITING FOR THE SUNSHINE

In the same way your light must shine before people, so that they will see the good things you do and praise your Father in heaven (Mt 5:16)

Christmas is a time of joy to the world, but there are thousands of people who suffer sorrow, yearning and loneliness during this time. The Lord expects of his children to share the joy they experience. We are called to heal the pain and bring sunshine to destitute lives.

Somewhere the story is related of a bed-ridden little boy in the slum area of London. He spent one dreary day after the other limited to the four walls of a small room with a single window through which the sun never shone. Both parents were away at work during the daytime, and his only companion was the sunless silence. With his little broken body shackled to his bed, one joyless day followed the other.

However, an ingenious young friend noticed that on each cloudless day, the sun shone for two hours on the wall opposite the sick child's room. Somewhere he found a piece of cracked mirror and every day the sun shone on that wall, he stood in the sunshine with loving patience and reflected the sunshine onto the bed of his friend.

In these days of joyful expectations our hearts go out to the unhappy people who live in the shadows. The Holy Spirit makes us aware of their need: the underprivileged; the aged; the sick; the addicts; the beggars; the sorrowing and the homeless. We must bear mirrors in the sunshine – even if they are cracked. The reflection of the Sun of Righteousness will bring untold joy to others.

Lord Jesus, You shine upon this earth as the Sun of Righteousness. Help me to reflect your sunshine into the lives of unhappy people living in the shadows.

December 7 — Luke 1:26-38

A CHILD ALLAYS OUR FEARS

The angel said to her, "Don't be afraid, Mary; God has been gracious to you" (Lk 1:30)

God wants to replace our fear with jubilant joy. This is indeed what the angel proclaimed on that first Christmas: "Don't be afraid! I am here with good news for you . . ." (Lk 2:10).

This world is saturated with fear! It has indeed become a labyrinth of anxiety. And it all started when Adam said to God after his fall into sin: "I was afraid and hid from You . . ." (Gen 3:10). On the day of judgement there will be a last desperate prayer meeting, when fearful humanity will try to hide from the wrath of God and pray for the mountains to fall upon them and the hills to cover them.

Fear is not a figment of man's imagination. From his cradle to his grave it is a real and terrifying presence.

We fear the unknown as little children fear the dark. We fear for the collapse of our health; loneliness; old age and the end of the road – death!

Everybody everywhere has this gnawing fear of a thousand different things.

But now, at Christmas, God once more sends his messenger with the glad tiding of great joy: The love of God drives out all fear, because sin has been conquered – and sin is the cause of all our fear.

In the storms of life He says to you as He once said to his anxious disciples: "Why are you frightened? Have you still no faith?" (Mk 4:40).

He is always Immanuel, God with us! Why then would we fear?

Immanuel, I thank You that I can say in the most desperate circumstances: Even if I go through the deepest darkness, I will not be afraid, Lord, for You are with me. And all this is true because it once was Christmas.

December 8   Luke 2:22-35

CHRISTMAS IS TIMELESS

Led by the Spirit, Simeon went into the Temple. When the parents brought the child Jesus . . . Simeon took the Child in his arms and gave thanks to God . . . (Lk 2:27-28)

Simeon was an old man, pious and righteous in all respects. He could talk to God and also listen to Him. In truth, the name Simeon means: "The one who listens". God blessed him because Simeon set great value on his meetings with Him. To him the greatest moment of his life was when he could take the child Jesus in his arms – Jesus, his Saviour and Redeemer!

Like Simeon, we must learn to wait upon the Lord, so that we can receive his wonderful gifts of grace. We dare not simply receive with a cold and untouched heart, but we must look forward to them with an expectant heart and accept them in faith. We must know: Christ was born also for me.

That is faith: to see the invisible. A faith so real that it will force you to proclaim the message of Advent even in your old age: "Christ is a light to reveal God's will to the nations."

This is God's action each Christmas: He places the Child of his love in your arms; and with Him you receive his love, redemption, his body and his blood – everything which is needed for your salvation. How amazing the Gift of God!

God does his part – but we also have a duty at Chistmas. Like Simeon took the Child in his arms, we must embrace Jesus and take Him to our hearts; accept Him as Lord and Saviour. Advent is the coming of God to man, and of the coming of man to God.

Help me, dear Lord, to take You in my arms like Simeon, but also into my heart. So Christmas will be a festival to the honour of Jesus Christ alone.

December 9   Luke 2:1-7

CHRISTMAS: FESTIVAL OF THE CHILD

She gave birth to her first Son, wrapped Him in strips of cloth and laid Him in a manger – there was no room for them to stay in the inn (Lk 2:7)

At Christmas-time we all become children again! In our hearts we relive the timeless adventure of unquestioned faith, when all things were immediately possible and where the Prince of Peace is the central figure. The manger in the stable, becomes a precious cot in the palace, and kings from the mystic East pay homage to the King of kings!

Like a glorious dream, we leave our predictable life-style and travel the road of imagination, wonder and excitement, while we rejoice without inhibitions, about the endless love of God. Even the stoic, spiritual realist feels the stirrings in his heart as the age-old story of the Star of Bethlehem; the song of angels upon the fields of Ephrathah; the surprise and joy of simple shepherds; the smell of frankincense and myrrh come back to our memory.

On the other hand, Christmas is as real as the presents we give and receive in love; as the candles we light and the decorations which fascinate us; as the bread we break with loved ones; as the festive joy and nostalgic songs which greet us at this joyous time of the year.

In our experience of the mystery surrounding Christmas, and the concrete reality of it, we are all deeply touched by the wonder of God's love. It causes the promise of peace and joy to be rekindled in our hearts.

If we have forgotten how to experience Christmas like a child, with joyful excitement, we must once again consecrate our lives to the Child in the manger. Christmas is a festival of the Child.

I praise your Holy name, o God, for loving me so that You sent your Son into this world to save sinners and to make me your child.

December 10   Matthew 2:1-12

CAN YOU TRULY CELEBRATE CHRISTMAS?
They brought out their gifts of gold, frankincense, and myrrh, and presented them to Him (Mt 2:11)

The astrologers from the East understood the message of Christmas: To give! God gave: his best; his most precious; his Son! He gave out of love (Jn 3:16). And Jesus gave – He gave Himself! Unto death even, He gave Himself.

You must learn to forget what you have given to other people and remember what others have done for you out of love. You must learn to forget what you expect of others and rather remember what you can do for others.

You must get away from the idea that the world owes you something, and start considering what you owe the world. You must be able to place your demands in the background and place your responsibilities prominently in the foreground.

You will have to discover that your fellow-man is just as sincere as you are, and beyond the exterior you must be able to see a heart hungering for love, friendship and joy. It is not what you can get out of life, but what you put into it of your noblest and best, which really matters.

You must be able to close the book of your complaints and look around you for a place where you can sow a few seeds of happiness and joy.

If you are willing to do all these things, even for one single day, then you have brought your gold, frankincense and myrrh – then you can truly celebrate Christmas!

Holy Lord Jesus, You became a tender child in Bethlehem. Teach me the deeper meaning of Christmas and make me more willing to give myself.

December 11 Isaiah 62:1-12

A SONG OF JOY WITH A FALSE NOTE
Tell the people of Jerusalem that the Lord is coming to save you, bringing with Him the people He has rescued (Is 62:11)

During advent we commemorate the coming of Jesus in the flesh to this world. We dare not, however, leave out of account the advent of Jesus Christ into our hearts and lives.

We dare not content ourselves with the physical appearance of Christ to this world, as if that is all that is of importance. We may not only confess with our mouths that He came into the world as the Lamb of God as a sacrifice for our sins. This is a glorious confession, but it is futile unless we have experienced his salvation personally.

Then we have a song of jubilation with a false note! It may be a time of festivity around us, but never within us! If we want to experience the joy of Christmas in its purest form, Christ has to occupy our lives with his salvation, peace and joy. Luther said: "Even though Christ were born a thousand times in Bethlehem, but not yet in my own heart, I am lost."

Christ came to earth so that his love and mercy could become a reality in the hearts of all who believe in Him. He came to seek and to save sinners and, according to John 1:12, He gave all those who accepted and believed in Him, unconditionally the right to become God's children.

Do you believe this? Do you believe that He comes to you in your lost state of sin? He comes with hands overflowing with mercy, forgiveness and blessing. He comes to change your sorrow to joy; He takes the false note out of your joy of Christmas and enables you to sing the perfect song of redemption.

Holy heavenly Father, I rejoice in the privilege and joy of a personal salvation through Jesus my Lord.

December 12   Micah 5:1-15

TO WORSHIP AT BETHLEHEM
The Lord says, "Bethlehem Ephrathah, you are one of the smallest towns in Judah, but out of you I will bring a ruler for Israel, whose family line goes back to ancient times (Mic 5:2)

As Micah prophesied, Christ was born in Bethlehem. Bethlehem – a little town about fifteen kilometres to the south of Jerusalem. At that time it was also known as Ephrathah. The name Bethlehem means "house of bread". The town is situated on the border of a fertile landscape with rich cornfields, which made this name very appropriate. This town had a long and renowned history: there Jacob buried his favourite wife, Rachel, and raised a memorial tablet to give concrete form to his deep sorrow. There Ruth lived and worked when she met Boas. From there, on a clear day, she could see the mountains of the land of her birth, Moab, across the rift-valley of the Jordan.

Bethlehem was the childhood town of David, the great king of Israel. When he was a lonely fugitive in the mountains, from the wrath of Saul, he longed for water from the well at the gates of Bethlehem. Out of his progeny the Son of God was born in Bethlehem to be the Redeemer of the whole world. He would be the Bread of life to millions; the Fountain of living water which would slake the eternal spiritual thirst of mankind.

When a pilgrim today wants to enter the Church of the Nativity in Bethlehem, he must bend very low to be able to go in. Thus all of us, especially during advent, will have to kneel in worship before Him who was born for our salvation. Glory be to God in the highest!

Jesus of Bethlehem, we are again setting out on our annual pilgrimage to the crib of Ephrathah. Feed us anew with the Bread and Water of life.

December 13   Malachi 3:13-4:6

THE SUN IS SHINING BUT I AM BLIND

But for you who obey Me, my saving power will rise on you like the sun and bring healing like the sun's rays (Mal 4:2)

On a bleak sunshine day in winter, a blind beggar sat at his regular corner, and on the cardboard placard hanging from his neck, were the touching words: "The sun is shining, but I am blind!"

The sun controls the heavens in majesty and glory, unapproachable in its sovereignty. The eye can't look at it unprotected, without being blinded.

Our God is like the sun. Elevated high above the noise of the earth, He reigns over the universe. Even though I try to protect my eyes against his glare – He is still there. As the sun brings light and warmth and growth by its rays, so God comes to us at Christmas-time. But, other than the sun, God is near to us, even in his unapproachable holiness.

We can't reach the sun, but yet the sun comes to us. God sends his light to enlighten our darkened minds, to warm our cold hearts, and to revert our night of sin to a glorious day of salvation.

In Jesus Christ the Sun of Righteousness came down to us. God of God and Light of Light! Zechariah rejoices in the Child of Bethlehem as the rising Sun who visited us to shine in the darkness for those who sit in the shadows of death. There are so many people wandering in the dark labyrinths of sin. The sun is shining, but they are blind. But, says Malachi, there is healing in his rays. He endured the suffering that should have been ours, the pain that we should have borne.

We must return from Christmas to everyday life and spread the Light of his glory in a world of darkness and sin.

Sun of Righteousness, I am reminded at Christmas-time of my responsibility to spread your light in this world. Help me in my ministry of reflecting your glory!

December 14   1 John 4:7-21

THE BASIC TRUTHS OF CHRISTMAS
And God showed his love for us by sending his only Son into the world, so that we might have life through Him (1 Jn 4:9)

The greatest truth of Christmas is that God loves us – because God is love! He loves us with a love which constantly gives; gives just the very best and the most precious – like at Christmas when He gave his Son!

He also loves us with a love which always forgives and a love which cares for us. On that first Christmas, God gave Himself to us in the person of his Son, Jesus Christ. We dare not leave such a love unrequited.

"Dear friends, if this is how God loves us, then we should love one another" (1 Jn 4:11). Love must triumph in our everyday lives: in our marriage; in our homes; in all our relationships, in each area of our lives. Not only in empty words, but in shining deeds of love.

However, it is also true that Jesus did not remain in the manger, but grew equal to his Via Dolorosa – his road of suffering; to Golgotha and Gethsemane; to the empty grave and his triumphant ascencion into heaven. Therefore we, his followers, dare not remain infants in our faith. We dare not be retarded to a stable-faith: we must grow to spiritual maturity.

We also have to be witnesses of the wonders of Christianity. "The shepherds went back, singing praises to God for all that they had heard and seen" (Lk 2:20). We must tell sinners that there is a way back to the Father's heart. We must witness to the miracles of forgiveness, salvation, mercy, peace and love! The portals are wide open for everyone who would enter.

Lord of Christmas-tide, I thank You that it has truly become Christmas in my life, because I found the way back to your heart and to all the wonders of salvation.

December 15   Luke 1:67-80

THE AFFLUENCE OF CHRISTMAS
He will cause the bright dawn of salvation to rise on us and to shine from heaven on all those who live in the dark shadow of death, to guide our steps into the path of peace (Lk 1:78-79)

At Christmas God opened his treasure-chambers to his children. The thought of Christmas had its origin in the loving heart of God and finds its culmination when sinful man opens his heart to the Child of Bethlehem. May all the events surrounding this festive season, bring abundant blessings for each day of the year ahead.

May it mean that you will open your life to the love of God; that you will consider his wonders with your intellect and open your ears to his tender voice calling you to commit your life to Him!

May you renew the assurance that faith is never disappointed. We learn to know true joy in Jesus Christ and we learn to know that we must care for each other; that we must witness to the gospel; that we must give so as to receive. The Word leads us to Christ, and through Christ we learn to know God as our Father!

May you travel your road with the sparkle of stars in your eyes; of true Christmas-joy in your heart; the spirit of Christmas visible in your actions; a faith in Christ in your soul; and the message of Christmas on your lips. Then you will live in the affluence of what God intended for you at Christmas.

May you remember throughout the year that Christmas is not simply a date on the calendar, but a way of life!

Thank you, Jesus of Bethlehem, for coming down to earth and opening the treasure-house of God to us, your children.

December 16 — Psalm 78:1-8

THE MAGNIFICENT DEEDS OF GOD
... we will tell the next generation about the Lord's power and his great deeds and the wonderful things He has done (Ps 78:4)

The Day of the Covenant – the day on which we remember the great deeds of God and not so much the achievements of men. This day reminds us that those who place their trust in God Almighty are never disappointed. It reminds us that one faithful person, with God on his side, is a majority.

That is why today is a day of thanksgiving in which we humbly honour God, who keeps the times and destinies of people and nations in his hand. We kneel before God in gratitude for more than three centuries of divine mercy. We think of the high price paid for freedom, and honour those who willingly made the sacrifice. We thank Him for faithful believers who carried the light of his Word into this dark continent.

On this day, so close to Christmas, we kneel in renewed worship and consecration before God, who controls the history of this world. We commit ourselves anew to the land we love and to the God of our ancestors. We reconsider our spiritual, cultural, social and economic heritage in the light of the demands of the Word of God.

We confess before God that we can't face the future in these confusing and trying times without his holy guidance. We plead for his support, even when we threaten to break away from Him in obstinate self-will.

Lord of the Covenant, as our fathers trusted, we too will trust and obey. Grant us the courage to follow bravely on the road You lead our country. Keep us from despondency and despair, knowing that our destiny is in your hands.

December 17 — John 1:1-18

NATURE, SCRIPTURE AND THE FLESH
The Word became a human being and, full of grace and truth, lived among us. We saw his glory, the glory which He received as the Father's only Son (Jn 1:14)

God revealed Himself to mankind in nature and in Scripture. And then He revealed Himself in the most wonderful way of all – in the flesh! This knowledge is the source of all true Christian joy.

The Christmas-drama reaches its climax when the wise men humbly kneel in worship before the new-born King. Now for the first time they see God revealed in the flesh. The enchantment of the stars is past. The Light of God breaks in their hearts triumphantly. For the first time they understand the mystery of the Word made flesh. The Child is now the Star – the Shining Morning Star – the Fairest of ten thousand!

Like the Wise Men, our eyes must look past the stars, to see the truth of the Word. We must reach the stable in Bethlehem where we too must kneel in adoration with our sacrifice in our hands: the gold of our love; the frankincense of our prayers; and the myrrh of our consecration.

In the stable we learn what the stars cannot teach us: that the world became the centre of the universe on Christmas Day!

And when the stars no longer shine, the new day of God will dawn. Then God will no longer speak to us by stars, or even by his Word – but eternally and unbrokenly by the Word made flesh – Jesus Immanuel!

Great and mighty God, lead me past the sparkling stars this Christmas, through your Holy Word, to the Child in the crib. I would worship the Word made flesh in spirit and in truth.

December 18   Luke 2:8-20

CHRISTMAS IS FOR THE FAMILY
So they hurried off and found Mary and Joseph and saw the Baby lying in the manger (Lk 2:16)
Our greatest desire is to be home with the family on Christmas day. It was so on that first Christmas: Joseph, Mary and the Baby.

Joseph, the father, was present. Even though it was under exceptional circumstances. He didn't seek escape in the teeming mass of humanity away from his loved ones. He is not in the inn next door, enjoying an evening at the pub. No, at this great moment he is with Mary and the Child – because they needed him and he loved them.

Man belongs with his wife: this is repeatedly the message of Christmas. There are times when they must close ranks against the outside world; when the family is the first priority of his life. He dare not neglect this responsibility.

How easily we allow the world to deprive us of these joyful and sanctified moments. We desperately want to do great and noble deeds in the outside world, while we should only be present where we are needed most – with our family.

Mary felt safe with her Child while Joseph was present. Joseph with his calloused carpenter's hands, clumsily holding the new-born Baby – but Joseph with a heart overflowing with love.

May we learn again from Christmas, that we can only attain to joy and bliss in marriage if we are willing to make sacrifices. Our marriage and family life can only gain in quality if we work at it with dedication and love.

Thank you, Child of Bethlehem, that You made it possible for the family to care for one another in love.

December 19 Psalm 94:12-23

TENDER COMFORT AT CHRISTMAS-TIDE
Whenever I am anxious and worried, You comfort me and make me glad (Ps 94:19)

There are many people who are seriously ill. Others again have to cope with the decay of old age. To many others Christmas can never again be the same, because the family circle has been broken. There is so much grief and sorrow because, especially at this time of the year, death callously carries on its work of destruction on our highways. There are parents who pine for their children who cannot be home at Yuletide: possibly due to military service; or because they are too far departed to be home during this time; or because there is estrangement which threatens to break the parent's heart.

There are many reasons why Christmas-time holds little joy to many people. Perhaps the worst is the utter loneliness of those who have to face this Christmas alone for the first time or by repetition, because death has separated them. Who will ever be able to fully understand this yearning if you have not had firsthand experience?

The Child of Bethlehem had to travel all these paths during his earthly life. He identifies with our sorrow and pain. He also felt Godforsaken and lonely, desperate and denied. He understands – and He cares. He has the power to touch your heart with comfort. Stay close to Him and you will experience victory over sorrow because you have persevered in love and obedience.

God of the lonely and the sorrowing, thank you for your comforting presence in our pain and bereavement. Christmas reminds us that You are Immanuel – God with us!

December 20 Luke 2:8-20

THE SIGN OF GOD'S LOVE
And this is what will prove it to you: you will find a baby wrapped in strips of cloth and lying in a manger (Lk 2:12)

As with the advent of a child into a home, there were many who were yearning for the coming of this Child: the prophets and faithful people of the Old Testament; his parents; pious people of his time – Simeon and Anna; Zechariah and Elizabeth; and also we look forward with longing to the celebration of his coming, with the prayer in our hearts: "Grant us a true festival of the Son!"

God talks to humanity with a thousand tongues: on Mount Sinai the thunder rolled; in Sodom and Gomorrah He spoke with fire and brimstone; in the life of Job He spoke through loss, sickness and affliction. God talks through nature and through his Holy Word.

At Christmas-time God speaks through a little Child in the crook of a mother's arm, from a manger in a stable, waving us back to Him with the hand of the Baby of Bethlehem. God became a Child to speak to us in a language which each human being would understand. The Child of Bethlehem tells us of God's undying love for us . . . God so loved the world . . .! Won't this love encourage us to love our children more dearly and to seek their salvation more sincerely?

Our children always present us with a choice: to love and cherish them; or to neglect and grieve them. The Child of Bethlehem presents us with precisely the same choice – shall we love Him, or grieve Him?

Eternal and loving Father, I accept your sign in love. The choice of my heart is that You shall be King of my life!

December 21　　　　　　　　　　　　　　　　　　　Luke 2:1-7

OPEN THE DOORS: THE SON OF GOD HAS ARRIVED
She gave birth to her first Son, wrapped Him in strips of cloth and laid Him in a manger – there was no room for them to stay in the inn (Lk 2:7)
If the people of Bethlehem had only known! If they had only known Who it was seeking a place to stay! However, we can't judge them. The place was so full – perhaps it wasn't that they did not want to make accommodation available for Joseph and Mary – and the Child! Like during holiday-times at the seaside. Nowhere can a room be found if you have not booked.

But if the inn-keeper had known who his visitors were, we wonder if he wouldn't have taken more pains to accommodate them. Shortly Mary would become the mother of the Messiah – He whom upon the whole of Israel was waiting with great expectation. Each devout Israelite would have willingly offered them a room.

However, God did not come to earth in strength and glory. He came in the humble form of a servant and was laid down in a manger. He became like one of us.

Will history repeat itself this Christmas? Will we have no place in our lives for Jesus? Then we will be much more guilty than the inhabitants of Bethlehem. We know, indeed, that He is Christ, the Lord!

The wonder of God's mercy is that He hasn't punished us for what we did to Him. Even though there was no place for Him on earth, He promised: "I am going to prepare a place for you" (Jn 14:2).

Our Christmas act of faith and worship should be to invite Jesus into our lives; throwing open the doors of each room and granting Him total dominion. Then we have nothing to fear – not even death!

Merciful Lord, this Christmas I want to open the doors of my heart as wide as possible to You. Thank you, that by your finished work, the house of the Father is open to me.

December 22 Matthew 2:1-12

CHRIST IS BORN! IMMANUEL!
Jesus was born in the town of Bethlehem in Judaea, during the time when Herod was king (Mt 2:1)

It is a historic fact. Jesus was born in Bethlehem, and by this physical birth God came to reveal Himself to mankind. Jesus Christ revealed the nature of God to this world. The fact that humanity accepted this with difficulty, does not retract from its truth. Even though there are thousands upon thousands who do not accept Him, there are millions who accept Him as their Lord and Master.

He who was born in Bethlehem more than 2 000 years ago, is still being born in the hearts and lives of modern men. This elementary, but at the same time overwhelming truth, is often lost in the rush and hurry of our lives.

In spite of the festivities of the world around Christmas, it is also true that, if you have not experienced the birth of Christ in your own life, you will never know the true peace and jubilation of Christmas. Only the presence of the living Christ can give a deeper meaning to Advent. That is why Luther said: "Even though Christ was born in Bethlehem a thousand times, but not born in your life, it is an empty occurrence, entirely missing its purpose in your life."

If you long to experience true Christmas joy, Christ must be at the centre of your whole life. With his entry into your life, it becomes a "Merry Christmas" in the truest sense of the word.

Thank you, Holy One of Bethlehem, that when You were born into my life, I became heir to your Spirit and that I have since experienced only joy as your disciple.

December 23 Matthew 1:18-25

GOD WITH US!
"... *and He will be called Immanuel*" *(which means, "God is with us")* (Mt 1:23)
Christmas reminds us of the glorious fact that God is with us to purify our imperfect love. Christmas teaches us what the essence of self-sacrificing love is.

Jesus Christ came to his own people, but they refused to receive Him. Nevertheless, those who did receive Him and believe in Him, He gave the right to become God's children (Jn 1:12).

There was no place for Him in the inn. Nevertheless, He guarantees us a place in his Father's house if we love and follow Him (Jn 14:3).

He was despised and rejected by man. Nevertheless He invites all who are tired and heavy laden, to come to Him for rest. He had the power to come down from the cross and destroy all those who scorned Him. But He refused to do so. He died on the cruel cross for the sins of the whole world. The vindictive world would not grant Him life, but He offers eternal life to all who accept his love.

There is so much hatred in this loveless world. Relationships are ruined between man and God; and between man and man. But God is love, He sent his Son to the world. If God so loved us, we must love one another. Confess this love again this Christmas: to God, to your parents, to your marriage partner, to your fellow-men.

Heavenly Father, I worship You in gratitude that You revealed your love for mankind in Jesus Christ at Christmas. Grant me more and purer love.

December 24 Titus 2:1-15

BEHOLD, YOUR KING IS COMING!
For God has revealed his grace for the salvation of all mankind (Tit 2:11)
We are reminded of "his grace for the salvation of all mankind" at Christmas-tide. It became our rich and personal heritage when the almighty God had compassion on us in his Son, Jesus Christ. Christmas confirms what Isaiah had prophesied so long ago: "Once again you will see a king ruling in splendour" (Is 33:17). God came down from heaven to live with us – Immanuel! His love and mercy was revealed to all people, while the choirs of heaven were singing their jubilant hymns over the fields of Ephrathah.

We already know God as a Father, a Father who cares for his children, sustains and protects them. He assures us: "Whoever goes to the Lord for safety, whoever remains under the protection of the Almighty, can say to Him, 'You are my defender and protector. You are my God; in You I trust'" (Ps 91:1-2).

On Christmas-day God appeared to us in the image of the Son and became equal to us in all things, except sin. He came to fix all the broken things in this sin-torn world. By his appearance He gave us total victory over sin and death. As the Master-Potter He remoulded our sinful lives into new people living to his honour and glory.

God also comes to us in these joyous days in the person of the Holy Spirit to gird us with power from on high; to equip us for service; to teach, to guide and to comfort us; to enlighten our minds; to warm our hearts; and to lift up our souls in worship. Immanuel – God with us: Father, Son and Holy Spirit.

Eternal God, and in Jesus Christ, my heavenly Father, thank you for the grace of salvation which became my heritage. Thank you for the Holy Spirit living in me. Fill my heart with genuine love for You.

December 25 Luke 2:8-20

FESTIVAL OF LOVE!
This very day in David's town your Saviour was born – Christ the Lord! (Lk 2:11)
All those who are burdened and heavy laden; all those who are desperate

and despondent and live in the shadow of pain and sorrow; all those who are trapped in sin and unrighteousness; all those who can't find joy or faith in God . . .

All those who are victims of injustice and suppression; all those who are hurt and want to take revenge; all those who fear death and hate life; all those whose children have forsaken them, who mourn through the night and can find no comfort or peace . . .

All those who labour in vain and find no satisfaction or meaning in what they do; all those who will die today or tomorrow and call out for an answer in vain . . .

All those who are without friends, without a home; all those who hate because of their affliction, and all those who hate out of blind jealousy; all those who are without love because they have never received love . . .

To all of you a Redeemer was born today! In love and mercy He will heal your wounds; give sight to the blind. He will release you of hatred and jealousy, pain and sorrow and grant you his comfort.

He comes to you – the Word made flesh – in love and mercy. All He asks for you is to love Him and follow Him.

Jesus we praise You, Jesus we glorify You! We join the angels in a hymn of praise. You are born today. We are lost no longer. Receive the gratitude and love of our hearts!

December 26   Luke 2:8-20

THE AFTERGLOW OF CHRISTMAS
The shepherds went back, singing praises to God for all they had heard and seen; it had been just as the angel had told them (Lk 2:20)

The shepherds in the fields of Bethlehem were witnesses of the miracles of that first Christmas night. We also experience the wonder of Christmas each year by way of carols, bright lights, loving gifts and meaningful worship. Everywhere we sense a spirit of love and benevolence.

A spirit of Christmas which is thrown on the rubbishdump together with the wilted Christmas tree, is useless. It makes a mockery of the deeper meaning of Christmas.

Wouldn't it be wonderful if we could preserve the singular spirit of Chirstmas in bottles, as we do with seasonal fruit, and then to open a bottle each week of the year to experience the exhilarating experience right through the year? One often hungers for the spirit of Christmas during the year. After the songs of the angels have fallen silent, the star had disappeared from the heavens, the kings of the Orient have returned home and the shepherds are back with their flocks – then the work of Christmas has only begun.

Because we were at the stable in Bethlehem and have relived the night of Christmas; because we have met the Child of Bethlehem again – that is why an afterglow of Christmas must hang over our lives. With this glow of love in our hearts, we must have sympathy with those who don't have it, rebuild the world, bring peace and reconciliation between man and man and fill the world with the eternal music of love.

Dear God of Christmas, but also of every day of the year, help me by the power of Jesus Christ to sing the everlasting song of love as a witness to the world.

December 27   1 John 2:7-17

WALK IN THE LIGHT
Whoever says that he is in the light, yet hates his brother, is in the darkness to this very hour (1 Jn 2:9)
If your love for Jesus Christ is genuine, his glory and beauty will become evident in everything you say and do. If your commitment is superficial, the reflection of the light of Christ in your life will be feeble. He reveals Himself in your life, only to the extent in which you allow Him to. If He becomes the light of your life, He will be a spiritual power in each situation you may find yourself.

There is only one way the world will see the light of Christ, and that is in the love his children reveal. If your love for Him is simply a front, it will lack quality. If your love for Him is genuine and sincere, people will involuntary be influenced by the Spirit which controls your life. Your strength is from a Source greater than yourself, and other people will be attracted to it.

Christ needs torches of light for his kingdom, which will expel the darkness of hate and sin from this world. Consecrated disciples bear his light into the dark places of life. They combat misunderstanding and hate simply by comprehension and love; ignorance with truth. This constructive and positive attitude is adhered to in spite of distrust and estrangement.

The light of Christ shines through these people and they experience joy and fulfilment.

Saviour and Lord, let your light be reflected in my life, so that the world will know that I belong to You.

December 28   1 John 3:1-10

CHILDREN OF GOD!
See how much the Father has loved us! His love is so great that we are called God's children . . . (1 Jn 3:1)
Does this proclamation sound somewhat far-fetched or sentimental? Indeed, it is one of the greatest truths imaginable and should fill each child of God with amazement and joy.

One can serve God in each area of life. There are children of God occupying positions of honour and responsibility; many of them hold authority. Thousands of others serve God in humility, away from the eye and the applause of the world. However varying our situations in life may be, we all have the blessed assurance that God is our Father and, in Jesus Christ, we are children of the King! It creates a joy in our lives which is beyond understanding.

To accept God as your Father and to rejoice in this glorious relationship, brings a very special dimension to your life. You realize that God loves you and guides you through the indwelling Holy Spirit. It is an exciting and fulfilling experience.

How high or how humble your position may be, you can face the world, because you know you are royalty – a child of the King of kings. Pride is buried in worship and love. There is a new dignity in your daily task. You know the joy of honest work as you labour in the cause of your Father and witness to his love.

Father! I kneel in speechless worship for the knowledge that I am your child through Jesus Christ, my Lord! Help me by your Spirit to work and live to your honour and glory.

December 29 — Psalm 139:1-24

LIBERATING INTROSPECTION

Examine me, O God, and know my mind; test me, and discover my thoughts. Find out if there is any evil in me and guide me in the everlasting way (Ps 139:23-24)

The time has come for us to take stock and do self-examination of our lives. Especially at this time of year this prayer of David is most appropriate.

Some prayers make no demands upon the one who prays. It is simply a salve for the conscience. To pray in a meaningful manner, acceptable to the Holy Spirit, our petitions must be absolutely honest and accompanied with a willingness to do whole-hearted self-examination.

To ask God to know your heart and mind, may be a recreating experience. It strips one of all superficiality and hypocrisy. You see yourself as God sees you. This picture is not flattering. It is humbling, but at the same time liberating.

Testing and evaluating are imperative in one's spiritual life. It is a condition for effective service: if we can't pass God's test, He cannot use us in his service. When the Holy Spirit forces us to self-examination, then and only then do we become serviceable instruments in his hand and we labour to his honour. Then we no longer work in our own strength and to our own honour. Fearless of the future, we place our hand into the almighty hand of God and approach the dawn of a new year with faith and courage.

Eternal Father, make me willing to be placed under the searchlight of your Holy Spirit. Mould my life into an object to your honour and service.

December 30 — Mark 7:31-37

GOD'S PERFECT WORK

"How well He does everything!" they exclaimed (Mk 7:37)

Most people have the desire to spend the dying moments of the old year in the presence of God and enter the new, unknown year with the assurance of his guidance.

God speaks to us in many ways, but most clearly He speaks to us through his Son and his eternal Word. In the light of this Word, we must look back over the whole road which we have come and plead for his kindly light for the road stretching out ahead of us.

We dare not consider only the transcience of life on Old Year's Eve. These negative thoughts can be very disturbing. The content of the year now behind us, is of far greater importance than its length.

During the past year, God has done so much to give content and quality to our lives. It is only undeserved grace. What we have achieved we do not deserve. We must confess: "How well He does everything!"

Paradoxically it is good that the year passing from us now, has not only brought joy and happiness. Sometimes God tests us with affliction to draw us closer to Him and to comfort us. All things work together for the good of those who love God.

When we have reached the end of our pilgrimage – as we now reach the end of the year – we will fold our hands in a prayer of amazement and confess: "How well He does everything!"

Leader and Finisher, I rejoice in the knowledge that everything You do is excellent and to my spiritual benefit.

December 31 — Revelation 1:4-20

GRACE TO THE END!
"I am the first and the last," says the Lord God Almighty, who is, who was, and who is to come (Rev 1:8)

So we come to the final day of the year. There is so much of which we are ashamed, but there is also so much to be grateful for. There is so much self-condemnation because of lost opportunities, but also so much grace we received from God every day. The passing year brought joy, but also sorrow; victory but also defeat; sunshine, but also storms.

However, we can still call God our Father – the greatest privilege a person can experience. Let us count our blessings on this day and know that our Lord is the same yesterday, today and for ever.

You are wealthier today than yesterday if you took time to see the hand of God in all things in life; if you have learnt the power of discrimination; if you forgave others, made new friends; if you had a little bit more patience with the faults of others.

You are very wealthy today if a little child has smiled with you; if you sought to cultivate the best in others; and have given the best and noblest of yourself to God and to your fellow-men.

Then you will praise Him today and every day. You will step out boldly into the new year, your hand in His, your heart in tune with his holy will, safe in his love and tender care!

Thank you, Eternal God, that You have brought me safely through another year. I praise your holy Name for the assurance that You will never leave me nor forsake me. Praise the Lord, o my soul!